The Development Dictionary @25

Few books in the history of Development Studies have had an impact like *The Development Dictionary – A Guide to Knowledge as Power*, which was edited by Wolfgang Sachs and published by Zed Books in 1992. *The Development Dictionary* was crucial in establishing what has become known as the Post-Development (PD) school. This volume is devoted to the legacy of *The Development Dictionary* and to discussing Post-Development.

The chapters in this book were originally published as a special issue of *Third World Quarterly*.

Aram Ziai studied sociology, history, and English literature in Aachen and Dublin, and received his PhD from the University of Hamburg, Germany. He has taught at the universities of Aachen, Hamburg, Magdeburg, Kassel, Amsterdam, Vienna, and Accra, and is currently Heisenberg Professor for Development and Postcolonial Studies at the University of Kassel, Germany.

ThirdWorlds

Edited by Shahid Qadir, *University of London, UK*

ThirdWorlds will focus on the political economy, development and cultures of those parts of the world that have experienced the most political, social, and economic upheaval, and which have faced the greatest challenges of the postcolonial world under globalisation: poverty, displacement and diaspora, environmental degradation, human and civil rights abuses, war, hunger, and disease.

ThirdWorlds serves as a signifier of oppositional emerging economies and cultures ranging from Africa, Asia, Latin America, Middle East, and even those 'Souths' within a larger perceived North, such as the U.S. South and Mediterranean Europe. The study of these otherwise disparate and discontinuous areas, known collectively as the Global South, demonstrates that as globalisation pervades the planet, the south, as a synonym for subalterity, also transcends geographical and ideological frontier.

For more information about this series, please visit: https://www.routledge.com/series/TWQ

The Development Dictionary @25

Post-Development and Its Consequences

Edited by
Aram Ziai

Routledge
Taylor & Francis Group

LONDON AND NEW YORK

First published 2019
by Routledge
2 Park Square, Milton Park, Abingdon, Oxon, OX14 4RN, UK

and by Routledge
52 Vanderbilt Avenue, New York, NY 10017, USA

First issued in paperback 2020

Routledge is an imprint of the Taylor & Francis Group, an informa business

© 2019 Global South Ltd

All rights reserved. No part of this book may be reprinted or reproduced or utilised in any form or by any electronic, mechanical, or other means, now known or hereafter invented, including photocopying and recording, or in any information storage or retrieval system, without permission in writing from the publishers.

Trademark notice: Product or corporate names may be trademarks or registered trademarks, and are used only for identification and explanation without intent to infringe.

British Library Cataloguing in Publication Data
A catalogue record for this book is available from the British Library

ISBN 13: 978-0-367-58397-2 (pbk)
ISBN 13: 978-1-138-32347-6 (hbk)

Typeset in Myriad Pro
by RefineCatch Limited, Bungay, Suffolk

Publisher's Note
The publisher accepts responsibility for any inconsistencies that may have arisen during the conversion of this book from journal articles to book chapters, namely the possible inclusion of journal terminology.

Disclaimer
Every effort has been made to contact copyright holders for their permission to reprint material in this book. The publishers would be grateful to hear from any copyright holder who is not here acknowledged and will undertake to rectify any errors or omissions in future editions of this book.

Contents

CONTENTS

Citation Information

The chapters in this book were originally published in *Third World Quarterly*, volume 38, issue 12 (December 2017). When citing this material, please use the original page numbering for each article, as follows:

For any permission-related enquiries please visit:
http://www.tandfonline.com/page/help/permissions

Notes on Contributors

Alberto Acosta is an Ecuadorean economist. He is an honorary Professor at Ricardo Palma University in Lima, Peru. He formerly occupied the following roles: Minister of Energy and Mines, President of the Constituent Assembly, and Candidate to the Presidency of the Republic.

Stefan Andreasson is a Senior Lecturer in Comparative Politics in the School of History, Anthropology, Philosophy and Politics, and a Fellow in the Centre for the Study of Risk and Inequality, at Queen's University Belfast, UK. He works in the areas of international and comparative politics with a primary interest in the political economy of development and energy markets in Sub-Saharan Africa.

Daniel Bendix is a Senior Researcher in the Department of Development and Postcolonial Studies at the University of Kassel, Germany. His research focuses on (post-)development policy, (post)colonialism, population and reproductive health policy, and global citizenship education. He does freelance work for *glokal*, a postcolonial education NGO based in Berlin, Germany.

Federico Demaria is a Researcher in Ecological Economics and Political Ecology at the Autonomous University of Barcelona, Spain. He is a member of Research & Degrowth (@R_Degrowth) and co-editor of *Degrowth: A Vocabulary for a New Era* (Routledge, 2014), a book translated into ten languages.

Arturo Escobar is Professor of Anthropology at the University of North Carolina, Chapel Hill, USA, and a Research Associate at Universidad del Valle, Colombia. His main interests are political ecology, ontological design, and the anthropology of development and social movements. Over the past 25 years, he has worked closely with several Afrodescendant social movements in the Colombian Pacific.

Gustavo Esteva is a Grassroots Activist and a Public Intellectual. He works independently and in conjunction with Mexican, Latin American, and international grassroots organisations. He was an advisor to the Zapatistas in their negotiations with the government. He has authored, co-authored, and edited many books and essays.

Wendy Harcourt is Professor of Gender, Diversity and Sustainable Development at the International Institute of Social Studies, Erasmus University in The Hague, the Netherlands. She joined ISS in November 2011 after 23 years at the Society for International Development, Rome, Italy, where she was the Editor of the journal *Development*, and Director of Programmes.

Ilan Kapoor is Professor of Critical Development Studies at the Faculty of Environmental Studies, York University, Canada. He teaches in the areas of global development and environmental politics. His research focuses on postcolonial theory/politics, participatory development and democracy, and ideology critique (drawing on psychoanalytic Marxism).

Ashish Kothari is one of the founders of Kalpavriksh, an Indian environmental non-governmental organisation; he coordinates Kalpavriksh's programme on Alternatives. Ashish has served on the Indian Government's Environmental Appraisal Committee on River Valley Projects, and Expert Committees to formulate India's Biological Diversity Act and National Wildlife Action Plan. He coordinated India's National Biodiversity Strategy and Action Plan process.

Sally Matthews is a Senior Lecturer in the Department of Political and International Studies, Rhodes University, South Africa. She teaches comparative politics, African studies, and development studies. Her current research focuses on the relationship between poverty, privilege, and social justice.

Wolfgang Sachs is Research Director Emeritus at the Wuppertal Institute for Climate, Environment and Energy in Germany. He has been Chair of the board of Greenpeace Germany and a member of the Intergovernmental Panel on Climate Change, and was a member of the Club of Rome. He used to teach at Schumacher College, UK, and as Honorary Professor at the University of Kassel, Germany.

Kalpana Wilson is a Lecturer in the Department of Geography, Birkbeck, University of London, UK. She writes about questions of race/gender, labour, neoliberalism, and development. She has also researched for many years on rural labour movements in India. She is the author of *Race, Racism and Development: Interrogating History, Discourse and Practice* (2012).

Aram Ziai studied sociology, history, and English literature in Aachen and Dublin, and received his PhD from the University of Hamburg, Germany. He has taught at the universities of Aachen, Hamburg, Magdeburg, Kassel, Amsterdam, Vienna, and Accra, and is currently Heisenberg Professor for Development and Postcolonial Studies at the University of Kassel, Germany.

Preface

Post-Development? Do we not have more pressing issues at hand? The rise of right-wing parties and racism, the ever-increasing material inequality leading to starving and dying children, the wars in which hundreds of thousands are killed and millions displaced? Given these circumstances, should we seriously engage in fundamental critiques of development theory and policy instead of in more constructive contributions to the SDGs?

I believe we should. Because I think that these pressing issues are – not wholly, but to a considerable extent – related to what most of us regard as a 'developed' society, a good life and a normal way of treating other human beings and nature: a society which is based on nation state units, the inhabitants of which share a common interest opposed to those of other units; an economic system based on competition and aiming at the infinite increase of individually owned consumer goods and the latest technology, no matter at what cost to humans and the environment they have been produced and whether everyone can be equally provided with them; scientific knowledge which discounts all other forms of knowl-edge as invalid and sees nature as something to be harnessed, controlled and exploited for the benefit of humans; and in general a Eurocentric perspective perceiving difference as backwardness. What is usually called the Western model of society, based on the ideas that each one of us is a profit-maximizing homo oeconomicus with unlimited needs, that the Cartesian rationality of dissecting the world into parts and a Baconian relation to nature are all there is, is not the only game in town – not even in the West. And although the attempt to spread this model throughout the world in the name of 'development' may have had positive as well as negative aspects, the latter have been ignored all too often by many. Certainly by most people in the 'development' industry, whose job it was to 'develop the underdeveloped' and help the poor without stepping on the toes of the rich and who natu-rally felt it difficult to believe that this task might be impossible.

When I started writing my PhD on Post-Development, I asked a professor for advice whom I – based on the poster of Emiliano Zapata in his office – imagined to share my values. He clearly and strongly advised me to look for a different topic: those involved in 'development' theory and policy would not listen to a critique questioning the ground on which they stood, and the other academics simply would not care about 'development' issues anyway. Of course I did not heed his advice, but for a long time I thought he had been quite right in his prediction. However, that in recent years more and more people are joining the degrowth movement for example and looking for alternatives, and that even within the 'development' establishment Post-Development increasingly arouses interest and curiosity, has made me more optimistic.

I would like to express my gratitude and give my heartfelt thanks to the following people: First of all to the authors who made this volume possible. Then, to Wolfgang Sachs and

Arturo Escobar for showing me and countless others the power involved in defining someone as underdeveloped and equally for being such warmhearted and down-to-earth intellectuals. To Friederike Habermann and Daniel Bendix for thinking about how Post-Development could look like in the North. To Sally Matthews, Kalpana Wilson and Ilan Kapoor for sharp critiques furthering the debate. To Katherine Gibson, Eduardo Gudynas and Gustavo Esteva for inspiring texts, to Kwesi Aikins, Christine Klapeer, Jacqueline Krause and my students in Kassel for inspiring discussions about Post-Development. To Megan Hiatt, Rhona Carroll, Laura Huxley and Sean Rothman at Taylor & Francis for their work and support. To Daniel for being so much more than a colleague. To my kids for being much more aware of injustice than I was at their age, to my sister for giving a new home to our mum, and to Franziska for everything. And most of all to those who are building another world which is based more on solidarity than on competition, more on humility than hubris, more on harmony than on domination.

INTRODUCTION

Post-development 25 years after *The Development Dictionary*

Aram Ziai

ABSTRACT
Few books in the history of development studies have had an impact
like *The Development Dictionary – A Guide to Knowledge as Power*,
which was edited by Wolfgang Sachs and published by Zed Books in
1992, and which was crucial in establishing what has become known
as the Post-Development (PD) school. This special issue is devoted to
the legacy of this book and thus to discussing PD.

The Development Dictionary started by stating: 'The last 40 years can be called the age of development. This epoch is coming to an end. The time is ripe to write its obituary.'[1] A few pages later, Gustavo Esteva referred to 'development' as an 'unburied corpse.'[2] Twenty-five years later, it can be observed that although the concept has been declared dead many times since then, the Sustainable Development Goals have provided a rejuvenating cure – or has it been only the last in a long line of cosmetic surgeries designed to let its object appear fresh and vigorous, but unable to mask the signs of decay? Eduardo Gudynas has recently called 'development' a 'zombie category', not really alive anymore, but not quite dead either.[3] As the contributions to the volume will show, there are differing views on the accuracy of this diagnosis.

A fundamental critique of 'development'

What distinguished Post-Development (PD) from previous critiques in development studies was that it did not intend to improve the attempts to bring about 'development', but questioned this very objective, advocated the 'rejection of the entire paradigm', and instead called for 'alternatives to development'.[4] But what exactly is meant by 'development' in this context? A close look reveals that the signifier is linked to different (yet connected) signifieds in PD.[5] (1) 'Development' is criticised as an ideology of the West, promising material affluence to decolonising countries in Africa and Asia in order to prevent them from joining the communist camp and maintaining a colonial division of labour.[6] (2) It is criticised as a failed project of universalising the way of life of the 'developed' countries on a global scale which has for the overwhelming majority of affected people led to the 'progressive modernization of poverty'.[7] (3) It is criticised as a Eurocentric and hierarchic construct defining non-Western, non-modern, non-industrialised ways of life as inferior and in need of 'development' (social

1

change as it has occurred in the 'developed' countries).[8] (4) It is criticised as an economic rationality centred around accumulation, a capitalist logic of privileging activities earning money through the market (and disvaluing all other forms of social existence), and the idea of the Homo oeconomicus (whose needs for consumption are infinite).[9] (5) It is criticised as a concept legitimising interventions into the lives of people defined as 'less developed' as justified in the name of a higher, evolutionary goal or simply the common good defined by people claiming expert knowledge.[10]

But why does PD argue that the epoch of 'development' has ended? Sachs gives four reasons: first, the evidence that the ecological consequences of the 'developed' way of life in terms of resource consumption and environmental destruction were such that this way cannot be treated as a model to be replicated. Second, after the end of the Cold War there was no geopolitical motivation for the West to uphold the 'promise of development' to countries in the South. Third, the increasing gap between rich and poor countries during the 'development decades' had rendered the promise implausible. And, fourth, more and more people would realise that successful 'development' entailed the Westernisation of the world, leading to a global monoculture.[11]

According to the PD school, 'alternative development' is not enough, because it repro-duces the idea that the majority of the world's population is 'underdeveloped' and needs to live like the West. So, what about the 'alternatives to development' that PD envisions? Esteva claims that because of the exclusion produced by the project of 'development', ordinary men and women would recover 'their own definition of needs' as well as 'autonomous ways of living'.[12] They would be creating alternatives to 'development', ie to the universal Western models of the economy, politics and knowledge, and reclaiming the commons, often falling back on indigenous or traditional concepts and practices. For him, the Zapatistas in Chiapas/ Mexico provide a good example of such alternatives. But when looking closely, one realises that alternative concepts of what a good society looks like and alternative practices of organ-ising it exist in almost every society: Buen Vivir in Ecuador and Bolivia, Ubuntu in South Africa, Swaraj in India, Gharbzadegi in Iran and Décroissance in France are only the most well-known among them.[13]

Noble savages: the debate on PD

In the ensuing debate[14] PD has been confronted with a number of criticisms, the most important of which shall be reiterated here.

Unconditional rejection of modernity and 'development': This rejection overlooks their successes and emancipatory elements, e.g. the rise in life expectancy and reduction in child mortality throughout the Third World. Instead of throwing the baby out with the bath water, it is necessary to differentiate between the positive and negative consequences of devel-opment projects and modern science – some of them did improve the lives of people in the South.[15]

Noble savages – romanticising the 'alternatives to development': The picture of traditional subsistence communities drawn by PD was romanticising because it ignores or downplays relations of domination and exploitation in these communities and because it assumes their inhabitants not to be interested in Westernisation and material goods. In this respect PD indeed provides the 'last refuge of the noble savage'. The marginalised in the South were interested in 'access to development', not its rejection.[16]

Cultural relativism: The relativist rejection of allegedly Eurocentric universal standards of a good society in PD leads, in the view of some critics, to indifference towards oppression and misery, and prevents critique 'from outside'. The promotion of traditional culture – conceived as static or even essentialist – allows local elites to frame their dismissal of modern practices challenging their privileges as anti-imperialist.[17]

Paternalism: PD has also been criticised for preaching an ethics of sufficiency from a paternalist affluent perspective, claiming to know better about the needs of the poor (and their legitimacy) than they themselves. So, in the end, again a certain model of society (traditional subsistence communities) is prescribed as the right one.[18]

Pontius Pilate politics: On the other hand, the opposite criticism has also been voiced: PD was lacking concrete alternatives, there was 'critique but no construction'. Instead of a political programme there was merely political agnosticism confined to supporting social movements in the South, thus washing its hands of political decisions and engaging in Pontius Pilate politics.[19]

Methodological deficits: The last point is concerned with the selective use of discourse analysis and the uncritical attitude exhibited towards grassroots movements. The emphasis of differences and discontinuities so dear to Foucault had been replaced by essentialisms and the construction of a monolithic discourse of 'development' in PD, turning discourse analysis from a method into an ideological platform.[20]

While this is not the place to thoroughly discuss these arguments, a more in-depth analysis concluded that all of these criticisms were justified in regard to some PD texts, but not to all.[21] Therefore, it is useful to differentiate: sceptical PD does not generally reject all elements of modernity and promotes cultural hybridisation, is critical towards cultural traditions, abstains from articulating desirable models of society and employs a dynamic, constructivist concept of culture. Neo-populist PD does reject modern industrial society altogether and promotes the return to (often idealised) subsistence communities, employing an essentialist concept of culture. Whereas sceptical PD thus leads to a radical democratic position, neo-populist PD potentially has reactionary consequences, as it is able to dismiss people's desire for 'development' as the results of ideology and manipulation, based on privileged knowledge of their 'real' needs – bringing the proponents in a position dangerously close to that of the 'development experts' they criticise so sharply. Yet while the quoted study links these two variants to different authors, it would be more precise to talk about a sceptical and a neo-populist PD discourse in the light of occasional arguments contradicting this distinction.

One last point of criticism has to be cited, as it is both significant and (in this form) rarely mentioned. It concerns the agency of the South and its ability to provoke and appropriate discourses. As Frederick Cooper argues: While 'development ideology was originally supposed to sustain empire, not facilitate the transfer of power', the discourse still provided 'something trade union and political leaders in Africa could engage with, appropriate, and turn back'. Therefore,

> Much as one can read the universalism of development discourse as a form of European particularism imposed abroad, it could also be read … as a rejection of the fundamental premises of colonial rule, a firm assertion of people of all races to participate in global politics and lay claim to a globally defined standard of living.[22]

It is noteworthy that this element, the vision of global social equality, has been quietly buried with the disillusionment over the 'lost decade of development', the ascent of neoliberalism and the abandonment of the 'development' promise in the neoliberal discourse of 'globalisation'.

Slaying the 'development monster': PD's response to the criticisms

Although PD authors concede that their proclamation about the end of the era of 'development' was premature, they reaffirm the necessity of performing a 'decolonization of the imagination'.[23] Responding to the criticism that PD had presented 'development' as monolithic while in fact it was heterogeneous and contested, Escobar concedes that the critics were right. But, he continues, they 'fail to acknowledge ... that their own project of analyzing the contestation of development on the ground was in great part made possible by the deconstruction of development discourse'. Post-development's project had been to 'slay the development monster', ie to break the consensus about 'development' being necessary, self-evident, positive and unquestionable, and thus pave the way for more nuanced analyses. Romanticisation, however, was an accusation used against any and all visions of societies which transcend the current model.[24]

Sachs also engages with the idea of contestation and admits:

we had not really appreciated the extent to which the development idea has been charged with hopes for redress and self-affirmation. It certainly was an invention of the West, as we showed at length, but not just an imposition on the rest. On the contrary, as the desire for recognition and equity is framed in terms of the civilizational model of the powerful nations, the South has emerged as the staunchest defender of development.[25]

This resonates with Cooper's criticism mentioned above, concerning the discourse of 'development' that could also (!) be read as a discourse of rights.

Another interesting response comes from Rist, who engages with the criticism of cultural relativism and supporting groups who disrespect human rights. He argues:

It may well be true that certain movements which oppose 'development' have scant regard for certain articles in the Declaration of Human Rights; or that they force boys to look after goats instead of going to school; or that, as in the case of our grandmothers in Europe, they do not allow women to go out of the house 'bareheaded'. Nevertheless, if respect for the values linked to modernity is the only criterion for judging the social order, what should be said of our own society, which amid general indifference is increasing the numbers of those excluded in the name of economic growth? And what of the wars that cause countless victims, especially civilians, in the name of democracy and human rights?[26]

The argument can of course be interpreted as countering the accusation of abusive practices in one group with a reference to abusive practices in some other group – not an entirely convincing argument. However, it could also be interpreted not as indifference towards abusive practices, but as a refusal to attribute these practices to the non-Western Other while exempting the Western Self, allowing us to affirm our 'civilisational superiority'.

The contribution of PD to development studies

I argue that the contribution of PD is twofold[27]: firstly, in a critique of different kinds of power relations and, secondly, in its potential contribution to a non-Eurocentric and more power-sensitive theory of positive social change.

PD points to the naturalisation of the universal scale: The first and maybe most fundamental achievement of PD is the insight that the categories and strategies of 'development'
imply a certain perspective which is contingent – in contrast to being the natural and normal
way of seeing things. That societies can be compared according to their 'level of development'; that there are 'developed' and 'less developed' countries; and that the latter can be
found in Africa, Asia and Latin America and are in need of 'development', development
experts, development projects and development aid provided by the former are assumptions
that are by no means self-evident.[28] They constitute a historically specific way of looking at
different societies and global inequality, naturalising the norms and historical processes of
the European Self.

It reveals the process of othering and the problematisation of deviance: The naturalisation
of the Self enables the problematisation of the Other as deviant. The universal scale allows
one to measure and compare according to a Eurocentric norm and to thus define the majority
of humanity as 'underdeveloped'. The Other is not seen as different, but as a deficient version
of the Self, which is why development discourse operates by identifying deviance from the
norm as inferiority ('underdevelopment', 'illiterate', 'unemployed', etc.).[29]

It shows how the promise of betterment functions as a mechanism of legitimation. Even
if the prescriptions of development discourse do not work, the development industry claims
to have learnt from its earlier mistakes, reaffirming its knowledge on how to improve other
people's lives, but now rendering visible a new aspect hitherto neglected (poverty, basic
needs, women, the environment, the market, good governance, ownership, etc.). Failures
thus lead only to a reformulation of the promise.[30]

It points to the hierarchisation of different types of knowledge (and sometimes also cultures and values), with one type (universally applicable expert knowledge, typically claimed
by trustees) being privileged and the other (local, 'unscientific' knowledge) denigrated.[31]

It highlights the depoliticisation which often takes place in the discourse of 'development'.
The discourse of 'development', at least the one employed by most development agencies,
assumes that 'development' is something that benefits everyone and therefore that no one
can object to, something removed from conflicts over political and economic questions,
portraying positive social change as a technical matter related exclusively to the presence
or absence of knowledge, technology and capital. Simply put, this discourse wants to help
the poor without hurting the rich (on a national and international level). It has to do so in
order to gain support and legitimacy, but in doing so neglects an analysis of the structural
causes of poverty and depoliticises the conflicts and divisions in society.[32]

PD's thin feminist current has revealed that 'development' is in fact not gender neutral:
its privileging of rationality, productivity, technology and mastery over nature has clearly
masculine connotations. According to Shiva, the 'treatment of nature as a resource which
acquires value only in exploitation for economic growth has been central to the project of
development' and is certainly not unrelated to the 'fundamental dichotomizing between
male and female, mind and matter, objective and subjective, the rational and the emotional'
which has been a central feature of European modernity at least since Bacon.[33]

This critical potential of PD can, by the way, be used also by persons not sharing PD's
commitment to 'alternatives to development', which is why it gained so much currency in
the discipline (see the final paper of this issue). However, PD's full potential unfolds only if
these alternatives are taken seriously, allowing it to contribute to a reformulation of a theory
of emancipatory social change beyond 'development'. The problem of development theory's

impasse lies in the fact that it has not sufficiently dealt with the implications of pluralism. Nederveen Pieterse correctly remarks: 'The idea of development as a single forward path ... or generalizing across developing societies lies well behind us'.[34] And he is also right in stating that since the crisis, '[m]ainstream approaches have coopted elements of alternative development like participation'.[35] But the implications of this rejection of 'development as a single path' have not been fully recognised. Kothari and Minogue agree with Nederveen Pieterse that 'forms of alternative development have become institutionalized as part of mainstream development', but argue that this type of alternative development 'does not redefine development, but instead questions its modalities, agency and procedures ... It is still ultimately about the achievement of Western modernity by developing and transitional countries'.[36] This means that alternative development merely looks for different roads to arrive at the same goal. However, if this goal is unambiguous and defined by modern, industrial capitalist societies, then even alternative development remains firmly grounded in the Western, or more precisely hegemonic, models of politics (nation state and liberal democracy), the economy (neoliberal, globalised capitalism) and knowledge (Western science). Thus, we are still assuming a single path forward to a good society, and the potential of non-Western alternatives to these models to improve human well-being remains untapped. If we take the imperative of 'development pluralism'[37] seriously, we need to consider these non-Western alternatives as well in order to redefine development, taking into account not only different paths to modernity but different ideas of a good life altogether. This is why the PD approach which questions these hegemonic models and promotes non-Western alternatives could play a central role in a reinvention of development theory beyond the impasse.

Of course, such a theory would have to embrace the plurality of knowledges (being aware of its limits and of other ways of knowing) and operate, in the words of Santos, as a 'rearguard theory'[38] – theorising the practice of social movements instead of prescribing it like vanguard theories used to do. However, PD can be used for different ends: for criticising discourses and practices imbued with Eurocentrism and relations of power and thinking about global inequality beyond the discourse of 'development', or for theorising contemporary struggles and envisioning different futures based on non-capitalist values, communal ownership and a humbler relation of human beings to nature.

The contributions of this issue

The first four contributions to the special issue are viewpoint articles by eminent participants in the debate on PD. In the opening article 'Post-Development at 25: on "being stuck" and moving forward, sideways, backward, and otherwise' Gustavo Esteva and Arturo Escobar engage in a powerful restatement of a radical PD position, rejecting 'development' as 'the slogan used by capital to facilitate the implementation of a neocolonial enterprise' and exploring what it might mean to live 'beyond development'. Reiterating the theses of Ivan Illich, they denounce the 'dictatorship of needs' in 'development' thinking, whose success has eliminated the art of autonomous living and created dependency on schools for learning, doctors for healing and cars for mobility. Taking inspiration from indigenous communities, but also from 'non-dominant Wests that exist within the West', they are envisioning a civilisational transition which brings us 'beyond development' towards more autonomous, convivial and non-capitalist forms of life, based on a more respectful relation to nature ('liberation of Mother Earth') and different notions of what it is to live well ('defence of the pluriverse').

In his contribution 'The Sustainable Development Goals and *Laudato si'*: varieties of Post-Development?', Wolfgang Sachs analyses the Sustainable Development Goals (SDGs) as a curious mix of noble ideals, capitalist *realpolitik* and self-delusion, but notes that 'the classical development narrative is conspicuously missing'. However, although the frame of reference has shifted from the promise of affluence to mere survival, and the myth of catching up with the North has been buried, for some, namely an emerging transnational middle class increasingly located in the South, the promise has actually become reality, yet at an enormous cultural and ecological cost. The SDGs, Sachs argues, still follow the script of development discourse in using quantitative data to enable comparisons constructing deficits between nations – and in the inability to imagine prosperity without economic growth. In contrast, the Encyclical *Laudato si'* of Pope Francis has renounced development discourse far more thoroughly, according to Sachs, emphasising relationships – to nature, to others, to oneself and to god – and interdependence. It does not shy away from talking about ecological debts and recommending degrowth to the affluent regions, from advocating a 'cultural revolution' to overcome the 'technocratic paradigm' and a human-centred conception of creation. Sachs sees both documents as testimony of a PD era, one promoting the globalisation narrative, the other a spirit of pluralist eco-solidarity.

The following two contributions are concerned with fleshing out the 'alternatives to development' of PD discourse. Federico Demaria and Ashish Kothari sketch '*The Post-Development Dictionary*: paths to the pluriverse' and the book project following in the footsteps of the original contribution of 1992. After criticising the shortcomings of a green economy/sustainable development approach, they outline two alternative worldviews differing from the anthropocentric and androcentric logic of capitalism (and also state socialism): *swaraj* (or radical ecological democracy) and degrowth. Ecological swaraj, emerging from Indian civil society, entails not only communal self-rule and self-reliance, but also a holistic vision of human well-being respecting the limits of the Earth and the rights of other species. Degrowth, an approach devised in the North, is seen by the authors as closely linked to the idea of sufficiency and an attempt to re-politicise environmentalism, calling for 'a downscaling of production and consumption in industrialised countries as a means to achieve environmental sustainability, social justice and well-being'.

Alberto Acosta's contribution 'Living well: ideas for reinventing the future' delves into another of the PD alternatives: the concept of *buen vivir*. Based in Andean and Amazonean indigenous traditions and experiences with capitalism and colonialism, buen vivir proposes a transformation towards biocentrism, recognising the rights of nature (instead of commodifying it) as well as a plurality of ways of living well within self-governed communities. Thus, it is not only about different ways of organising life, but equally about different ways of understanding the world – a new cosmovision. Yet although buen vivir has been incorporated into the constitutions of Ecuador and Bolivia, this has not prevented their governments from engaging in practices of extractivism and neo-developmentalism.

The first of the research papers, by Daniel Bendix, entitled 'Reflecting the Post-Development gaze: the degrowth debate in Germany', is, like its predecessors, also concerned with environmentalism and sustainability and a particular alternative concept. Focusing on the debate around *Postwachstum* in Germany, it shows that degrowth appears in conservative, liberal, sufficiency-oriented, anti-capitalist and ecofeminist variants, exhibiting significant differences. However, they all to some extent reflect the 'development gaze', perceiving the North as in need of transformation or even intervention. The debate thus furthers the PD agenda in that 'its focus on Western wealth creation re-centres the North as the problem for global economic, ecological and social transformation', but needs to question the myth of Northern supremacy by taking into account the coloniality–modernity–development nexus.

The next two articles turn away from the North and towards the South, but to a region curiously neglected in PD debates: Africa. The contribution by Stefan Andreasson, 'Fossil-fuelled development and the legacy of Post-Development theory in twenty-first century Africa', argues that in spite of PD's aspirations, economic growth, industrialisation and material affluence are still the guiding objectives of policy in Africa, and that thus the project of 'development' is by no means outdated or exhausted. This is exemplified in the energy sector where reliance on fossil fuels and desire for access to electricity, according to Andreasson, cast doubt on PD's hypotheses.

Sally Matthews' article, 'Colonised minds? Post-Development theory and the desirability of development in Africa', similarly is sceptical about PD on the grounds of an analysis which sees not Western-style modernisation (in terms of hospitals, housing, water, electricity, sanitation and education) but its absence as more linked to problems of poverty and political struggles in Africa. Problematising neo-populist PD's notion of the desire for 'development' being a manifestation of colonised minds, the author asks: 'What happens when Post-Development theorists' desire to celebrate "the otherness of the other" is confronted with "others" who insist on their sameness with "us" and assert their right to live as "we" do?' – assuming, of course, that 'we' do in fact enjoy the comforts of a privileged position in industrial modernity. Matthews thus proposes building on those aspects of PD theory which evade judging the objectives of political struggles by the marginalized, and recognises that the desire for 'development' is often tangled up with that for dignity.

Opposing PD from a different angle, Ilan Kapoor's 'Cold critique, faint passion, bleak future: Post-Development's surrender to global capitalism' engages in a psychoanalytical reading of the approach. It argues that PD fails to recognise that the power of development discourse, how it takes hold, expands and persists, cannot be explained without the unconscious emotions and desires of its subjects. According to Kapoor, this leaves PD with few resources beyond localised resistance to address the structural challenges of global capitalism, which, from the perspective of psychoanalysis, 'appears to manifest ... an unconscious acceptance of capitalism'.

Kalpana Wilson, in her article 'Worlds beyond the political? Post-Development approaches in practices of transnational solidarity activism', shows that the image of the noble savage persists in some of today's civil-society protests. She argues that this is linked to the tendency of neo-populist PD discourses to 'rearticulate racialised constructions of unspoiled and authentic "natives" requiring protection', and illustrates her claim with examples from a campaign to prevent bauxite mining in the Niyamgiri hills in Odisha (India). These constructions, according to her, silence local activists and their complex engagements with ideas of 'development', and depoliticise opposition to neoliberal policies.

Wendy Harcourt's contribution, 'The making and unmaking of development: using Post-Development as a tool in teaching development studies', shifts back from the critique to the application of the ideas of *The Development Dictionary*. The author reflects on her experiences in teaching post-graduate students in development studies in a manner consistent with PD, encouraging them to use their own experiences with 'development' as a basis instead of textbook knowledge. This experiment yielded strong positive and negative reactions among the author's students and colleagues at the Institute of Social Studies, showing, according to the author, 'how difficult it is to unsettle truths of mainstream development' and to create spaces of transgression even in progressive institutions at the interface of activism and academia.

The last contribution, '"I am not a Post-Developmentalist, but…" The influence of Post-Development on development studies', investigates the reception of PD in development studies textbooks. It concludes that these textbooks are often characterised by a mix of rejecting and integrating PD – by an explicit critique of its alleged failures and shortcomings, coupled with a (mostly implicit) reproduction of at least some of its core arguments. Therefore, the typical reaction to PD can be described by the sentence: 'I am not a Post-Developmentalist, but the discourse of development is Eurocentric, paternalist and imbued with relations of power'.

The variety of topics and plurality of positions illustrates that even within critical development studies there is no consensus regarding the patient 'development': is it alive and well, rotting away or already undead? What is clear is that the problems often referred to under the heading of 'underdevelopment' – misery and inequality, violence and hunger, to name but a few – have not disappeared, even after the MDGs have been declared more or less successful. Yet the displacement of 'development' from 'its centrality in representations and discussions about conditions in Asia, Africa and Latin America'[39] is well underway. This does not need to be reason for joy; it depends what becomes hegemonic in its stead. But I would like to think that this issue testifies to the critical and creative energy of academics and activists alike. May it not only be used for changing the discourse, but also for building and enriching the new commons *The Development Dictionary* envisioned.

Disclosure statement

No potential conflict of interest was reported by the author.

Funding

This work was supported by Deutsche Forschungsgemeinschaft [grant number ZI 759/8-2].

Notes

1. Sachs, *Development Dictionary*, 1992, 1.
2. Esteva, "Development," 6.
3. Gudynas, "Buen Vivir: Today's Tomorrow," 441.
4. Escobar, *Encountering Development*, 1995, 215.
5. See Ziai, Post-Development: Premature Burials.

6. Rahnema, "Towards Post-Development," 379.
7. Esteva, "Development: Metaphor, Myth, Threat," 79.
8. Esteva, "Development," 7.
9. Esteva, "Development," 17–9.
10. Sachs, *Planet Dialectics*, 7.
11. Sachs, *Development Dictionary*, 1992, 2–4.
12. Esteva, "Development," 21.
13. For a cautious attempt at a limited comparison, see Ziai, "Post-Development Concepts."
14. For an overview of the debate see Simon, "Separated by Common Ground"; Sidaway, "Spaces of Postdevelopment"; Ziai, *Exploring Post-Development*; McGregor, "New Possibilities"; Gudynas, "Postdevelopment and Other Critiques." For a general introduction to PD see Ziai, "Post-Development and Alternatives to Development."
15. Corbridge, "Beneath the Pavement Only Soil," 144f.
16. Kiely, "Last Refuge of the Noble Savage," 44; Storey, "Post-Development Theory," 42.
17. Knippenberg and Schuurman, "Blinded by Rainbows," 95; Nanda, "Who Needs Post-Development?," 11.
18. Knippenberg and Schuurman, "Blinded by Rainbows," 95; Cowen and Shenton, *Doctrines of Development*, 69ff.
19. Nederveen Pieterse, "My Paradigm or Yours," 366; Nederveen Pieterse, "After Post-Development," 182; Kiely, "Last Refuge of the Noble Savage," 45f.
20. Nederveen Pieterse, "My Paradigm or Yours," 363; Nederveen Pieterse, "After Post-Development," 180.
21. Ziai, "Ambivalence of Post-Development."
22. Cooper, "Modernizing Bureaucrats, Backward Africans," 84.
23. Rist, *History of Development*, 273; see also Sachs, *Development Dictionary*, 2010, vi, ix; Escobar, *Encountering Development*, 2012, vii.
24. Escobar, "Beyond the Search for a Paradigm," 12f.
25. Sachs, *Development Dictionary*, 2010, viii.
26. Rist, *History of Development*, 276.
27. For a longer version of the arguments in the first part of this section, see Ziai, *Contribution of Discourse Analysis*; and Ziai, *Development Discourse and Global History*.
28. Escobar, *Encountering Development*, 1995, 12, 39.
29. Escobar, *Encountering Development*, 1995, 41.
30. Sachs, "Archaeology of the Development Idea," 6; Escobar, *Encountering Development*, 58.
31. DuBois, "Governance of the Third World," 7.
32. Ferguson, *Anti-Politics Machine*, 256; Escobar, *Encountering Development*, 45.
33. Shiva, "Resources," 211.
34. Nederveen Pieterse, *Development Theory: Deconstructions/Reconstructions*, 214.
35. Ibid., 184.
36. Kothari and Minogue, *Development Theory and Practice*, 9f.
37. Nederveen Pieterse, *Development Theory: Deconstructions/Reconstructions*, 214.
38. Santos, *Epistemologies of the South*, 44.
39. Escobar, *Encountering Development*, 2012, xii.

Bibliography

Cooper, F. "Modernizing Bureaucrats, Backward Africans, and the Development Concept." In *International Development and the Social Sciences. Essays on the History and Politics of Knowledge*, edited by F. Cooper and R. Packard, 64–92. Berkeley and Los Angeles, CA: University of California Press, 1997.

Corbridge, S. "'Beneath the Pavement Only Soil': The Poverty of Post-Development." *Journal of Development Studies* 34, no. 6 (1998): 138–148.

Cowen, M. P., and R. W. Shenton. *Doctrines of Development*. London: Routledge, 1996.

DuBois, M. "The Governance of the Third World: A Foucauldian Perspective on Power Relations in Development." *Alternatives* 16, no. 1 (1991): 1–30.

Escobar, A. *Encountering Development. The Making and Unmaking of the Third World*. Princeton: Princeton University Press, 1995.

Escobar, A. "Beyond the Search for a Paradigm? Post-Development and beyond." *Development* 43 (2000): 11–14.

Escobar, A. *Encountering Development. The Making and Unmaking of the Third World*. 2nd ed. Princeton: Princeton University Press, 2012.

Esteva, G. "Development: Metaphor, Myth, Threat." *Development: Seeds of Change* 3 (1985): 78–79.

Esteva, G. "Development." In *The Development Dictionary. A Guide to Knowledge as Power*, edited by Wolfgang Sachs, 6–25. London: Zed Books, 1992.

Ferguson, J. *The Anti-Politics Machine. 'Development', Depoliticization and Bureaucratic Power in Lesotho*. Minneapolis, MN: University of Minnesota Press, 1994.

Gudynas, E. "Buen Vivir: Today's Tomorrow." *Development* 54, no. 4 (2011): 441–447.

Gudynas, E. "Postdevelopment and Other Critiques of the Roots of Development." In *The Essential Guide to Critical Development Studies*, edited by Henry Veltmeyer and Paul Bowles, London: Routledge, forthcoming.

Kiely, R. "The Last Refuge of the Noble Savage? A Critical Assessment of Post-Development Theory." *The European Journal of Development Research* 11, no. 1 (1999): 30–55.

Knippenberg, L., and F. Schuurmann. "Blinded by Rainbows: Anti-Modernist and Modernist Deconstructions of Development." In *Current Issues in Development Studies. Global Aspects of Agency and Structure*, Nimegen Studies in Development and Social Change, 21 vols, edited by F. Schuurman, 90–106. Saarbruecken: Verlag fuer Entwicklungspolitik Breitenbach, 1994.

Kothari, U., and M. Minogue, eds. *Development Theory and Practice. Critical Perspectives*. Houndmills: Palgrave, 2002.

McGregor, A. "New Possibilities? Shifts in Post-Development Theory and Practice." *Geography Compass* 3, no. 5 (2009): 1688–1702.

Nanda, M. "Who Needs Post-Development? Discourses of Difference, Green Revolution and Agrarian Populism in India." *Journal of Developing Societies* 15 (1999): 5–31.

Nederveen Pieterse, J. "My Paradigm or Yours? Alternative Development, Post-Development, Reflexive Development." *Development and Change* 29 (1998): 343–373.

Nederveen Pieterse, J. "After Post-Development." *Third World Quarterly* 20, no. 1 (2000): 175–191.

Nederveen Pieterse, J. *Development Theory: Deconstructions/Reconstructions*. 2nd ed. London: Sage, 2010.

Rahnema, M. "Towards Post-Development: Searching for Signposts, a New Language and New Paradigms." In *The Post-Development Reader*, edited by Majid Rahnema with Victoria Bawtree, 377–403. London: Zed Books, 1997.

Rist, G. *The History of Development. From Western Origins to Global Faith*. 4th ed. London: Zed Books, 2012.

Sachs, W. "The Archaeology of the Development Idea." *Interculture* 23, no. 4 (1990): 1–37.

Sachs, W., ed. *The Development Dictionary. A Guide to Knowledge as Power*, London: Zed Books, 1992.

Sachs, W. *Planet Dialectics. Explorations in Environment and Development*. London: Zed Books, 1999.

Sachs, W. ed. *The Development Dictionary. A Guide to Knowledge as Power*, 2nd ed. London: Zed Books, 2010.

Santos, B. d. S. *Epistemologies of the South. Justice against Epistemicide*. Boulder: Paradigm Publishers, 2014.

Shiva, V. "Resources." In *The Development Dictionary. A Guide to Knowledge as Power*, edited by Wolfgang Sachs, 206–218. London: Zed Books, 1992.

Sidaway, J. D. "Spaces of Postdevelopment." *Progress in Human Geography* 31, no. 3 (2007): 345–361.

Simon, D. "Separated by Common Ground? Bringing (Post)Development and (Post)Colonialism Together." *The Geographical Journal* 172, no. 1 (2006): 10–21.

Storey, A. "Post-Development Theory: Romanticism and Pontius Pilate Politics." *Development* 43, no. 4 (2000): 40–46.

Ziai, A. "The Ambivalence of Post-Development: Between Reactionary Populism and Radical Democracy." *Third World Quarterly* 25, no. 6 (2004): 1045–1060.

Ziai, A., ed. *Exploring Post-Development. Theory and Practice, Problems and Perspectives*. London: Routledge, 2007.

Ziai, A. "Post-Development: Premature Burials and Haunting Ghosts." *Development and Change* 46, no. 4 (2015): 833–854.

Ziai, A. *The Contribution of Discourse Analysis to Development Studies.* Working Paper No. 1. University of Kassel, Development and Postcolonial Studies, 2015.

Ziai, A. "Post-Development Concepts? Buen Vivir, Ubuntu and Degrowth." In *Epistemologies of the South: South–South, South–North and North–South Global Learnings. Other Economies*, edited by Boaventura de Sousa Santos and Theresa Cunha, 143–154. Coimbra: CES, 2015.

Ziai, A. *Development Discourse and Global History. from Colonialism to the Sustainable Development Goals.* London: Routledge, 2016.

Ziai, A. "Post-Development and Alternatives to Development." In *Introduction to International Development: Approaches, Actors, and Issues.* 3rd ed, edited by Paul Haslam, Jessica Schafer, and Pierre Beaudet, 65–83. Oxford: Oxford University Press, 2016.

Post-Development @ 25: on 'being stuck' and moving forward, sideways, backward and otherwise

Gustavo Esteva and Arturo Escobar

ABSTRACT
Escobar and Esteva engage in a retrospective conversation on Post-Development, reassessing the critiques and discussing openly the meaning of 'living beyond development' today. Some of the topics covered include: how the development discourse has shaped mentalities and practices; the tensions and contradictions in the institutional world, trapped in their compulsion for development in the face of the multiple crisis plaguing the world; the new manifestations of the resistance to development; and the relevant experiences that anticipate the new worlds beyond development and patriarchal capitalist modernity and towards the pluriverse.

Arturo

It's been almost 30 years since that memorable week of September 1988, when we sat around the convivial table at Ivan Illich's house on Foster Avenue in University Park (where Penn State University is located), summoned by Wolfgang Sachs and Ivan. Out of the intense and enjoyable discussions of those days there emerged the task of writing our respective chapters for what a few years later would emerge as *The Development Dictionary*. The book made a 'splash' of sorts when it made its debut in print. For some, the splash has been enduring and one of the most essential elements behind what came to be known as the Post-Development school. Other, less generous, retrospective analyses of the *Dictionary* (and Post-Development) argue that it was interesting but ineffective and that, in any way, it is superseded by now since development has certainly not died, as the *Dictionary* appeared to prognosticate. Many mainstream scholars and development practitioners, harsher in their appraisal, consider it to have been a terribly misguided endeavour and a disservice to the poor.

Aram Ziai's invitation comes at an auspicious time to take stock of what has gone 'under the bridge' of the *Dictionary* and Post-Development waters in the intervening years, and to renew our understanding and critique. You were not only one of the pioneers of the critique but your position regarding development has, if anything, become even more radical than in 1992 – at least that's how I read your most recent texts on the subject.[1] To remain for now on a historical register, I would like to ask you, to start this conversation: How do you see now the intellectual-political ferment of those early days, when the radical problematisation of development was first launched, as compared with the conditions that exist today for radical critiques? Is there something you think that our group could have done differently? Where do you hear echoes from those conversations in current debates?

Gustavo

'Development' is no longer an unquestionable category. At the grassroots, I have seen in recent years open resistance and opposition to development itself, not only to certain forms of development – and some have a long history. Such opposition is now fully incorporated in people's discourses, something they did not dare to do before. In my contribution to the *Dictionary*, I celebrated the emergence of new commons, which I saw as an alternative to development. *The Ecologist* described such emergence that very year. And the commons movement is today in full swing, everywhere, in what we can legitimately call a post-economic society, not only beyond development.

Salvatore Babones' classification of the current development panorama is very effective. He associates it with three Sachses.[2]

The 'Goldman Sachs' approach expresses a pretty general consensus that dominates in governments and international institutions. It defines development through their commodities trading desks, their infrastructure projects and their exploration units. It means an oil platform located 10 km offshore, safe from harassment by local indigenous militants.

The 'Jeffrey Sachs' approach blindly believes in development and capitalism but is concerned with massive hunger and misery, which they see not as consequences but as insufficiencies of both. Well-meaning people like Sachs, Gates and major US and European NGOs focus on the alleviation of obvious suffering – they stand for a chicken in every pot, a mosquito net over every bed and a condom on every penis.

The 'Wolfgang Sachs' approach circulates in critical development studies circles and departments and among indigenous leaders, independent intellectuals and a motley group of people basically ignored by academia and the 1%. In my view, this approach corresponds today to the awareness and experience, not necessarily the discourse, of millions, perhaps billions, of ordinary men and women around the world who are increasingly 'beyond' development.

The adventure of the *Dictionary* started for me a few months before that meeting in Foster Avenue. Ivan invited us to his house in Ocotepec, Cuernavaca, Mexico, to talk about 'After development, what?' Majid Rahnema, Jean Robert and Wolfgang were there. One of the things that I remember very well of that meeting was that we abandoned the expression 'after development', with an implicit periodisation that Wolfgang retained. We knew that the developers were still around and would continue their devastating enterprise. We wanted to explore how *to be* beyond development.

As you know, I am not a scholar. I read a lot, but my ideas, my words, my vocabulary, my inspiration, come from my experience at the grassroots, in my world of *campesinos*, *indios* and urban marginals. Ivan knew that. At one point in the conversation, he asked me: 'Gustavo, if you had only one word to express what is to be beyond development, which is the word you will use?' My immediate answer was 'hospitality'. Development is radically inhospitable: it imposes a universal definition of the good life and excludes all others. We need to hospitably embrace the thousand different ways of thinking, being, living and experiencing the world that characterise reality.

This was not an occurrence: it came from my experience. In the early 1980s those classified as 'underdeveloped' were frustrated and enraged with always being at the end of the line. We knew by then that 'development' as the universalisation of the American Way of Life was impossible; that we would not catch-up with the developed, as Truman promised; that we would be permanently left behind. For many of us such awareness became a revelation; we still had our own notions of what is to live well and they were feasible. Instead of continuing the foolish race to nowhere, we should reorient our effort. In my experience, it was not dissident vanguards attempting development 'alternatives' or alternatives to development, but many grassroots groups reaffirming themselves in their own path, in many cases for sheer survival in the dramatic 1980s, what was later called 'the lost decade' in Latin America. For me, they were already beyond development.

I bought into underdevelopment when I was 13 years old. That implied that I fully assumed my 'lacks': I wanted development for me, for my family and for my country, in order to satisfy all the 'needs' suddenly created. Let me clarify this. When I was a child the word 'need' had only one practical application: shitting. It was used when my mother told us: 'Once you arrive at your uncle's house, ask him where you can make your needs'. We *made* the 'needs'; we did not *have* them. This way of talking applied to everything: our 'needs' were defined by our own capacity, our tools and the way we used them, and were strictly personal, imponderable and incommensurable. It was in the course of my lifetime that all current 'needs' were created and we were transmogrified into needy, measured and controlled people. Professionals defined the needs and we were classified according to them.

When I was a child, people were talking to me. Words were symbols, not representations or categories, and only one of every 10 of them addressed me as an undifferentiated member of a crowd. As I grew, words became categories and I was addressed as a member of a class of people: children, skinny, underdeveloped … according to our 'needs': education, nutrition, development.

As you know very well, in the early 1970s, the recognition that the development enterprise was causing hunger and misery everywhere produced the Basic Needs Approach. The goal became to satisfy a package of 'basic needs'. There was no consensus about the definition of those needs, but such orientation still characterises most development efforts … and shaped the UN Millennium Goals and the Sustainable Development Goals (SDGs) today.

In 1976, I was in the immediate danger of becoming a minister in the new administration of the Mexican government, after my success as a high officer for more than 10 years in conceiving and implementing great development programmes. I quit. I started to work autonomously with people at the grassroots. By then I knew that instead of 'development' the people looked for autonomy, as expressed in the name of an independent organisation I created with some friends (*Autonomía, Descentralismo y Gestión*). I also knew that the 'State' was a mechanism for control and domination, useless for emancipation. After observing the damages done by professionals, as the transmission belts for the creation of 'needs' and dependence, I began the complex process of deprofessionalising myself.

In the early 1980s, there was increasing awareness of the failures of the development enterprise and the foolishness of adopting a universal definition of the good life. The idea of Post-Development started to circulate: people were reclaiming their own, feasible, ways of living well. In the 1985 conference of the Society for International Development in Rome, invited by Wolfgang to discuss the future of development studies, I suggested it lay in archaeology: only an archaeological eye could explore the ruins left by development. I was seeing development in my past, not in my present and even less in my future. I was exploring those ruins in my own world and already looking for hospitality for our ways of being … the ways captured in the expression *buen vivir* now coming from your area of the world.

A few years ago, when Salvatore Babones approached me with a proposal to write a book about development, he observed that 'we' in the Post-Development School don't use statistics. He was right; we hate them. Salvatore is a quantitative sociologist, well acquainted with development statistics. He wanted to incorporate them to our analysis. He also observed that people studying development are often concerned with the real problems of the world, interested in making a difference. But we closed the door on them by proclaiming a firm 'No' to development. Can we open a decent door to them? He was right. And he appeared at a time when I was adopting, with many others, the position of 'One No and Many Yeses', following the Zapatista suggestion to create a world in which many worlds can be embraced. Yes, I agreed, we can share a common 'No' to development but be open to a thousand 'Yeses': the many paths people are following around the world beyond development; people studying development can accompany and support them. That is why we wrote and published *The Future of Development: A Radical Manifesto*.

Arturo

There are so many interesting dimensions to your answer, Gustavo. I would like to explore a few, and perhaps provide a counterpoint on some of them (as in the musical counterpoint, where a theme is developed in various directions). But first there is something I remembered as I read your comment on 'needs', something I heard Ivan saying once, I am not sure whether it was at Penn State or perhaps at Berkeley in the early 1980s when he came to do his, then, controversial lectures on *Gender*. *Homo faber*, he said, had given way to *homo miserabilis* (the 'man of needs') which eventually gave rise to *homo oeconomicus*. The history of needs was one of Ivan's long-term interests, and it still has to be worked on, for instance, in today's digital age and given the expansion of middle classes in many world regions, for whom 'needs' have seemingly skyrocketed. How do we treat needs 'postdevelopmentally'?

Here I arrive at my first substantive question. It is a question often asked of me, so I thought we ought to give it our best answer. I think it is a significant obstacle in getting many people to embrace the thinking of Post-Development. And it is: You speak about the grassroots as the space par excellence to explore how *to be* beyond development. In doing so, are we not romanticising the grassroots (in your case) or ethnic communities and social movements (in mine)? Are they not also, now and increasingly, the subject of needs and desires, including those that 'development' and capitalist modernity promise and eventually delivers (though in limited ways; cheap cell phones, more consumer goods, second-rate overcrowded schools and health services)? Let me give you my answer to this issue, and then I would like to hear yours. The first part of my answer is a simple reversal: faced with the social and ecological devastation brought about by patriarchal capitalist modernity, coupled with the fact that things are not getting better (skyrocketing inequality, climate change), isn't it more romantic to think that 'more of the same', in whatever guise (new World Bank recipes, green economy, SDGs or the new 'Green Revolution for Africa' advocated by J. Sachs), is going to lead to lasting improvement? In this context, more genuinely realist and less romantic are the alternatives emerging at the grassroots and with social movements. I would rather bet on them than on the world bankers and mainstream NGOs.

This links up with the historical dimension of my reply to the 'romanticism' charge. I was remembering Walter Benjamin's injunction: 'To articulate the past historically … means to seize it as it flashes up at a moment of danger'. He associates this moment with 'the politicians' stubborn faith in progress'.[3] Are we not going through one of these moments again, with technology promising humans anything they wish, from unlimited information and imme-diate communication to eternal life, a 'life beyond biology'? At the same time, we are, as Boaventura de Sousa Santos puts it, at a juncture where we are facing modern problems for which there are no longer modern solutions. And yet the slogan of the moment seems to be: 'Everything for the corporations! Everything for the super-rich!' What is the danger, then? That of an even more profound ontological occupation of people's territories and lives. Land grabbing and extractivism are the ugliest heads of it, but they also include growing con-sumerism and individualism. It is not romantic, in my mind, to be on the side of those who oppose these tendencies, especially when Earth itself is 'on our side', considering the warn-ings she is giving as we wound her ever more deeply and extensively.

Finally, on the theoretical side, I am pondering the question of how to understand 'really existing communities' without falling into the trap of endorsing or re-enacting modernist traps. Here I find the recent debates on autonomy and the communities (or 'communalitarian' as you would say) that have emerged in Chiapas, Oaxaca and the Norte del Cauca in Colombia's southwest new and hopeful. Both of us have written about this recently (though largely in Spanish).[4] Here we might also locate the intense South American debates on *buen vivir* of the last decade. This is not the place to even try to summarise these currents of thought and action. But I'd like to refer, however briefly, to recent works that conceptualise communities in all of their entanglement with global forms of capital and modern technology without reducing them to the terms of capitalism or modernity. I am referring to the recent work by Silvia Rivera Cusicanqui and Veronica Gago.[5] As they show, communities are also the site of intense forms of capitalist exploitation, patriarchal domination and consumerism. They are significantly affected by globalisation and yet they are not completely determined by it. Rivera Cusicanqui points at this feature of many of today's indigenous and popular communities by referring to their capacity to define their own forms of modernity, more convivial than the dominant ones precisely because they also find nourishment in their own histories, intricately weaving indigenous and local practices with those which are not and resulting in worlds made up of different cultural strands without nevertheless fusing into one. They find sustenance in the complementarities among diverse worlds without over-looking the antagonisms, articulating with market economies while anchored in indigenous knowledge and technologies. 'There is no "post" nor "pre" in this vision of history which is not linear nor teleological but rather moves in spirals and cycles, that always traces a path but never fails to return to the same point. *The indigenous world does not conceive of history as linear; the past-future are contained in the present*', she says (emphasis added).[6]

I would say that social groups in struggle, at their best, move in several directions at once: adding to and strengthening their long-standing practices, while engaging selectively and effectively with the 'modern world' and its practices and technologies. This ability is crucial for deepening the autonomous and communalitarian foundations of social life. I suspect you'll have much to add in this regard.

The second aspect of your reply that caught my attention was the idea of 'opening a door' to those genuinely concerned with the world's problems. You go on to state that what you mean is one No to 'development' and many Yeses to 'the many paths people are following around the world beyond development; people studying development can accompany and support them'. Are you here suggesting opening a door to those working with progressive development organisations? Could you please clarify? I want to offer a reflection that came to mind recently as I was responding to an interview on 'development cooperation' in Barcelona. I came up with three paths for thinking about cooperation as follows: (1) *Cooperation as development aid*: this is the standard form of cooperation, practiced by institution such as US AID, the World Bank and mainstream NGOs. It takes for granted the dominant world (in terms of markets, individual actions, productivity, etc.). Cooperation under this rubric might lead to some improvements for some people but it can only reinforce colonialist understandings of development and, so, dispossession. To this I'd say: let's keep the doors tightly closed on them; (2) *cooperation as, or for, social justice*: this is the kind of cooperation practiced with the intention of fostering greater social justice and environmental sustainability; it embraces human rights (including gender and ethnic diversity), environmental justice, the reduction of inequality, direct support for grassroots groups, and so forth. Oxfam might serve as paradigm for this second trajectory. In this case I'd say: let's keep the door open, while applying pressure on them to move towards the third trajectory; (3) could go under several names, such as *cooperation for civilizational transitions* or *cooperation for autonomy*. Those practicing this option would be, in my view, radical Post-Development's natural allies. What is interesting is that this form would go beyond the binary of 'us' (who have) and 'them' (who need), and embrace all sides in the same, though diverse, movement for civilizational transitions and inter-autonomy, that is, coalitions and meshworks of autonomous collectives and communities from both the Global North and the Global South. There are no ready-available models for this third kind of solidarity cooperation, but there are groups here and there that approach it (like a few I know in Catalunya).

Do you see any value in this distinction? Is it helpful to raise the question of 'allies' for the project of moving beyond development?

Gustavo

My hope, Arturo, is that some readers may enjoy our conversation as much as I am enjoying it!

You are right, of course: we still have a lot of work to do about 'needs'. A good starting point is the chapter on 'Needs' by Ivan Illich for the *Dictionary*. He clarifies how, for thousands of years, 'human' implied communal submission to the rule of necessity in a particular place and time. He explains the transition to prescribed universal needs, to the needy addict, and tells the story of *homo miserabilis*.

We must remember that in classical political economy, for Malthus, Ricardo or Marx, a vague 'standard of living' alluded to an acceptable subsistence income, the cost of the reproduction of labour force. That notion, however, was transmogrified into a *desired* form of living presented as a condition to reach, and finally a normalised definition of a *necessary* standard defined by basic needs. In that process, the idea of the good became a quantity. The very different ways of the art of living vanished and were substituted by standards that homogenised individual searches. Serge Latouche, also in the *Dictionary*, urges us to view with scepticism this fetishistic object 'standard of living', and to rediscover the multidimensionality of life.

To discuss 'needs' today requires acknowledging that more than ever they are created through dispossession, in the classical tradition of the enclosure of the commons that marked the beginning of capitalism. The commoners, dispossessed of their means of subsistence, became people in need of jobs, shelter, food, everything. As Illich explained in the *Dictionary*, development changed the human condition by transmogrifying necessities and desires into prescribed 'needs'. For the dominant mind it is difficult to understand that the commoners, before the enclosures, were eating, learning, healing, settling ... within the limits imposed by nature and their culture to their desires and necessities.

We should also explore questions like those examined by Agnes Heller in her critical analysis of the notion of 'needs' in Marx. What she and others observed in the Soviet Union as the dictatorship of needs[7] can be applied today to the functioning of contemporary societies, through other means, like compulsory schooling, marginalisation of alternative ways of healing, repression of the art of dwelling, elimination of self-mobility in a world organised to create dependency of the automobile and other vehicles, and so forth.

In exploring what grassroots people are doing we must carefully draw a line between market and State imposed needs and people's own uses of technology. Around the year 2000, more than half of people on Earth had never made a phone call. Even when phone booths came to their villages, many people never used them because they did not have anybody to call: their family and friends had no phones. Today the situation is entirely different. Even the poorest people have access to a cellular phone and use them intensely. Yes, as we all know, many young people are now pathologically plugged into this technology and alienated from their communities. But there are people of all ages that are effectively using it for their own purposes in their own way. In a conversation with David Cayley, Ivan Illich observed that the change he anticipated took finally the form of millions of people 'misusing' or tweaking for their own purposes the failing counterproductive institutions as well as the market.[8]

Of course, we must resist any romanticisation of the people at the grassroots. 'Don't idealise us', insists the Zapatista Subcomandante Moisés all the time. All kinds of horrors happen at the grassroots. If women are taking the lead in many communities, in a very radical post-patriarchal attitude, it is because for them the combination of traditional patriarchy and modern sexism has become a kind of hell.

At the same time, we must acknowledge that these communities, particularly the Indigenous communities, are today a source of inspiration for all of us. They have been struggling for centuries with the predicaments we are facing today; they have the experience. They know well how to deal with 'modernity'. Many of them successfully resisted modernisation and were able to protect their own traditional ways. We need to seriously explore the hypothesis that we will not have modern solutions to modern problems ... because modernity itself already collapsed. We are in the transition to another era (which is not postmodernism), with the uncertainty created by the fact that old rationalities and sensibilities are obsolete and the new ones are not yet clearly identified. Using the experience of similar periods in the past, we must turn to the artists – which often smell the new era and produce their creations not with the old logic but with new insights.

THE DEVELOPMENT DICTIONARY @25

The communities were never isolated; this was an invention of British anthropology. We can find all the global forces affecting and infecting the communities and *barrios* everywhere. But what we also observe is the creative construction of a contemporary art of living. The Zapatistas are amazingly autonomous and self-sufficient. They don't get any funds from the government. They don't need the market or the state to live their lives. If a total siege were suddenly imposed on them, their way of life will basically remain the same. But they have X-rays and ultrasound equipment in their health clinics and they buy in the market equipment for their community radios, mobile phones, computers, bikes, vehicles and so on, but they know how to use those technologies instead of being used by them.

An increasing number of people are resisting old and new enclosures, thus preventing the creation of new needs. Yes, they are exposed to all kind of pressures and many times surrender to old or new dependencies. But what I am increasingly observing at the grassroots is how people dismantle the 'need' for state apparatuses or the goods and services offered by the market. Many people are producing their own food (small farmers, mainly women, feed 70% of the people on Earth); learning in freedom (beyond the school system, escaping from education); 'healing from health' (trusting again their own healers and their own notions and traditions of how to be sane or heal … with a little help from modern technologies); recovering the art of dwelling (building by themselves their houses and buildings), and so forth. This is, in my view, to live beyond development. It is not going back to the Stone Age, but saying no, for sheer survival or in the name of old ideals, to a tragic path destroying Mother Earth, dissolving the social fabric and dooming millions to hunger, misery and homelessness … even in prosperous societies like the US.

Silvia is right, of course. If you live among Indigenous people, sometimes you don't know if what they are talking about is happening now, happened yesterday or a thousand years ago or will happen tomorrow. Time is not real for them. They pack into the present as much past and future as they can. They live in cycles, natural and social cycles, and the image of the spiral of the Zapatista *caracoles* may represent changes in which they come back to the same place but at a different level.

I agree with all your reflections on aid and cooperation. In 1994 and 1995 there was a flow of people and goods coming to help the Zapatistas. At one point, the famous subcomandante Marcos produced a communiqué in which he stated that he was now forced to carry in his backpack a red high heel, just to remember what was happening. In one of the many boxes with charity for the communities came that red high heel, just one, not the pair, for the jungle. It was for him a symbol of what was happening. 'If you want to offer help to these poor Indians, struggling against a bad government, thanks … but no thanks. We don't want or need your help. However, if you think that our struggle is also your struggle, please come. There are plenty of things we need to talk about … and to do together'. Yes, we need more than ever alliances and coalitions. There are many things that we can do together with people that want to make a difference in this tragic world in which we all live today, people that also want to resist the horror, the destruction of Mother Earth and culture and social fabric and hunger and misery. We can join forces with them.

After the US election on 8 November 2016, it seems evident that very diverse groups in the US should join forces and find new forms of articulation. Instead of issue struggles –for the environment in the face of climate change, against racism or racist police violence, against all forms of *machismo* and sexual discrimination, against chronic debt, unemployment or homelessness – what is needed is to struggle together: to resist the horror – to resist specific measures, policies, decisions, behaviour, offensive language; to construct a better society, more humane and sensible. This is the time to come together, to hold each other tight, both inside every country and between people of different countries.

I don't see a lot of conventional developers around me these days. Public developers no longer have large enough budgets. Private developers are increasingly concentrated on grabbing and dispossession, not really on development. The rich are accumulating more money than ever, but that money is not transformed into capitalist social relations, into hiring workers. Many of us are increasingly becoming, as the Zapatistas warned, disposable human beings. What we are calling *extractivismo* in Latin America (mining, urban, financial *extractivismo* but also labour and services *extractivismo*) cannot be described as development … with any notion of that concept of monumental emptiness, as Wolfgang used to say.

The long agony of development as a myth and as an enterprise is clearly ending. Do we really think that the 'American dream' is intact? That the American Way of Life is still the universal definition of the good life?

In my view, development is no longer a myth, a taboo, a promise or a threat. It is an obsession, an addiction, a pathological mania that some people suffer, in their minds, their emotions or their behaviour … and also a tool of domination and control. I don't see people mobilised to get development in all its masks and shapes as they were in the past. Of course, we still have capitalism. But can we really call capitalism this society in which we have many zombies – capitalist enterprises blaming anyone for falling profits, whether the banks, the state, immigrants, or what have you – controlled and mined by a group, a very small group, of vampires, sucking from them and from all of us the blood of profit, income, goods, everything? As everybody knows, the vampires are not only devastating the planet to the point of endangering the survival of the human species. They are also killing the goose of the golden eggs … by accumulating through extraction and speculation, instead of production; by reducing both salaries and employment and exhausting resources, thus preventing or limiting the reproduction of the very system in which they thrive.

We are no longer in the time of TINA (There Is No Alternative). There are now thousands of alternatives and a new one emerges every day; many of them, perhaps most of them, are alternatives to development or express conditions beyond development, in spite of the ominous March of vampires and do-gooders in governments, international institutions, NGOs and academia still threatening or harassing the social majorities and the planet itself.

Arturo

Your answers pose many challenges, Gustavo. I shall take two of them only, for the sake of space: the idea that modernity has already collapsed, and what you so insightfully refer to as 'the creative construction of a contemporary art of living' by many communities resisting capitalism and development. They are inter-related, and there is a reason why I want to take on the question of modernity here, and this is the angst that the 'death of modernity' causes among so many friends and potential allies, particularly otherwise critical academics in both the North and the South.

I have found the following paraphrase to be true: that it is easier to imagine the end of the world than the end of modernity. I would like to attempt two displacements of modernity's centrism, starting with Ashis Nandy's telling reversal that the pathologies of science-driven modernity have already proven to be more lethal than the pathologies of tradition.[9] And yet we seem utterly unwilling to consider the creative retrieval of traditions' history making potentiality, a task that Nandy's 'critical traditionalism' embraces. Beyond a handful of philosophical treatises, critical academics rarely entertain seriously the end of modernity; most scholars react disdainfully against such proposition, disqualifying it as utopian or even reactionary. It is, however, implicit (though rarely stated out loudly) in most discourses that speak of the need for civilizational transitions. The revered Buddhist teacher Thich Nhat Hanh has spoken openly about it in his critique of consumerism (he could well be referring to development as addiction): '[T]this civilization of ours will have to end one day. But we have a huge role to play in determining when it ends and how quickly … Global warming may be an early symptom of that death'.[10] He goes further, inviting us to actively accept the end of our civilization by meditating on this thought: 'Breathing in, I know that this civilization is going to die. Breathing out, this civilization cannot escape dying'.[11] He is calling us to move beyond a civilization that has become antithetical to the ontology and ethics of interexistence.[12]

For us, moderns (I include myself here) actively facing the ontological challenges posed by the idea of the end of modernity – of a world significantly different than the current one – is not easy; it induces a type of fright that is deeply unsettling. How do we articulate this civilizational anxiety in effective ways? After all, most other worlds have had to exist (still do) with the fright and, not infrequently, the reality of their vanishing.

I have found two responses among European and Latin American academic friends: first, that what they perceive as a condemnation of modernity is not fair because the West itself is plural, inhabited by dissenting voices and plural modernities. This is an important corrective to the tendency, in our critiques, to homogenise the West/modern. We need to acknowledge the many non-dominant, peripheral and alternative forms of modernity, the non-dominant Wests that exist within the West. At the same time – I say to these colleagues – we need to do it decolonially and post-developmentally, in other words, without disavowing the privileges accorded to all things European (especially white European), and without reinforcing Western modernity as the de facto (naturalised) site of reason, progress, civility and so forth in contrast to the alleged barbarism or unviability of other worlds. And, in my view, the best way to do so is to see clearly how we are all in this together, that is, that the Liberation of Mother Earth (as the indigenous *Nasa* people of Colombia put it) and the defence of the pluriverse ('a world where many worlds can be embraced', in the Zapatista dictum) is a project we should all embrace, from wherever we are, whether in the Lacandon forest or in the heart of Europe or Cali or Mexico City.

Our critique is in not really 'anti-European' or 'anti-West', but in pro of the Liberation of Modern Earth and the pluriverse, and the Earth and the pluriverse are all of us, not just 'indigenous peoples'. These concepts have not been created by indigenous and ethnic movements just for them, but for all. They apply to all. It is incumbent upon those of us 'in the belly of the beast' who would like to defend those other non-dominant modernities to set into motion *effectively* their differences with the dominant West, thus joining forces with those opposing the assemblages of patriarchal, Eurocentric and racist capitalist modernity from the peripheries of the Global South, those struggling daily to construct territories for re-existence in mutually enriching ways with the Planet. This is the meaning, for me, of inhabiting ethically and politically the civilizational crossroads in which we are enmeshed at present. And this means that we all need to make serious efforts at *vivir entre mundos*, to live in-between, with and from multiple worlds, as we attempt the re-communalisation of our daily existence.

Said differently, we need to resist endowing 'modernity' with the ability to fully and naturally occupy the entire field of the social, making invisible or secondary other ways of instituting it, including what has been called 'traditions'. This brings me to the second aspect of your answer I want to comment on, that of constructing other forms of re-existence. This would include the question of how we might cultivate ourselves as subjects who desire non-capitalist, non-liberal and non-modern forms of life – more autonomous, convivial and communal. In the field of transition visions and narratives, re-localisation (of food, energy, transportation, health, etc.) and the re-communalisation of social life (reconnecting with other humans and non-humans, including the spiritual worlds) are emerging as two principal criteria for moving in this direction; these are the sine qua non conditions for living beyond development. *Autonomía* is the name given by Latin American grassroots struggles to this attempt at creating conditions for re-existence and a thoroughly contemporary art of living. Again, this concept is not just for those in the peripheries, but for all. How do we think about autonomous living and communities everywhere, and perhaps particularly in the densest and most consumption-oriented liberal worlds, namely, those of today's middle classes worldwide? This is one of today's greatest challenges, and debates on degrowth and Post-Development have lots to contribute to making it tangible and realisable.

Gustavo

The end of modernity, in my view, comes first in the form of dis-illusionement, as Wolfgang Dietrich brilliantly describes in his *Call for Many Peaces*.[13] Modern people increasingly doubt the universal truth of the modern paradigm – a societal project characterised by Newtonian physics, Cartesian reductionism, the nation-state of Thomas Hobbes and the capitalist world system. This doubting comes from everyday experience. The subsequent scholarly reflection has not been very productive. As a consequence, we have confusion, a loss of values and orientation, or the insight of a pluriverse: instead of dissolving plurality, the idea is to celebrate it, to demand respect for and coexistence with difference, as expressed in the Zapatista dictum you already mentioned: a world in which many worlds can be embraced.

Many academics and universities are already engaged in the search for a new unitary system of reference, as a substitute for the exhausted modern paradigm. But such a search is becoming something like the old definition of metaphysics: the search in a dark room for a black cat that does not exist. As Einstein observed, we cannot find a solution for a problem within the frame that created it. Some of us are beginning to believe that the new paradigm already exists, not in academic rooms but in reality – in the form of an alternative practice that is in itself a theory. The Zapatistas are the best example, but many groups are engaged in the same path. It is not the impossible attempt of going back in history or of discarding everything that modernity has brought about. It is the autonomous construction of a contemporary art of living. Instead of cutting a head off the capitalist hydra, only to see how it regenerates other heads, people are drying up the soil on which the hydra can grow, that is, escaping from the habit of 'needs' and thus dissolving their dependence on the market and the State.

That is the very nature of autonomy for many in Latin America. And this is the attitude, by the way, that the so-called 'progressive governments' in Latin America don't want to understand.

Indigenous peoples have a long experience in dealing with modernity and they are a source of inspiration for those imagining its end. I see again a very creative alliance with those inside modern thinking looking for alternatives. Foucault, for example, talked repeatedly about the insurrection of the great diversity of subjugated knowledges, when erudite knowledge is juxtaposed with empirical knowledge to generate historical knowledges of struggle. Similarly, the commons movement is today everywhere, not only in the so-called Global South. Everywhere, people exposed to hyper-individualism, consumerism, exploitation and climate change seem to have had enough. They are rescuing old terms to give them new meanings to name their contemporary social constructions – even if often in contradictory ways – which in my view are clearly beyond development … and the conventional, modern, capitalist paradigms.

A recent UN report, prepared for the Quito Conference Habitat III in October 2016, called *Urbanisation and Development: Emerging Futures,* has some pertinent gems, buried in the mass of bureaucratic jargon. It mentions the failure of urban policies that can be translated as the failure of development policies – entirely visible and of devastating consequences. For the report, prosperity was described as a tide rising all vessels and boats … but it is clear now that it raises only the yachts. I can adopt without reservation that kind of obituary for development. I don't think we said in the *Dictionary* (nor today) that developers are dead; they continue their destructive enterprise. What is dead is its promise. We can no longer argue seriously that development may bring justice, sustainability, dignity or a good life, or that eliminates hunger and misery; that it is a tide raising all vessels.

Of course, we must continue exploring the conditions that shaped the desire to be led and to have others legislate life, which generates a herd instinct, massively displayed in the 1930s and still at work today. Foucault made these observations 50 years ago, in his preface of the *Anti-Oedipus* of Deleuze and Guattari.[14] They are today more pertinent and urgent than ever, given the increasingly destructive ethos of the dominant economic and political system we now suffer. We need to resist the current horror, and the best way to resist is to construct a new society, in the many shapes it will take in our pluralist world.

Arturo

Unfortunately, Gustavo, we must bring this conversation to an end … for now. To conclude, could you summarise succinctly how your views on development have changed over the past 25 years?

Gustavo

Have I changed my views about 'development' in the last 25 years? Yes, and no.

Today, I am insisting in my call to public debate and action to stop the current madness still packaged as 'development' or 'progress'. Today, like 25 years ago, I denounce the cynicism of those still promoting 'development', even when they pose as 'do-gooders' and pretend to help the poor.

But there is a change. Twenty-five years ago we were not explicit enough in showing how 'development' was just the slogan used by capital to facilitate the implementation of a neo-colonial enterprise. We all know well that capitalism has permeated the whole society through every pore.

I am fully aware that today there are still many millions whose desires are shaped by the belief that 'development' defines a universal norm of the good life. Many people still believe in the Western or American way of life, no matter how much they experience its consequences: the immense price to be paid by adopting it in terms of decency, joy, freedom and humanity; the radical impossibility of extending it to all people on Earth; the measure in which it endangers the survival of life on the planet.

I am also aware that the current ecological, economic, social and political limits to that irresponsible race are stimulating violent and blind reactions, of a fundamentalist character. We are living in a moment of extreme danger that was not so clear 25 years ago.

Yet today, most of all, I am enjoying the surge of a new hope. I wrote, 25 years ago, that it was 'time to recover a sense of reality, time to walk with one's own feet, on one's own path, in order to dream one's own dreams, not the borrowed ones of development'. Millions, perhaps billions, are following that path and experiencing what is to be beyond development. Capitalism is not an almighty and omnipresent monolith. The current wave of violence and destruction is fostering struggles against capital, which involve the heart, the head, and the hands of people increasingly discontent with the situation. A new social force, transforming rebellion and indignation into a political revolution, is thus beginning to take shape.

There is no place for optimism, in this tragic circumstance of the world, in this transition to a new era. Many of those millions are struggling for sheer necessity and everywhere the struggle requires lots of courage and lucidity. But there is room for hope, the opposite to the expectations defining the economic society, 'development' and capitalism; hope is not the conviction that something will happen in a certain way, but the conviction that something makes sense, whatever happens. What makes sense today, like always, is to reclaim our human condition and decency.

Disclosure statement

No potential conflict of interest was reported by the authors.

Notes

1. Esteva, Babones, and Babcicky, *The Future of Development*.
2. Esteva, Babones, and Babcicky, *The Future of Development*, 22–23.
3. Benjamin, *Illuminations*.
4. Escobar, *Sentipensar con la Tierra*; Esteva, "Para sentipensar la comunalidad."
5. Rivera Cusicanqui, *Hambre de Huelga*; Gago, *La razón neoliberal*.
6. Rivera Cusicanqui, *Hambre de Huelga*, 57.
7. Feher, Heller, and Markus, *Dictatorship over Needs*.
8. Cailey, "The Rivers North."
9. 'The pathology of relatedness has already become less dangerous than the pathology of unrelatedness', ecologically at least, this seem an incontrovertible statement; Nandy, *Traditions, Tyrannies, and Utopias*, 51.
10. *The World We Have*, 43, 44.
11. *The World We Have*, 55.
12. This idea has found a recent lucid expression in the domain of insurrectionary politics: 'The biggest problem we face is a philosophical one: understanding that this civilization is *already dead* … [its end] has been clinically established for a century'; Invisible Committee, *To Our Friends*, 29. For this group, it is the West that is the catastrophe – nobody is out to 'destroy the West', it is destroying itself.
13. http://www.friedensburg.at/uploads/files/wp7_97.pdf
14. Foucault, "Preface."

Bibliography

Benjamin, Walter. *Illuminations*. New York: Schocken Books, 1968.
Cayley, David. *The Rivers North of the Future. The Testament of Ivan Illich*. Toronto: House of Anansi Press, 2005.
Escobar, Arturo. *Sentipensar con la Tierra* [Thinking-Feeling with the Earth]. Medellín: UNAULA, 2014.
Esteva, Gustavo. "Para sentipensar la comunalidad." [To Think-Feel the Communal.] *Bajo el Volcán* 16, no. 23 (2015): 171–186.
Esteva, Gustavo, Salvatore Babones, and Philip Babcicky. *The Future of Development. A Radical Manifesto*. Chicago: Policy Press, 2013.
Feher, Ferenc, Agnes Heller, and Györgi Markus. *Dictatorship over Needs*. Oxford: Blackwell, 1986.
Foucault, Michel. "Preface." In *Anti-Oedipus, Capitalism and Squizophrenia*, edited by Gilles Deleuze and Felix Guattari, xi–xiv. Minneapolis: University of Minnesota Press, 1983.
Gago, Verónica. *La razón neoliberal* [On Neoliberal Reason]. Buenos Aires: Tinta Limón, 2014.
Invisible Committee. *To Our Friends*. Cambridge: MIT Press, 2015.
Nath Hanh, Thich. *The World We Have*. Berkeley: Parallax Books, 2008.
Nandy, Ashis. *Traditions, Tyrannies, and Utopias*. New Delhi: Oxford University Press, 1987.
Rivera Cusicanqui, Silvia. *Hambre de Huelga* [Hunger for the Strike]. Querétaro: La Mirada Salvaje, 2014.

The Sustainable Development Goals and *Laudato si'*: varieties of Post-Development?

Wolfgang Sachs

ABSTRACT

Comparing the Agenda 2030 of the United Nations and the *Laudato si'* by the Pope, both authored in 2015, one point stands out: the Development enthusiasm of the twentieth century is gone. In its place, we are now dealing with the demise of expansive modernity. The motto of the previous century (playing on words of the Lord's Prayer), 'on Earth as in the West', now seems like a threat. The world is in crisis roundabout: the biosphere is being shattered and, in more ways than one, the gap between the rich and the poor is widening. While both publications agree that the global economic model can now be considered old iron, there are equally significant differences. While the Agenda 2030 seeks to repair the existing global economic model significantly, the encyclical calls for a pushing back of economic hegemony and for more ethical responsibility on all levels. While the Agenda 2030 envisions a green economy with social democratic hues, the encyclical foresees a post capitalist-era, based on a cultural shift towards eco-solidarity.

How naive we were to pompously declare the 'End of the Age of Development'! In autumn 1988 in Barbara Duden's house at the Pennsylvania State University, we had invited our friends to 'living room consultations'. Accompanied by spaghetti, red wine and roll-mats, we conceived the heady idea to publish a 'Development Dictionary'.[1] It was to be no ordinary handbook; it had to be critical and dissect 'Development', a key term in world politics of the twentieth century, in a Foucauldian manner. According to Foucault, knowledge and power are inseparable, although power does not necessarily refer to repression, rather to – canalised – freedom. As a consequence, 'Development', in our understanding, was the matter from which plans, forecasts and dreams were made – basically, a view of the world that wields power by social consensus. Moreover, the history of the idea of 'Development' is typical for many ideas: a once historic innovation became a convention in time, eventually ending in frustration. Our *spiritus rector* who sat in our midst, Ivan Illich, realised that the idea would fit perfectly in the Archaeology of Modernity he was planning to write. For Illich, one could only talk about 'Development' in the gesture of an obituary.

In retrospect, it is surprising what we didn't know or at best guessed back then. For instance, the fall of the Berlin Wall and the end of the Cold War and its implications for the idea of Development that President Truman had brandished against Communism; the sieve-like perforation of the nation-state system by the globalisation of markets; an increasingly polycentric world order that is disarranging the hierarchy of nations and undermining espe-cially the USA's hegemony; the Internet and later the smartphone that is creating a global communication space; and, finally, the rise of newly industrialised countries that has rele-gated the usual categories such as 'Third World' and 'donor countries' to the rubbish heap of history.

All in all, we were opposed to the idea of Development,[2] in chronopolitical, geopolitical and civilisational terms.[3] Chronopolitically, it seems as though all of humanity is moving forwards on a single path while, ultimately, the goal of social and economic progress is never fully attained. On the other hand, geopolitically, the first movers (the developed nations) are leading the way of Humanity. The once confusing global diversity of humanity has been clearly ranked into rich and poor nations. Finally, from a civilisational perspective, the 'Development' of a nation is measured by its degree of economic performance, ie the gross domestic product. Societies that have just emerged from colonial rule are required to place themselves under the custody of the economy.

So what happened to the idea of Development? It became a plastic word, an empty word that lends positive valence to the most contradictory of intentions.[4] Nevertheless, 'Development' has survived as a worldview which has been embedded in an international network of institutions; the United Nations (UN), ministries, and even non-governmental organisations (NGOs). However, it is possible to trace Development's extraordinary transfor-mation up to the present day. In 2015 there was a noticeable consolidation of the Development discourse: there was the papal Encyclical *Laudato si'* in June, the Sustainable Development Goals of the United Nations in September and, lastly, the Paris Climate Agreement in December. Are these international statements still obliged to Development? Or can one, to the contrary, consider them proof of Post-Development thinking?

The transformation of 'Development' in the SDGs

By agreeing to the Sustainable Development Goals (SDGs) and adopting the Agenda 2030, the General Assembly of the United Nations initiated a programme that is expected to guide world politics for the next 15 years.[5] The SDGs were a result of two processes: the Millennium Goals of 2000, and the documents of the 2012 Rio+20 Summit that had continued where the Agenda 21 of the 1992 Rio Earth Summit had left off. The SDGs had a relatively long forerun with consultations in 88 countries, intergovernmental consultations, a high-ranking, prestigious panel and a notably high participation of civil society. Eventually, 17 goals and 169 sub-goals ranging from 'No Poverty' to 'Education for All' to 'Renewable Energy' were agreed upon. As a result, the SDGs are a complex matter, a comprehensive manual that is at once ponderous and visionary but that is non-binding, and lacks a sanction mechanism. It is no wonder that some say its vague demands and inflated goals could well be an invita-tion to inaction for governments.[6]

Admittedly, perennial noncommittal avowals are indispensable for the governments of the world. The Paris Climate Agreement of December 2015, which combined a formidable goal with vague obligations, is the latest example. Who does not remember the frequent UN campaigns against hunger and climate change? These have been mere rhetorical pawns, at least since the 1963 World Food Conference in Washington and the 1972 UN Conference on Human Development in Stockholm. Even benevolent governments find themselves in an awkward position. On one hand, they have to give in to the objective urgency of the problem and the strength of civil society, but on the other hand, they are simultaneously obliged to both the capitalist markets and the consumption wishes of their respective societies. It follows that a certain degree of simulative potential is inherent in the declarations of the UN.[7] They act as if … while the market logic already shines through. A considerable amount of self-illusion rather than chicanery is at play here. Unfortunately, the UN is a perfect stage from which to declare noble goals top down, and then retreat to *realpolitik* when push comes to shove. As a result, a disconnect between international rhetoric and national measures has become a structural trait of politics. How else can the declaration 'We commit ourselves to working tirelessly for the full implementation of the Agenda 2030'[8] be understood other than as a practice in simulation when the same governments support coal mining, land grabbing or the international finance industry?

Survival instead of progress

The time when Development was still a promise, when 'young' and 'aspiring' nations were on the Road to Progress, is long gone. Indeed, the chronopolitical, geopolitical and civilisational politics of development constituted a monumental historical promise, a promise that eventually all societies would be able to close the gap between the rich and the poor and to reap the fruits of industrial civilisation.

Development thought suffered two setbacks from which it has not quite recovered yet: the persistence of poverty and the finitude of nature. Development aid, conceived especially for the purpose of fighting poverty, is confronted by the enduring reproduction of poverty at an alarming rate even after the expiry of the MDGs. Of course, the number of people suffering from absolute poverty has gone down in emerging economies; however, it has remained constant in poorer countries. Additionally, the politics of poverty reduction often comes at the price of increasing inequality and environmental degradation. Secondly, global warming, the drastic loss of biodiversity and the latent poisoning of oceans and landmasses have tarnished the belief that developed nations are at the head of social evolution. On the contrary, progress has often turned out to be regression, since the economic system of the Global North cannot do without systematic exploitation of nature. Analyses, from 'Limits to Growth' in 1972 to 'Planetary Boundaries' in 2009, are crystal clear: Development-as-Growth is leading to a planet that is inhospitable to human life.[9]

Indeed, the SDGs make do without high-flying plans for sky-high growth; instead, they try to secure a minimum for a dignified life universally. The 'call to action' of the SDG document reads: 'We can be the first generation to succeed in ending poverty; just as we may be the last to have a chance of saving the planet. The world will be a better place in 2030 if we succeed in our objectives.'[10] Apart from the obtrusive use of the word 'we' (who is being addressed? Governments? Well-wishers? Or Humanity?), the appeal is elated and noble. However, it still fails to hide the fact that the once-rousing model 'Development' is more or less narrowed down to requirements for survival. Seven goals are dedicated to human vulnerability (ending poverty, ensuring food security, universal health, universal education, gender equality, universal access to water and sanitation, and access to sustainable energy sources) and five goals to ecological vulnerability (sustainable cities, sustainable methods of production and consumption, tackling climate change, conservation of oceans and landmass ecosystems). This constitutes nothing more than a due appropriation of human rights obligations and ecological imperatives highlighted with specified targets. The classical development narrative is conspicuously missing.

Conflating Development with security has been commonplace since the 1990s, a time during which a change in perception of poor countries by the old industrialised countries occurred. Previously hailed as bearers of hope for catch-up Development, they were now seen as risk zones that were dealt with accordingly, by the use of crisis prevention strategies. They were perceived as points of origin for job seekers and refugees, or as hotbeds of destabilisation and terror. Every reasonably rich country tried to protect itself through conflict prevention projects in poorer countries. The German Chancellor Angela Merkel's remarks on the refugee crisis, that posit Africa's well-being as being in the interest of Germany,[11] and Bayer boss Walter Baumann's claims that the merger with Monsanto was meant to fight global hunger[12] are some recent examples of the crisis prevention mode described above. Be that as it may, the *development* in SDGs is a semantic delusion. The *Sustainable Development Goals* should more fittingly have been called SSGs – *Sustainable Survival Goals*.

One world in lieu of North–South

In hindsight, the 2000 Millennium Summit was merely a commemoration of the twentieth century, not an anticipation of the twenty-first century. In New York all those years ago, the pattern of the last 50 years was reproduced: the world neatly divided into North and South, where donors hand down capital, growth and social policies to beneficiary countries to recondition them for the global race. This pattern is a familiar sediment of colonial history and was, just like the catch-up imperative, omnipresent in the post-war years. What happened to catching up, an idea so fundamental to the idea of Development?

For a possible answer, it is necessary to quote a passage from the SDG proclamation document:

> This is an Agenda of unprecedented scope and significance. It is accepted by all countries and is applicable to all, taking into account different national realities … These are universal goals and targets which involve the entire world, developed and developing countries alike.[13]

The SDGs stress their globality and universality. The mental rupture could not have been formulated more clearly: The geopolitics of development embodied by the old-industrialised countries serving as an example for poorer countries to follow was ceremoniously disposed of. All the planning and passion, the amount of resources and romance that went into realising the dream of catching up! Secular eschatology became a thing of the past. Just as the Cold War era withered away in in 1989, the myth of catching up followed suit in 2015. Myths have rarely been buried as quietly and informally as this one. What sense would development make, if there is no country that can justifiably be called developed? All of a sudden, it was no longer a provocation to call industrialised nations developing countries.

All of this did not fall from heaven. Paragraph §7 of the 1992 Rio Declaration enshrines the principle of *common but differentiated responsibilities* in environmental policy. On the basis of this principle, developing countries were not required to reduce emissions in accordance to the Kyoto Protocol. Twenty years on, due to the changes in the economic geography of the world, this exemption could no longer be upheld.[14] At the 2011 Durban climate conference as well as the Rio+20 conference, developing countries had to get used to the idea that they had a responsibility to bear with regards to biospheric damage. Likewise, developed countries could not escape the fact that their economic system, from global agri-business to labour markets and even climate impact, had repercussions on poorer countries. After long and intricate political beating around the bush, there was no denying that the sustainable goals were to be valid for all countries alike.

This is a late manifestation of the replacement of the Development era by the Globalisation era. Across nation states, a transnational world emerged, a world connected by value chains, similar consumption patterns and globalist thought. The rise of emerging economies and the strengthening of the global middle classes bear witness to this turn of events. Most spectacular remains of course the rise of China, and the speed at which it rose. As of 2014, China was the best-performing economic power in the world, although the USA's economy was double its size as recently as 2005. The seven largest emerging economies have since superseded the old-industrial countries who enthuse over global economic hegemony as the G7. The creation of the G20 was politically cognisant of the changing dynamic of the global economy.

Additionally, a new transnational middle class has emerged. Between 1990 and 2010, members of the middle class based in the Global South rose from 26 to 58% and will probably rise to 80% by the year 2030.[15] They also shop in shopping malls, buy high-tech gadgets, watch similar films and TV series, regularly travel for leisure and have access to a crucial homogenising medium: money. They are an integral part of a transnational economic complex that is developing its markets globally. Samsung supplies them with gadgets, Toyota with automobiles, Sony with TV sets, Siemens with refrigerators, Burger King with fast food and Time-Warner with movies. This is an enormous success for the development industry, a success that has come not only at an enormous cultural cost, but at an ecological cost as well. Currently, the only way out of poverty and powerlessness is a direct simultaneous entry into the ecological robber economy.

Social indicators instead of GDP

In the post-war decades, there were a number of critical inquiries into whether the civilisational politics of Development was misleading. But the gross domestic product (GDP) as the magic number retained predominance. It also birthed the Development idea by allowing the conception of a hierarchy of the world on supposedly objective terms.[16] Based on an economic world view and a statistical toolbox, experts conceptualised 'Development' as growth of production and per-capita income. Since the 1970s a dichotomisation of development discourse occurred that saw development-as-growth confronted with development-as-social-policy. Institutions such as the World Bank, IMF (International Monetary Fund) and the World Trade Organization (WTO) revered the idea of development-as-growth while the UNDP (United Nations Development Programme) and UNEP (United Nations Environment Programme) as well as a majority of the NGOs subscribed to the idea of development-as-social-policy. In this way, the term 'Development' became an all-purpose adhesive which could refer to building an airport or to drilling a borehole. The Millennium Development Goals and the SDGs are rooted in this legacy.

Over and over again, the relationship between social indicators and economic growth has revealed itself to be a thorny issue. On the one hand, the Agenda 2030 recognises the decline of ocean-ecosystems and the increasing social inequality, but on the other hand, it calls for economic growth[17] (at the rate of at least 7% for the poorest countries), and affirms the WTO trade regime.[18] To overcome the strain, or rather the contradiction between growth and sustainable goals, 'inclusive growth' and 'green growth' have often been called upon. This disregards the fact that, for a while now, it has been clear that inclusive growth driven by the financial markets is an impossibility, as it constantly reproduces inequality. The same can be said for the slogan of green growth. Even at the highest echelons of the G7 Summits, the fact that fossil-fuelled economic growth is not feasible in the medium run has done the rounds. Although the decarbonisation of the global economy was unanimously proposed in 2015, nobody seems to know how it would work without further depleting biodiversity. All recipes for green growth rely on decoupling environmental degradation from growth even as absolute decoupling (increasing growth while decreasing environmental degradation) has never been achieved in history.[19] The Agenda 2030 fails to speak about prosperity without growth, even for the old industrialised countries. This was simply off the table.

Regardless, the development idea has proven its resilience. Social indicators have replaced GDP in determining the performance of a country in various dimensions. This is one of the reasons why statisticians all over the globe have joined hands to declare the *data revolution*. Citing the UN Secretary General during the preparation phase of the SDGs:

> Data are the lifeblood of decision-making. Without data, we cannot know how many people are born and at what age they die; how many men, women and children still live in poverty; how many children need educating; how many doctors to train or schools to build; how public money is being spent and to what effect; whether greenhouse gas emissions are increasing or the fish stocks in the ocean are dangerously low; how many people are in what kinds of work, what companies are trading and whether economic activity is expanding.[20]

The data revolutionaries are operating under Lord Kelvin's maxim, reckoning that one can only improve what one has previously measured ('If you cannot measure it, you cannot improve'). Thanks to digital technology, the monitoring of several areas of life is currently undergoing a transformation in terms of the amount, the degree of detail, and the speeds at which the data is exchanged. Complex fields such as education, health, oceanology or food security can now be summarised into indices and easily compared with other data sets.

Political actors, governments and NGOs have learnt to take advantage of the simplification and complex reduction that numbers and quantification offer and regularly use these as short formulas.[21] But beneath these short formulas there is history, a plethora of social struggles and cultural world views and practices. As a result, numbers have an enormous homogenising effect: all the diversity and difference in the world boils down into a scale of numbers. Additionally, the data revolution has not been successful in emerging from the shadows of the development creed; on the contrary, the development idea has been living off of the dictatorship of comparison. Wherever one looks, quantitative data serve to enable comparison in time and space that constructs deficits along the time axis between groups as well as nations. Ironically, this very deficit-creation dynamic has given the development idea a purpose to exist for the last 70 years. The Human Development Index, like the GDP, is a deficit index; it categorises countries according to a hierarchy, thereby presupposing that there is only one kind of social evolution. The SDGs, with the scales and indices of the 17 goals and 169 sub-goals, follow in this legacy. Because numbers now constitute the framework of multi-dimensional development, the Agenda 2030, aside from all the noble goals, is an attempt at measuring the world.

Laudato si' – renouncing the development discourse

Pope Francis' greeting *buona sera*, as he emerged from the loggia of St. Peter's Cathedral on the evening of 13 March 2013, surprised the crowd of thousands of people, for it was neither ceremonial nor in Latin. The newly elected Pope had hit the ground running with his modesty and brotherhood. In his second, rather gawky sentence, he went the long way around, speaking in a way that would mark his pontificate: 'It seems that my fellow Cardinals have gone to the ends of the Earth to get one ... but here we are'.[22] As a matter of fact, Francis is Argentinian and the first non-European (and from the southern hemisphere at that) to occupy the chair of St. Peter. He brings a Latin American perspective to the church and to the world. His nonchalance towards dogma and church law, his emphasis on compassion towards the poor, refugees and other marginalised communities, and his outspokenness on environmental degradation cannot be understood without his Latin American background.

With the Encyclical *Laudato si'* of June 2015, the Pope declared and celebrated his view of the world, and the wider global public paid attention. It is worth remembering that his stance in the encyclical constituted a first step of the diplomatic offensive that led to a thawing of relations between Cuba and the USA where the Pope, the son of immigrant parents, urgently warned against xenophobia in Congress and subsequently also at the UN General Assembly, where the SDGs were enacted on the same day. *Laudato si'* covers a lot of ground, spanning from the destruction of creation to the unjust global order to the individual responsibility that each of us bears. Can one classify the Pope's sentiments under the heading of Post-Development?

A declaration of mutual dependency

It is well known that the Pope successfully carried out a significant coup with this encyclical, especially amongst environmentalists. For the first time ever, the epochal environmental crisis was the subject of an encyclical. Once more the adage that the church thinks in centuries, or at least half-centuries, turned out to be true. Indeed, 50 years lie between the *Communist Manifesto*[23] and the Encyclical *Rerum Novarum*[24]. A similar span is identifiable between the wake-up call that was Rachel Carson's *Silent Spring* and the *Laudato si'*.[25] The wait seems to have been worth it: the *Laudato si'* is a forceful, stylistically elegant document, and, most importantly, a timely one.

From the perspective of a development expert, the encyclical makes for a paradoxical read: the experts are affirmative even as the idea of development does not seem to play a role. The unconventional language might be surprising, but the fact that the chronopolitics of Development are conspicuously absent from the encyclical is inescapable. Progress, and other promises for the future, are non-existent in the document and one gets the impression that the arrow of time that has shaped historical perception for two centuries has simply been done away with. Instead of progressive optimism, linear improvement and thrilling expectations for the future, only sober, nuanced contemplations on the present await readers.

It was different in the encyclical *Populorum Progressio*[26] during the reign of Paul VI in 1967. Back then, the magisterium trailed behind the development discourse, claiming that the poorer parts of the world were on their way towards the richer parts of the world, towards true human development. As a side note, the environment did not feature anywhere in said encyclical. Contrastingly, in *Laudato si'* the rejection of the arrow of time is so extreme that evolution is completely absent, even as nature is prominently discussed. With this implicit rejection, the encyclical denies itself the opportunity to speak to a cosmological interpretation of the belief in creation in the way that French theologian and natural scientist Teilhard de Chardin or the US-American theologian and cultural historian Thomas Berry did in the early and late twentieth century, respectively.

Instead, the papal circular replaces the arrow of time with spatial consciousness. Space has been able to garner more prominence than time in the current global mindset: the combination of things in virtual or geographical space appears to be more important than their sequence in time. This epochal change of consciousness is partly responsible for the demise of the development idea. Even so, the encyclical is decidedly space focused, a position clearly demonstrated in the subtitle 'On Care for our Common Home', the pivotal element being the vulnerability of creation. The document further criticises the various threats to nature and the mass vilification of human life, thus speaking out on issues that the SDGs are intended to address. Additionally, it hears 'both the cry of earth and the cry of the poor'[27] and prefers healing to management. Above and beyond all physicality, it conceives of the exploitation of nature and humanity as irreverent of the systemic connection all living things – including human beings – share.

It is not accidental that the encyclical places emphasis on relationships: the relationship to nature, to others, to oneself and to God.

> It cannot be emphasized enough how everything is interconnected. Time and space are not independent of one another, and not even atoms or subatomic particles can be considered in isolation. Just as the different aspects of the planet – physical, chemical and biological – are interrelated, so too living species are part of a network which we will never fully explore and understand.[28]

While the Agenda 2030 bureaucratically logs the unpleasant state of affairs in detail, the papal encyclical proposes a wholesome view, seeking to arrive at a transformatory and engaging narrative.[29] Indeed the encyclical can be read as a *declaration of interdependence* replacing the *declaration of independence* of the nation-state era. Irreverence of the life context is not only a sin; it has cumulative side effects that destabilise the whole. Adding the dimension of time, one can say that the encyclical is indeed a warning against a hostile future. In that way, the development idea has been flipped on its head.

No sufficiency, no justice

Much like chronopolitics, geopolitics is also conspicuously absent from the document. In the encyclical, the North–South scheme is only visible between §170 and 175, where the international compensation and financing modalities for global climate policy are discussed. In the rest of the document, the guiding principle is that 'Interdependence obliges us to think of one world with a common plan'.[30] Upon favourable interpretation, this stance would appear to be very close to that of the SDGs, as both documents appear to distance themselves from the geopolitics of Development.

However, in contrast to the SDGs, the encyclical presumes that the looting of the planet has already exceeded the ecological limits without solving the problem of poverty.[31] This, the major dilemma of our day, is far from being addressed by the Agenda 2030. The document recognises neither the boundaries nor the limits that a number of scientists have demonstrated, for instance in *Limits to Growth (1972)* and *Planetary Boundaries* 2009.[32] Instead terms such as 'risk' and 'scarcity' are preferred. According to calculations by the Global Footprint Network, the planet is already being drastically strained, with humanity consuming 1.6 times the available resources in the biosphere annually. Overfished oceans, extinct plant and animal species and the climate chaos bear witness to this state of affairs.[33] By ignoring the status quo, the Agenda 2030 is protecting the growth model, a model which has always been prioritised over protection of nature. This turn of events is traceable to the 1972 UN environmental conference, the 1987 Brundtland Report and now the Agenda 2030 as well. The Pope chooses the path less trodden by clearly mentioning both ecological and social limits, and by holding the industrial growth model accountable for its various shortcomings. At one point, he even goes as far as recommending degrowth for the more affluent parts of the world.[34] In other words, he advocates a reductive rather than an expansive modernity.[35]

When more and more people live on a limited planet, social inequality becomes an ecological problem. Usually, the rich consume resources that are then no longer available to the poor. For instance, high meat consumption occupies land where food for human consumption would otherwise have grown, full motorisation means less space for pedestrians and cyclists, and more oil and ore mining and mass use of smartphones and computers are contingent on supply of electricity, rare earth elements and other materials that are linked to land alienation and precarious working conditions. In summary, the global middle and upper classes are leading an imperial lifestyle[36] which is why the encyclical links poverty and the environment, as 'both everyday experience and scientific research show that the gravest effects of all attacks on the environment are suffered by the poorest'.[37] Goal 12 of the Agenda 2030 seeks to *Ensure sustainable consumption and production patterns* by emphasising efficient use of resources, a demand which falls behind a document from 1992: the Agenda 21. *Laudato si'* suggests a strategy of sufficiency embedded in cultural change: it is indeed the rich who have to change, not the poor; it is wealth that needs to be alleviated, not poverty. By requiring the rich to refrain from appropriating the surroundings of the poor, the powerless are accorded more freedom. This is made especially clear over a couple of pages of the encyclical where the term 'ecological debt' is used.[38] Though the wealthy of the Global North have accumulated significant ecological debts, they have suppressed consciousness of this fact because the Global South seems distant, geographically, temporally and socially. More than anyone else, the poor are paying the price for the wealth of the Global North. In light of this, sufficiency could perhaps already be defined as mere refusal to live at the expense of others.

Common good against technocracy

The common good is the great unknown of neoclassical economics. In a pluralistic democracy, the search for the common good is a permanent process. As long as one subscribes to the idea that society ought not to be the plaything for power- and individual interests, the term 'common good' is indispensable. As a consequence, the term has dominated political philosophy in various shades since antiquity, and reappears emphatically in the encyclical. From a civilisational perspective, the encyclical argues that the common good – as political and social well-being but also as ecological well-being – should be brought to fruition in various societies.

By citing well-being as a normative principle, the encyclical also gained some ground for criticism. It declares that:

> The failure of global summits on the environment makes it plain that our politics are subject
> to technology and finance. There are too many special interests, and economic interests easily

end up trumping the common good and manipulating information so that their own plans will not be affected.[39]

Here again, the encyclical attacks the power-interests of the economic and financial systems that perforate and disregard the common good. This is in stark contrast to the Agenda 2030, which fails to explain the reasons for the constant reproduction of poverty and the decline of the biosphere that have made the SDGs necessary. Neglecting the root causes is typical for UN documents and comfortable for governments, but fatal for any therapy.

The encyclical drills deep and reprimands the technocratic paradigm that has proven to be fatal for modernity. In a chapter entitled 'Human Roots of the Ecological Crisis', the Pope accuses modernity of inner contradictions: while science and technology have brought humans unprecedented power, humans have repeatedly proven themselves to be unable to deal with it accordingly. The immense increase in power has been largely void of responsibility and foresight:

> The technocratic paradigm also tends to dominate economic and political life. The economy accepts every advance in technology with a view to profit, without concern for its potentially negative impact on human beings. Finance overwhelms the real economy. The lessons of the global financial crisis have not been assimilated, and we are learning all too slowly the lessons of environmental deterioration.[40]

An instrumental gaze has transformed too many things, humans and other living things alike, into mere means for achieving ever more specific goals. According to the Pope, this is the reason for rapid degradation of the world and the systematic lack of focus on the 'whole' during societal decision-making. Save for an explanation of their more abstract ideas, one finds traces of the phenomenological and critical philosophy of the twentieth century, such as Heidegger and Horkheimer, in the encyclical.

Can the technocratic paradigm be overcome? According to the Pope, it can: by way of a brave 'cultural revolution'.[41] Human freedom only has to limit technology and orient it towards life-serving goals. One finds examples in the encyclical: renewable energy, clean production, social investments, fair trade, modest lifestyles. The encyclical touts for reflexive action that constantly incorporates a responsibility to wholeness (of humanity and nature). It dismisses institutional routines such as the habitual blindness of decision makers that prevent it. Prudence and foresight paired with empathy are the markers of non-technocratic behaviour. One must instinctively think about a feature of many religions, the perpetual struggle between good and bad. It appears in a more contemporary form in the encyclical, not in a dogmatic form but in an endearing one full of vivid imagery:

> An authentic humanity, calling for a new synthesis, seems to dwell in the midst of our technological culture, almost unnoticed, like a mist seeping gently beneath a closed door. Will the promise last, in spite of everything, with all that is authentic rising up in stubborn resistance?[42]

The creation and universal brotherhood/sisterhood

When Francis of Assisi (1181–1225) – whose name the Pope chose – called all animals and plants, even matter itself, his brothers and sisters, he meant it in a literal sense. As children of one God, all creatures have godly roots and dignity and are connected to each other as siblings. With *Laudato si'*, Pope Francis propagated a Franciscan version of the theology of creation which implies that the actual focus of ecology is the fellowship of all living things and the responsibility of human beings towards this fellowship. Undeniably influenced by the Brazilian Leonardo Boff,[43] the Pope's horizontal conception of creation rejects the hierarchical conception that puts humans at the centre of all creation.

But first, the spoil pile that has gathered over the centuries has to be done away with. God's word in Genesis 1:28, 'fill the earth and subdue it', can no longer be an ethical justification of the present. This blessing from the Old Testament has been used to legitimise a number of grotesque things in the modern era: from René Descartes'[44] declaration of humanity as 'lord and possessor', to American republicans who defended coal mining and fracking on the basis of this bible verse. Pope Francis was left with no other choice than to dispose of *dominium terrae*.[45] It certainly helps that there are two creation stories in the Bible. In Genesis 2:4ff, humankind is required to 'cultivate and care for' the garden of Eden. In this account, humankind is required to show brotherly and sisterly love to all fellow creatures. The fact that all are created by the same God underlies the inherent connection of all living things on a planetary and evolutionary scale. In light of this fact, the 'cry of nature and the cry of the poor' ought to be heard in all corners of the earth physically and spiritually, as it is an offence to our common fraternity and sorority. Injuries also have spiritual feedback effects, more so than physical ones.

Additionally, many interpretations of the creation are double coded, theologically and scientifically.[46] Scientists have a systematic view of life based on the assumption that networks constitute the basic unit of organisation of living things.[47] Nature is no longer seen as a machine, but as a network of relationships, physical, chemical, mental and communicative. The relationships between the parts constitute the whole. The connectedness of all manifestations of life, bacteria, chimpanzees and human consciousness alike, is emphasised by both science and the encyclical.

At least two ethical consequences can be drawn from this kind of creation theology. First, nature is understood as commons, belonging to all living things. How else could it be when nature is a gift from God and is systematic in character? Individual and national ownership of the biosphere only come second to the fact that the gifts of the earth are for all to enjoy. Private ownership of land has always been viewed critically in Catholic social teaching; accordingly, ownership of ground water, the ocean and the atmosphere is not legitimate. As the encyclical reiterates, 'The climate is a common good, belonging to all and meant for all'.[48] Although the Pope emphasises that 'The natural environment is a collective good, the patrimony of all humanity and the responsibility of everyone', he keeps himself away from the potentially subversive consequences of his comments.[49] In this context, mining, oil mining, air pollution and landscape destruction come to mind.

Secondly, plants, animals and human beings, like all living things in nature, are worthy in their own right, independent of their utilisable worth for humans. Nature is not primarily a resource like it is in the modern era; it is primarily a gift of God, or for non-believers, it constitutes the commons. A strong propensity towards anti-utilitarianism is recognisable throughout the encyclical. It pillories 'excessive anthropocentrism' and denies humans the exclusive right of use over the earth, a right which ants, monkeys, oceans and deserts possess as well. All living things have the right to exist independent of human purposes. 'We can speak of the priority of being over that of being useful … each creature possesses its own particular goodness and perfection'.[50] All creatures are dignified; the idea of an existence value (as opposed to a use and exchange value) has strong Christian roots.

Outlook

Comparing the Agenda 2030 of the United Nations and the *Laudato si'* by the Pope, both authored in 2015, one point stands out: the Development enthusiasm of the twentieth century is gone. In its place, we are now dealing with the demise of expansive modernity. The motto of the previous century (playing on words of Lord's Prayer), 'on Earth as in the West', now seems like a threat. The world is in crisis roundabout: the biosphere is being shattered, and in more ways than one, the gap between the rich and the poor is widening. While both publications agree that the global economic model can now be considered old iron, there are equally significant differences. While the Agenda 2030 seeks to repair the existing global economic model significantly, the encyclical calls for a pushing back of economic hegemony and for more ethical responsibility on all levels. While the Agenda 2030 envisions a green economy with social democratic hues, the encyclical foresees a post-capitalist era, based on a cultural shift toward eco-solidarity.

The era of expansive modernity is over. The more this insight sinks in globally, the more the talk of development and thus also of Post-Development will fade. Mental frameworks will shift, problems that societies face will no longer be conceived as development problems. Currently, thinking in fortress terms is popular, even as the globalisation narrative and an eco-solidary ethic line up in resistance.[51] Fortress thinking feeds on a mixture of nationalism, xenophobia, authoritarianism and a proper dose of wealth chauvinism. Often, it serves the longing for a strongman with whom the marginalised parts of society can identify. On the other hand, the globalisation narrative continues to wield the promise of economic growth and more well-being worldwide despite all limitations. But it provides multilateral governance and politics generally with more space for manoeuvre than in neo-liberal times. The Agenda 2030 largely follows this thinking. The ethics of eco-solidarity opposes fortress thinking as well as the globalisation narrative. It advocates cultural change at both the local and the global level that is based in cooperative economics and politics for the common good. For the sake of fairness, it is about undeveloping, about winding up the imperial lifestyle of the transnational middle classes. Doubtlessly, the papal encyclical belongs in this category. The paradigmatic debates in the coming decades will revolve around this discourse, while Development, just like monarchy and feudalism, will disappear into the haze of history. Consequently, it is about time that someone declared the end of the Post-Development era, some 25 years after we declared the end of the Development era.

Disclosure statement

No potential conflict of interest was reported by the author.

Acknowledgments

I am grateful to Eric Otieno for the translation.

Notes

1. Sachs, *The Development Dictionary*.
2. Esteva, "Development: Metaphor, Myth, Threat"; see also Rist, *The History of Development*.
3. Sachs, "Development. Rise and Decline of an Idea."
4. Pörksen, *Plastikwörter*.
5. United Nations, *Transforming our World: The 2030 Agenda for Sustainable Development*.
6. Easterly, "The Trouble with the Sustainable Development Goals"; Rivera, *Wieviel Entpolitisierung Vertragen Die SGDs?*
7. Blühdorn, *Simulative Demokratie*.
8. UN, *Transforming our World: The 2030 Agenda*; see also Ziai, *Development Discourse and Global History*.
9. Rockström et al., "A Safe Space for Human Operations."
10. UN, *Transforming our World: The 2030 Agenda*, §50.
11. http://www.zeit.de/2016/42/afrika-fluechtlingspolitik-angela-merkel
12. http://www.faz.net/agenturmeldungen/dpa/bayer-chef-monsanto-uebernahme-hilft-bei-hungerbekaempfung-14441046.html
13. UN, *Transforming our World: The 2030 Agenda*, §5.
14. Pauw et al., *Different Perspectives on Differentiated Responsibilities*.
15. UNDP, *Human Development Report 2013*, 14.
16. Speich-Chassè, *Die Erfindung des Bruttosozialprodukts*; Fioramonti, *Gross Domestic Problem: The Politics Behind the World's Most Powerful Number*; Lepenies, *Die Macht der einen Zahl*.
17. UN, *Transforming our World: The 2030 Agenda*, §8.1.
18. Ibid., §68.
19. Jackson and Webster. *Limits Revisited*.
20. UN Secretary-General's Independent Expert Advisory Group, *A World That Counts*.
21. Fioramonti, *How Numbers Rule the World*.
22. http://w2.vatican.va/content/francesco/en/speeches/2013/march/documents/papa-francesco_20130313_benedizione-urbi-et-orbi.html
23. Pope Leo XIII, *Encyclical Letter*.
24. Carson, *Silent Spring*.
25. Marx and Engels, *The Communist Manifesto*.
26. Pope Paul IV, *Encyclical Letter: Populorum Progressio*.
27. Pope Francis, *Laudato si'*, §49.
28. Ibid., §138.
29. Hickel, "Pope vs UN: Who Will Save the World First?"
30. Pope Francis, *Laudato si'*, §164.
31. Ibid., §27.
32. Rockström et al., "Safe Space for Human Operations."
33. WWF, *Living Planet Report 2016*.
34. Pope Francis, *Laudato si'*, §193.

35. Sommer and Welzer, *Transformationsdesign*.
36. Brand and Wissen, *Imperiale Lebensweise*.
37. Pope Francis, *Laudato si'*, §48.
38. Ibid., §51f.
39. Ibid., §54.
40. Ibid., §109.
41. Ibid., §114.
42. Ibid., §112.
43. Boff, *Cry of the Earth, Cry of the Poor*.
44. Descartes, *Discourse on Method*.
45. Pope Francis, *Laudato si'*, §67.
46. Bals, *A Successful Provocation for a Pluralistic Global Society*.
47. Capra and Luisi, *The System View of Life*.
48. Pope Francis, *Laudato si'*, §23.
49. Ibid., §95.
50. Ibid., §69.
51. Raskin, *Journey to Earthland*.

Bibliography

Bals, Christoph. *A Successful Provocation for a Pluralistic Global Society. The Encyclical Laudato si' – A Magna Carta of Integral Ecology as a Reaction to Humanity's Self-Destructive Course*. Bonn: Germanwatch, 2016. http://germanwatch.org/en/12697

Blühdorn, Ingofuhr. *Simulative Demokratie – Neue Politik nach der postdemokratischen Wende*. Berlin: Suhrkamp, 2013.

Boff, Leonardo. *Cry of the Earth, Cry of the Poor*. Maryknoll, NY: Orbis, 1997.

Brand, Ulrich und Markus Wissen. *Imperiale Lebensweise*. Munich: Ökom, 2017.

Capra, Fritjof, and Pier Luigi Luisi. *The System View of Life: A Unifying Vision*. Cambridge: Cambridge University Press, 2014.

Carson, Rachel. *Silent Spring*. Boston, MA: Houghton-Mifflin, 1962.

Descartes, René. *Discourse on Method*. Vol. XXXIV, Part 1. The Harvard Classics. New York: P.F. Collier & Son, 1909–14 (org, 1637).

Easterly, William. "The Trouble with the Sustainable Development Goals." *Current History* 114, no. 775 (2015): 322–324. http://www.currenthistory.com/Easterly_CurrentHistory.pdf

Escobar, Arturo. *Encountering Development: The Making and Unmaking of the Third World*. Princeton, NJ: Princeton University Press, 1995.

Esteva, Gustavo. "Development: Metaphor, Myth, Threat." *Development* 3 (1985): 78–79.

Fioramonti, Lorenzo. *Gross Domestic Problem: The Politics Behind the World's Most Powerful Number*. London: Zed Books, 2013.

Fioramonti, Lorenzo. *How Numbers Rule the World: The Use and Abuse of Statistics*. London: Zed Books, 2014.

Hickel, Jason. 2015. "Pope vs UN: Who Will Save the World First?" *Guardian*, June 23. https://www.theguardian.com/profile/jason-hickel

Jackson, Tim, and Robin Webster. *Limits Revisited. A Review of the Limits To Growth Debate*. London: APPG, 2016. limits2growth.org.uk/revisited

Lepenies, Philipp. *Die Macht der einen Zahl. Eine politische Geschichte das Bruttoinlandsprodukts*. Berlin: Suhrkamp, 2013.

Marx, Karl, and Friedrich Engels. *The Communist Manifesto*. London, 1848.

Pauw, Pieter, et al. *Different perspectives on Differentiated Responsibilities. A State-of-the-Art Review of the Notion of Common but Differentiated Responsibilities in International Negotiations*. Discussion Paper 6/2014. Bonn: DIE.

Pope Paul IV. *Encyclical Letter: Populorum Progressio*. Vatican City, 1967.

Pope Francis. *Encyclical letter: Laudato si'. On Care of our Common Home*. Vatican City, 2015. http://w2.vatican.va/content/francesco/en/encyclicals/documents/papa-francesco_20150524_enciclica-laudato-si.pdf

Pope Leo XIII. *Encyclical Letter: Rerum Novarum*. Vatican City, 1891.

Pörksen, Uwe. *Plastikwörter: die Sprache einer internationalen Diktatur*. Stuttgart: Klett, 1988.

Raskin, Paul. *Journey to Earthland. The Great Transition to Planetary Civilization*. Boston, MA: Tellus, 2016. http://www.greattransition.org/publication/journey-to-earthland

Rist, Gilbert. *The History of Development: From Western Origins to Global Faith*. London: Zed Books, 1997.

Rivera, Manuel. *Wieviel Entpolitisierung Vertragen Die SGDs?* IASS Working Paper, Potsdam, 2015. www.iass-potsdam.de/sites/.../working_paper_agenda_2030.pdf

Rockström, Johan, et al. "A Safe Space for Human Operations." *Nature* 461, no. 24 (2009): 472–475.

Sachs, Wolfgang, ed. *The Development Dictionary. A Guide to Knowledge as Power*. London: Zed Books, 1992 (reprint with a new preface, 2009).

Sachs, Wolfgang. "Development. Rise and Decline of an Idea." In *Encyclopedia of Global Environmental Change*, 4 vols, edited by Ted Munn. London: J. Wiley, 2001. https://epub.wupperinst.org/files/1078/WP108.pdf

Sommer, Bernd und Harald Welzer. *Transformationsdesign. Wege in eine zukunftsfähige Moderne*. Munich: Ökom, 2014.

Speich-Chassè, Daniel. *Die Erfindung des Bruttosozialprodukts. Globale Ungleichheit in der Wissensgeschichte der Ökonomie*. Göttingen: Vandenhoeck & Ruprecht, 2013.

UN Secretary-General's Independent Expert Advisory Group. *A World That Counts. Mobilizing Data Revolution for Sustainable Development*. New York, 2014. www.undatarevolution.org/report/

UNDP. *Human Development Report 2013. The Rise of the South: Human Progress in a Diverse World*. New York: UNDP, 2013.

United Nations. *Transforming our World: The 2030 Agenda for Sustainable Development*. New York: United Nations, 2015. https://sustainabledevelopment.un.org/post2015/transformingourworld

WWF. *Living Planet Report 2016. Risk and Resilience in a New Era*. Gland: WWF, 2016. wwf.panda.org/lpr

Ziai, Aram. *Development Discourse and Global History: From Colonialism to the Sustainable Development Goals*. Abingdon: Routledge, 2016.

The Post-Development Dictionary agenda: paths to the pluriverse

Federico Demaria ⓘ and Ashish Kothari

ABSTRACT
This article lays out both a critique of the oxymoron 'sustainable development', and the potential and nuances of a Post-Development agenda. We present ecological swaraj from India and Degrowth from Europe as two examples of alternatives to development. This gives a hint of the forthcoming book, provisionally titled *The Post-Development Dictionary*, that is meant to deepen and widen a research, dialogue and action agenda for activists, policymakers and scholars on a variety of worldviews and practices relating to our collective search for an ecologically wise and socially just world. This volume could be one base in the search for alternatives to United Nations' 2030 Agenda for Sustainable Development, in an attempt to truly transform the world. In fact, it is an agenda towards the pluriverse: 'a world where many worlds fit', as the Zapatista say.

1. Introduction

The year 2017 marks the 25th anniversary of *The Development Dictionary* edited by Wolfgang Sachs.[1] While the *Dictionary* might have fallen short of its intention to write the obituary of development, it did send shock waves through the activist, policy and scholarly worlds, and became an influential text. The relevance and impact of Sachs' book are still felt today. At the same time, there is no dearth of newly revitalised hegemonic notions, of which 'the green economy' (GE) might be best known, with the 'amoeba concept' (meaning its high malleability) of sustainable development still floating,[2] and indeed have been given new life by the global intergovernmental agreement on Sustainable Development Goals in 2015. In this context, we are working on a volume that, while emulating the spirit of the original *Dictionary*, brings both reincarnated worldviews and fresh alternatives to 'development' sharply into view. The starting point is the need to go beyond critique and concentrate efforts on articulating the narratives of those struggling to retain or create diverse ways of life against the homogenising forces of development. There is a need for radical Post-Development practices, ideas and worldviews to become an agenda for activists, policymakers and scholars, to help in truly 'transforming our world', and therefore be an alternative to the 2030 Agenda for Sustainable Development.[3]

ⓘ http://orcid.org/0000-0003-4939-8243

The concept of 'Post-Development' emerges from the confluence of four main books: first, *The Development Dictionary*, edited by Wolfgang Sachs; second, *Encountering Development*, by Arturo Escobar; third, *The History of Development*, by Gilbert Rist; fourth, *The Post-Development Reader*, edited by Rahnema and Bawtree.[4] Two decades later, our book, provisionally titled *The Post-Development Dictionary*, focuses more upon alternatives to, rather than the critique of, development.

Post-Development is generally meant as an era or approach in which development would no longer be the central organising principle of social life. Even as critiques of development increase in academic spaces, they are equally powerfully arising amongst indigenous peoples, other local communities, womens' rights movements, and other civil society arenas, most prominently amongst the victims of development. Across the world this is resulting in the resurfacing of ancient worldviews with current relevance, or new frameworks and visions that present systemic alternatives for human and planetary well-being. It is also forcing the decolonisation of knowledge systems and epistemologies, breaking down many of the dualisms that Western patriarchal paradigms have engendered, such as between humans and nature.

Post-Development is related to at least three other emerging imaginaries, those of post-capitalism (questioning capitalism's ability to fully and naturally occupy the economy, with the concomitant visualisation of an array of diverse economic practices), post- or de-growth (decentring growth from the definition of both the economy and social life) and post-patriarchy (challenging the primacy of masculinist approaches to political leadership, moral authority, social privilege and control of property). The current mood is 'to search for alternatives in a deeper sense, that is, aiming to break away from the cultural and ideological bases of development, bringing forth other imaginaries, goals, and practices'.[5]

Therefore, we argue that the time is ripe to deepen and widen a research, dialogue and action agenda on a variety of worldviews and practices relating to our collective search for an ecologically wise and socially just world. These should be transformative alternatives to the currently dominant processes of globalised development, including its structural roots in modernity,[6] capitalism, state domination, patriarchy, and more specific phenomena, like casteism, found in some in parts of the world. Plus, they should go beyond the false solutions that those in power are proposing in an attempt to 'greenwash' development, including variants of the GE, market remedies and technofixes. The Post-Development agenda should investigate the what, how, who and why of all that is transformative, and what is not. Equally, though, proponents of Post-Development need to go beyond a number of weaknesses in their narrative, acknowledge that development as an idea has not been buried, and sharpen their focus on the structural changes needed to deal with issues of inequity, injustice, deprivation and ecological collapse.[7]

The exploration of alternatives to development already finds concrete expression in a panoply of new or re-emerging concepts and practices such as *buen vivir*, degrowth, ecological *swaraj*, radical feminisms of various kinds, *ubuntu*, commoning, solidarity economy, food and energy sovereignty. These are perhaps the most visible examples of an emergent post-developmentalist epistemic-political field towards a pluriverse.[8] These radical alternatives are becoming not only more visible but, increasingly, genuinely credible and viable. And yet they are still marginal in comparison to the dominant narrative and practice of development. Thus, it seems a good moment to make such alternatives more widely known, and to facilitate bridges amongst them while respecting their geopolitical and epistemic specificities. It is also critical to build bridges between constructive alternatives and peoples' movements resisting the dominant economic and political systems.[9]

The article is structured as follows. First, we present a critique of development in its recent reincarnations, like 'sustainable development' and the GE, outlining the road from Stockholm 1972 to Rio+20, or the road from the critique to the defence of economic growth. Second, we introduce the origins and importance of transformative alternative worldviews and practices to development. Third, we outline the purpose and conceptualisation of the *Post-Development Dictionary*, with a set of questions at the core of the agenda for transformation that we are proposing.

2. Sustainable development, the green economy and their false solutions

'Everything must change in order to remain the same'.
Giuseppe Tomasi di Lampedusa,
The Leopard (1963)

In 1987, the United Nations (UN) World Commission on Development and the Environment presented the report *Our Common Future* (better known as the Brundtland report), coining the concept 'sustainable development', then launched at the Rio Summit on Environment and Development in 1992 (Principle 12 of the Summit Declaration). Within such a framing, the push towards growth and economic liberalisation was taken further at subsequent global events relating to sustainable development, though partially concealed behind the rhetoric of environmental sustainability. Compared to the United Nations Conference on Environment and Development in Stockholm in 1972, the later conferences involved an overall reframing of both the diagnosis and prognosis in relation to the ecological crisis (see Table 1). The focus supposedly became poverty in developing countries, instead of affluence in developed countries, along the lines of the post-materialist thesis of Inglehart (you first need to be rich, in order to be an environmentalist; critiqued by Martinez-Alier).[10] In so doing, economic growth was freed of the stigma, and reframed as a necessary step towards the solution of environmental problems.[11] This watering down of the initial debates of 1970s influenced by the Limits to Growth report[12] constitutes the core of the GE, a kind of Green Keynesianism with new millennium proposals such as a Green New Deal, and the 2030 Agenda for Sustainable Development.

At the UN Conference for Sustainable Development in 2012 (the so called Rio+20 Summit) the concept of GE played a key role as the guiding framework of the multilateral discussions

Table 1. A comparison of United Nations Environment Conferences: Stockholm 1972 and Rio 1992.[a]

	Stockholm 1972	Rio 1992
Prescription for the environmental crisis	Detailed enumeration of biotic and physical resources that should be preserved.	More abstract notion of 'sustainable development'.
Causes of environmental degradation	Resource extraction and existing relations of economic exploitation.	Poverty in developing countries.
Main actors	Governments.	Private initiatives: corporations and non-governmental organisations; Agenda 21 for municipalities (the lowest administration level).
Instruments	Political demands; Territorial and resource planning.	Legislation (eg environmental impact assessment); Market instruments.

[a]Based on Gómez-Baggethun and Naredo, "In Search of Lost Time."

(though resistance from many Southern nations meant it was not as central as its proponents may have wished). In preparation for the summit, The United Nations Environment Programme (UNEP) published a report on GE, defining it 'as one that results in improved human well-being and social equity, while significantly reducing environmental risks and ecological scarcities'.[13] In consonance with the pro-growth approach of sustainable development, the report by-passed any trade-off between economic growth and environmental conservation, and conceptualised natural capital as a 'critical economic asset' opening the doors for commodification (so-called green capitalism). In fact, it clearly stated that 'the key aim for a transition to a green economy is to enable economic growth and investment while increasing environmental quality and social inclusiveness'.[14]

As Gómez-Baggethun and Naredo report, in the Rio+20 final declaration, advocacy for economic growth is recalled in more than 20 articles. For example, Article 4 states that 'We also reaffirm the need to achieve sustainable development by: promoting sustained, inclusive and equitable economic growth'. This approach is based on neoclassical economic theory (environmental economics), leading to the belief that economic growth will de-link (or decouple) itself from its environmental base through dematerialisation and de-pollution because of the improvement in eco-efficiency (increased resource productivity and decreased pollution). In this conceptual framework, market prices are considered the appropriate means for solving environmental issues, and exogenous rates of technological progress are expected to counterbalance the effects of resource exhaustion. However, the conflict between a growth-dominated economy and the environment cannot be solved with appeals to 'sustainable development', 'eco-efficiency', 'ecological modernisation', 'geo-engineering', 'smart agricultures' or 'cities', 'circular' or GE. These are false solutions.

For instance, while the GE approach could be seen as an improvement over the conventional neoliberal economic model, it remains fundamentally flawed on a number of counts. For instance, the final objective for a New Green Deal is the creation of 'resilient low carbon economies, rich in jobs and based on independent sources of energy supply'.[15] While on this end there might be general agreement, controversy remains on the means to adopt. Among the flaws or weaknesses of the GE/Sustainable development (SD) approach as articulated thus far in various UN or UN-sponsored documents, including the declaration for *Transforming our World: The 2030 Agenda for Sustainable Development*,[16] are the following[17]:

1. Absence of an analysis of the historical and structural roots of poverty, hunger, unsustainability and inequities, which include centralisation of state power and capitalist monopolies;
2. Inadequate focus on direct democratic governance (decision-making by citizens and communities in face-to-face settings), beyond the stress on accountability and transparency;
3. Inability to recognise the biophysical limits to economic growth;
4. Continued subservience to private capital, and inability or unwillingness to democratise the economy;
5. Modern science and technology held up as panacea, ignoring their limits and marginalising other forms of knowledge;
6. Culture, ethics and spirituality side-lined;
7. Unbridled consumerism not tackled head-on;
8. Global relations built on localisation and self-reliance missing; and,

9. No new architecture of global governance, with a continued reliance on the centrality of nation-states, denying true democratisation.

These weaknesses outline why and how we consider the solutions that emerge out of SD and GE to be false. In the next section we instead present the alternatives that go beyond development, embedding a real potential for transformation.

3. Transformative alternatives to development: worldviews and practices

3.1. Critique of development and origins of alternative worldviews

A range of different and complementary notions or worldviews have emerged in various regions of the world, that seek to envision and achieve more fundamental transformation than that proposed by GE/SD approaches. Some of these are a revival of the longstanding worldviews of indigenous peoples; some have emerged from recent social and environmental movements in relation to old traditions and philosophies. Arising from different cultural and social contexts, they sometime differ on the prescription (what shall be done how), but they share the main characteristics of the diagnosis (what is the problem and who is responsible for it) as well as similar or equivalent *Weltanschauungen* (worldviews). *The Post-Development Dictionary* aims to illuminate pathways towards a synergic articulation of these alternatives to development.[18]

Unlike sustainable development, which is a concept based on false consensus,[19] these alternative approaches cannot be reduced to any single one and therefore do not aspire to be adopted as a common goal by the United Nations, the Organisation for Economic Co-operation and Development (OECD) or the African Union. These ideas are born as proposals for radical change from local to global. In a post-political condition,[20] they intend to re-politicise the debate on the much-needed socio-ecological transformation, affirming dissidence with the current world representations and searching for alternative ones. Along these lines, they are a critique of the current development hegemony, meaning a critique of the homogenisation of cultures due to the widespread adoption of particular technologies and consumption and production models experienced in the Global North.[21] The Western development model is a mental construct adopted by the rest of the world that needs to be deconstructed.[22] Development might therefore be seen as a toxic term to be rejected,[23] and, thus, 'sustainable development' as an oxymoron.

Deconstructing development opens up the door for a multiplicity of new and old notions and worldviews, or else a matrix of alternatives.[24] This includes *buen vivir*, a culture of life with different names and varieties in various regions of South America; *Ubuntu* with its emphasis on human mutuality in South Africa and several equivalents in other parts of Africa; *Swaraj* with a focus on self-reliance and self-governance, in India; and many others.[25] What is important is that while they are ancient, they are re-emerging in original or modified forms as a part of the narrative of movements that are struggling against development and/or asserting alternative forms of well-being. Ecofeminist arguments represent a further strand in this Post-Development rainbow.[26]

These worldviews are not a novelty of the twenty-first century, but they are rather part of a long search for and practice of alternative ways of living forged in the furnace of humanity's struggle for emancipation and enlightenment *within* (rather than outside of) the womb of nature. What is remarkable about these alternative proposals, however, is that they often arise from traditionally marginalised groups. These worldviews are different from dominant Western ones as they emerge from non-capitalist communities, or from non-capitalist spaces such as the household sector in the Global North.[27] They are therefore independent of the anthropocentric and androcentric logic of capitalism, the dominant civilisation, as well as of the various state socialist (effectively state capitalist) models existing until now. Other approaches emerging from within industrialised countries – the belly of the beast, so to speak – can also break from the dominant logic, such as is the case with degrowth (an example of a non-occidentalist West).[28]

These worldviews differ sharply from today's notion of development. It is not about applying a set of policies, instruments and indicators to exit 'underdevelopment' and reach that desired condition of 'development'. In any case, how many countries have achieved development? Decades after the notion of 'development' was spread around the world, only a handful of countries can be called 'developed', others are struggling to emulate them, and all are doing this at enormous ecological and social cost. The problem is not in the lack of implementation, but rather in the concept of development as linear, unidirectional material and financial growth. The world experiences a widespread 'bad development', including those countries regarded as industrialised, ie countries whose lifestyle was to serve as a reference beacon for backward countries. The functioning of the global system is itself a 'bad developer'.

In short, it is urgent to dissolve the traditional concept of progress in its productivist drift and of development (as well as its many synonyms) as a unidirectional concept, especially in its mechanistic view of economic growth. However, it is not only about dissolving it; different views are required, much richer in content as well as in complexity. As Kallis explains:

> Sustainable development and its more recent reincarnation 'green growth' depoliticize genuine political antagonisms between alternative visions for the future. They render environmental problems technical, promising win–win solutions and the impossible goal of perpetuating economic growth without harming the environment.[29]

Therefore, these alternative approaches are necessary to challenge the ideas of GE and SD and the associated belief in economic growth as a desirable path in political agendas. They are also important in presenting to us a set of ethical values and principles that underlie positive, transformative action, such as diversity, solidarity, commons, oneness with nature, interconnectedness, simplicity, inclusiveness, equity and non-hierarchy, pluriversality and peace.

Hereafter we briefly describe two of these transformative alternatives coming from the contexts in which we, the authors, live: ecological swaraj (or Radical Ecological Democracy) from India and Degrowth from Europe.

3.2. Ecological swaraj or Radical Ecological Democracy

Emerging from the grassroots experience of communities and civil society practising or conceiving of alternatives across the range of human endeavour in India, ecological swaraj (loosely, self-rule including self-reliance), or Radical Ecological Democracy (RED) is a framework that respects the limits of the Earth and the rights of other species, while pursuing the core values of social justice and equity. With its strong democratic and egalitarian impulse, it seeks to empower every person to be a part of decision-making, and its holistic vision of human well-being encompasses physical, material, socio-cultural, intellectual and spiritual dimensions.[30] Rather than the state and the corporation, it puts collectives and communities at the centre of governance and the economy, an approach that is grounded in real-life initiatives across the Indian subcontinent (see www.alternativesindia.org).

This approach rests on the following intersecting spheres: ecological wisdom and sustainability, social well-being and justice, economic democracy, direct political democracy, and cultural diversity. Fundamental to it is a set of values that include diversity, autonomy, cooperation and solidarity, rights with responsibilities, equity and justice, inclusion, simplicity and sufficiency, respect for all life, non-violence, interconnectedness, dignity of labour, and others.

Ecological swaraj is an evolving approach, not a blueprint set in stone. In its very process of democratic grassroots evolution, it forms an alternative to top-down ideologies and formulations, even as it takes on board the relevant elements of such ideologies.

3.3. Degrowth: not less of the same, but simply different

Degrowth calls for a rejection of the obsession with economic growth as a panacea for the solution of all problems. It should not be interpreted in its literal meaning (decrease of the gross domestic product) because that phenomenon already has a name: it is called recession. Degrowth does not mean 'less of the same'; it is simply different.[31] It was born in the Global North, and it is being developed for that context, though the questioning of a one-way future consisting only of economic growth is also inspired by – and relevant for – the Global South.[32]

The term was proposed by political ecologist André Gorz in 1972. In Australia, Ted Trainer was urging the public to *Abandon Affluence!* in 1985; in Germany, ecofeminists Maria Mies and Veronica Bennholdt-Thomsen argued *The Subsistence Perspective* in 1993.[33] Other European environmental activists used degrowth in 2001 as a provocative slogan or *mot-obus*, a missile word to re-politicise environmentalism. It springs from the hypothesis that we can live well with less and offers a frame that connects diverse ideas, concepts and proposals.[34]

Generally, degrowth challenges the hegemony of growth and calls for a democratically led redistributive downscaling of production and consumption in industrialised countries as a means to achieve environmental sustainability, social justice and well-being. Degrowth is usually associated with the idea that smaller can be beautiful. However, the emphasis should not only be on 'less', but also on 'different'. Degrowth signifies a society with a smaller metabolism (the energy and material throughput of the economy), but, more importantly, a society with a metabolism which has a different structure and serves new functions. In a degrowth society everything will be different from the current mainstream: activities, forms and uses of energy, relations, gender roles, allocations of time between paid and non-paid work, and relations with the non-human world.

Hereafter, we outline the purpose and conceptualisation of *The Post-Development Dictionary* that aims to collect and articulate the transformative alternatives to (sustainable) development.

4. *The Post-Development Dictionary* agenda: towards the pluriverse

At a time when neoliberal governments and rampant extractivism brutalise the everyday life of citizens across the world and in particular the Global South, it is crucial that opposi-tional voices and people's movements engage in a concentrated effort of research, outreach, dialogue and action, informed by and informing grassroots practice. Resistance is crucial, but it is not enough. We need our own narratives. Acts of resistance and regeneration offer hope in the here and now. This is what *The Post-Development Dictionary* is all about. It is meant to be a process of research, writing and dialogue that will culminate in a comprehen-sive book in early 2018. The dictionary format of the book comprises a series of keyword entries, with one or more expert scholars or practitioners writing each. The book has three main sections, provisionally titled as follows: (1) 'Global Reflections on an Old Idea: Development'; (2) 'False Solutions'; and (3) 'Transformative Alternatives: Worldviews and Practices'. It is co-edited by the two authors of this article in collaboration with Ariel Salleh, Arturo Escobar and Alberto Acosta.

In sum, the book aims to, first, present a rich variety of worldviews and practices relating to the collective search for an ecologically wise and socially just world, with well-known ones like eco-socialism, *buen vivir* or ecofeminism, but also with those rarely heard of like kyosei, minobimaatisiiwin and Nayakrishi. A vast range of approaches of indigenous peoples, peas-ant and pastoral communities, peoples' movements and urban communities are covered. It also offers critical essays on a number of false solutions that those in power are proposing in an attempt to 'greenwash' development, such as efficiency, techno-fixes, smart cities, lifeboat ethics, (neo)extractivism, GE and eco-modernism. The second aim is to consolidate a 25-year-long debate on the criticism of and alternatives to development, beyond the current fragmentation, presenting both its state of the art and future challenges, with con-tributions from influential international authors from different disciplines and continents. The third aim of the book is to be a guide to understanding the most important concepts of Post-Development for readers interested in grasping its nuances, and along the way help to clarify and overcome common misunderstandings and criticisms, and provide a basis to further advance both intellectual research and political practice of the alternatives to devel-opment. And, fourth, it aims to be a small but significant contribution to a worldwide con-fluence of alternative cultural, economic, social, political and ecological visions and practices.

5. Conclusions

This article has attempted to briefly lay out both the critique of (sustainable) development and the potential and nuances of a Post-Development agenda. *The Post-Development Dictionary* is meant to deepen and widen a research, dialogue and action agenda for activists, policymakers and scholars on a variety of worldviews and practices relating to our collective search for an ecologically wise and socially just world. These are meant to be truly transform-ative, and may be distinguished from the false solutions in a number of ways: firstly, their attempts to transform the structural roots of a problem, along political, economic, social, cultural, and ecological axes; secondly, in their explicit or implicit questioning of the core assumptions of the development discourse (eg growth, material progress, instrumental rationality, the centrality of markets and economy, universality, modernity and its binaries, and so forth); and, third, in encompassing a radically different set of ethics and values to those underpinning the current system, including diversity, solidarity, commons, oneness with nature, interconnectedness, simplicity, inclusiveness, equity, non-hierarchy, pluriversality and peace.

In conclusion, these alternatives to development practices and worldviews intend to re-politicise the debate on the much-needed socio-ecological transformation, affirming dissidence with the current world representations (ie sustainable development) and searching for alternative ones. They highlight the necessity to overcome the modern ontology of one world and expand on the multiplicity of worlds possible. As Escobar argues:

> The modern ontology presumes the existence of One World – a universe. This assumption is undermined by discussions in Transition Discourses, the buen vivir, and the rights of Nature. In emphasizing the profound relationality of all life, these newer tendencies show that there are indeed relational worldviews or ontologies for which the world is always multiple – a pluriverse. Relational ontologies are those that eschew the divisions between nature and culture, individual and community, and between us and them that are central to the modern ontology. Some of today's struggles could be seen as reflecting the defence and activation of relational communities and worldviews … and as such they could be read as *ontological struggles*; they refer to *a different way of imagining life*, to an other mode of existence. They point towards the pluriverse; in the successful formula of the Zapatista, the pluriverse can be described as 'a world where many worlds fit'.[35]

Along these lines, *The Post-Development Dictionary* will hopefully be an exciting volume of essays on transformative alternatives to the currently dominant processes of globalised development, including its structural roots in modernity, capitalism, state domination, patriarchy and other forces. The book is meant to help in the steps towards an equitable, just and ecologically wise world. When the language in use is inadequate to articulate what begs to be articulated, then it is time for a new dictionary – *The Post-Development Dictionary*: *An Agenda towards the Pluriverse*.

Disclosure statement

No potential conflict of interest was reported by the authors.

Funding

Federico Demaria and Ashish Kothari acknowledge the support of the European Research Council for the EnvJustice project [GA 695446], and Federico also of the Spanish government for the SINALECO project [CSO2014-54513-R].

Acknowledgements

The authors acknowledge useful comments on a previous draft by Ariel Alleh, Alberto Acosta and Arturo Escobar, and kind support by the Editor Aram Ziai. Special thanks to grass-roots activists who continue to be an incredible source of inspiration. Ashish Kothari also acknowledges links to the ACKnowl-EJ project [TKN150317115354] of the International Social Science Council.

Notes

1. Sachs, *Development Dictionary*.
2. Words like 'development' or 'strategy' have been called 'amoeba concepts' or 'plastic words' because of their malleability and the uncanny way they are used to fit every circumstance; Poerksen, *Plastic Words*. Like plastic Lego blocks, they are combinable and interchangeable. In the mouths of experts – politicians, professors, corporate officials and planners – they are used over and over again to explain and justify any type of plans and projects.
3. United Nations, *Transforming our World: The 2030 Agenda*.
4. Sachs, *Development Dictionary*; Escobar, *Encountering Development*; Rist, *History of Development*; Rahnema and Bawtree, *Post-Development Reader*.
5. Gudynas and Acosta, "La renovación," 75.
6. Note that a critique of 'modernity' does not imply a rejection of all that is 'modern', nor an uncritical acceptance of all that is 'traditional'; we are well aware that traditional societies had (and have) many aspects of inequity and injustice, and that elements of what has emerged in contemporary times have been liberating for those previously suppressed. It is the hegemonising, unidirectional, Western-centricism of modernity we are pointing to.
7. Ziai, "Post-development: Premature Burials."
8. See Walter Mignolo, "On Pluriversality," available at: https://waltermignolo.com/on-pluriversality/, accessed March 9, 2017.
9. Kothari, Demaria, and Acosta, "Buen Vivir," 362–75.
10. Inglehart, *Culture Shift*; Martinez-Alier, *Environmentalism of the Poor*.
11. Gómez-Baggethun and Naredo, "In Search of Lost Time."
12. Meadows et al., *Limits to Growth*.
13. UNEP, *Towards a Green Economy*.
14. Ibid.
15. UNEP, *Towards a Green Economy*; NEF, *A Green New Deal*.
16. SDSN, *Action Agenda for Sustainable Development*; UNEP, *Towards a Green Economy*; United Nations Secretary-General's High-level Panel on Global Sustainability, *Resilient People, Resilient Planet*; United Nations, *New Global Partnership*; United Nations, *Transforming our World: The 2030 Agenda*.
17. Adapted from Kothari, "Missed Opportunity?"
18. For earlier attempts, see Salleh, *Ecofeminism as Politics*; Kothari, Demaria, and Acosta, "Buen Vivir," 362–75; Escobar, "Degrowth, Postdevelopment, and Transitions."
19. Shiva, *Staying Alive*; Hornborg, "Zero-Sum World."

20. Swyngedouw, "Impossible/Undesirable Sustainability."
21. Escobar, *Encountering Development*; Rist, *History of Development*.
22. Latouche, *Farewell to Growth*.
23. Dearden, "Is Development Becoming a Toxic Term?"
24. Latouche, *Farewell to Growth*.
25. Gudynas, "Buen Vivir: Today's Tomorrow," 441–7; Metz, "Ubuntu as a Moral Theory," 532–59; Kothari, "Radical Ecological Democracy," 36–45.
26. Shiva, *Staying Alive*; Salleh, *Ecofeminism as Politics*.
27. Mies, *Patriarchy and Accumulation*; Salleh, *Ecofeminism as Politics*.
28. Sousa Santos, "Non-Occidentalist West?"
29. Kallis, "Degrowth Alternative."
30. Shrivastava and Kothari, *Churning*; Kothari, "Radical Ecological Democracy," 36–45.
31. D'Alisa, Demaria, and Kallis, *Degrowth*.
32. Demaria et al., "What Is Degrowth?"
33. Trainer, *Abandon Affluence!*; Mies and Bennholdt-Thomsen, *Subsistence Perspective*.
34. Demaria et al., "What Is Degrowth?"
35. Escobar, "Sustainability: Design for the Pluriverse," 139, quote in original.

Bibliography

D'Alisa, G., F. Demaria, and G. Kallis. *Degrowth: A Vocabulary for a New Era*. London: Routledge, 2014.

Dearden, Nick. 2014. "Is Development Becoming a Toxic Term?" *The Guardian*, January 22. https://www.theguardian.com/global-development-professionals-network/2015/jan/22/development-toxic-term?CMP=share_btn_tw

Demaria, F., F. Schneider, F. Sekulova, and J. Martinez-Alier. "What Is Degrowth? From an Activist Slogan to a Social Movement." *Environmental Values* 22 (2013): 191–215.

Escobar, A. *Encountering Development*. Princeton: Princeton University Press, 1995.

Escobar, A. "Sustainability: Design for the Pluriverse." *Development* 54, no. 2 (2011): 137–140.

Escobar, A. "Degrowth, Postdevelopment, and Transitions: A Preliminary Conversation." *Sustainability Science* 10, no. 3 (2015): 451–462.

Gómez-Baggethun, E., and J. M. Naredo. "In Search of Lost Time: The Rise and Fall of Limits to Growth in International Sustainability Policy." *Sustainability Science* 10, no. 3 (2015): 385–395.

Gudynas, E. "Buen Vivir: Today's Tomorrow." *Development* 54, no. 4 (2011): 441–447.

Gudynas, E., and A. Acosta. "La renovaclón de la crítica al desarrollo y el buen vivir como alternativa." [The Renovation to the Critique to Development and Buen Vivir as an Alternative.] *Utopia y Praxis Latinoamerica* 16, no. 53 (2011): 71–83.

Hornborg, A. "Zero-Sum World." *International Journal of Comparative Sociology* 50, nos. 3–4 (2009): 237–262.

Inglehart, R. *Culture Shift in Advanced Industrial Societies*. Princeton: Princeton University Press, 1990.

Kallis, G. 'The Degrowth Alternative', Great Transition Initiative, 2015. https://www.greattransition.org/publication/the-degrowth-alternative

Kothari, A. *Missed Opportunity? Comments on Two Global Reports for the Post-2015 Goals Process*. Pune: Kalpavriksh and ICCA Consortium, 2013. https://www.un-ngls.org/IMG/pdf/Kalpavriksh_and_ICCA_Consortium_-_Post-2015_reports_critique_-_Ashish_Kothari_July_2013.pdf

Kothari, A. "Radical Ecological Democracy: A Way for India and beyond." *Development* 57, no. 1 (2014): 36–45. doi:10.1057/dev.2014.43.

Kothari, Ashish, Federico Demaria, and Alberto Acosta. "Buen vivir, Degrowth and Ecological Swaraj: Alternatives to Development and the Green Economy." *Development* 57, no. 3 (2015): 362–375.

Latouche, S. *Farewell to Growth*. London: Polity, 2009.

Martinez-Alier, J. *The Environmentalism of the Poor: A Study of Ecological Conflicts and Valuation*. Cheltenham: Edward Elgar, 2002.

Meadows, D. H., D. L. Meadows, J. Randers, and W. W. Beherns III. *The Limits to Growth*. New York: Universe Books, 1972.

Metz, T. "Ubuntu as a Moral Theory and Human Rights in South Africa." *African Human Rights Law Journal* 11, no. 2 (2011): 532–559.

Mies, M. *Patriarchy and Accumulation on a World Scale*. London: Zed, 1986.

Mies, M., and V. Bennholdt-Thomsen. *The Subsistence Perspective*. London: Zed, 1993.

NEF. *A Green New Deal: Joined-up Policies to Solve the Triple Crunch of the Credit Crisis, Climate Change and High Oil Prices*. Green New Deal Group, New Economics Foundation, 2008. https://b.3cdn.net/nefoundation/8f737ea195fe56db2f_xbm6ihwb1.pdf.

Poerksen, U. *Plastic Words: The Tyranny of a Modular Language*. University Park: Penn State University Press, 2004.

Rahnema, M., and V. Bawtree. *The Post-Development Reader*. London: Zed Books, 1997.

Rist, G. *The History of Development: From Western Origins to Global Faith*. Expanded ed. London: Zed Books, 2003.

Sachs, W. *The Development Dictionary: A Guide to Knowledge as Power*. London: Zed Books, 1992.

Salleh, A. *Ecofeminism as Politics*. London: Zed Books/New York: Palgrave, 1997.

SDSN. *An Action Agenda for Sustainable Development*, Report for the Secretary General. Sustainable Development Solutions Network, 2013.

Shrivastava, A., and A. Kothari. *Churning the Earth: The Making of Global India*. Delhi: Penguin Books India, 2012.

Shiva, V. *Staying Alive: Women, Ecology and Development*. London: Zed Books, 1989.

Sousa Santos, B. "A Non-Occidentalist West? Learned Ignorance and Ecology of Knowledge." *Theory, Culture and Society* 26, nos. 7–8 (2009): 103–125.

Swyngedouw, E. "Impossible/Undesirable Sustainability and the Post-Political Condition." In *The Sustainable Development Paradox*, edited by J. R. Krueger and D. Gibbs, 13–40. New York: Guilford Press, 2007.

Tomasi di Lampedusa, G. *The Leopard*. Milan: Feltrinelli, 1958.

Trainer, T. *Abandon Affluence!* London: Zed, 1985.

UNEP. *Towards a Green Economy: Pathways to Sustainable Development and Poverty Eradication*, A Synthesis for Policy Makers. Nairobi: United Nations Environment Programme, 2011. www.unep.org/greeneconomy.

United Nations. *A New Global Partnership: Eradicate Poverty and Transform Economies through Sustainable Development*, The Report of the High-Level Panel of Eminent Persons on the Post-2015 Development Agenda. New York: United Nations, 2013.

United Nations. *Transforming Our World: The 2030 Agenda for Sustainable Development*. New York: United Nations, 2015. https://sustainabledevelopment.un.org/post2015/transformingourworld/publication.

United Nations Secretary-General's High-level Panel on Global Sustainability. *Resilient People, Resilient Planet: A Future worth Choosing*. New York: United Nations, 2012.

Ziai, Aram. "Post-Development: Premature Burials and Haunting Ghosts." *Development and Change* 46, no. 4 (2015): 833–854.

Living Well: ideas for reinventing the future

Alberto Acosta[†]

ABSTRACT

In various parts of the world, growing and serious problems, especially economic, social and environmental, are increasingly calling into question the conventional ideas of progress. The lives of human beings are in danger. We are in 'the age of survival', a sort of crossroads in which the future of the human species is defined. That is why alternatives that exceed the dominant concepts typical of Modernity are arising from many sectors and places. Above all, natives are determined to recover their origins and even to strengthen their ancestral practices, from their past to project into the future. And there are those who try to build bridges between these different shores, from which it may be possible to build other worlds where life with dignity for all beings existing on the planet is a possibility.

As the concept of 'Living Well' takes root in our collective imagination, it not only strives to remind the world that other ways of living are possible … it also posits another way of understanding the world.
    Enrique Leff

Origins of a concept

Conventional ideas of progress, together with its main offspring, development, are increasingly coming into question throughout the world. This is due to growing resistance in the face of the world's worsening economic, social and environmental problems. Bubbling up from the wellspring of memory, a memory that in many communities throughout the world goes back very far, the ideas, values, experiences and practices of Living Well are sowing themselves in this landscape.

[†]Translator's note: This article was originally titled 'El Buen Vivir' in Spanish. This is an Ecuadorean indigenous concept that is difficult to translate exactly into English. An approximate translation, which has now become widely accepted as the standard translation, is 'Living Well'. This is the term used throughout the translation of this article. A similar concept exists in Bolivia, under the name 'Vivir Bien'. As these concepts are considered almost identical, and as neither of them is straightforward to translate into English, they are both conflated to have the same English translation, namely 'Living Well'. In some instances, the author refers to both the Ecuadorean and the Bolivian variants in the same sentence. In the English translation, these are condensed into a single use of the term 'Living Well'.

As human life comes under increasing threat, we must rediscover those groups of humans who have sought to live in harmony and equilibrium with the world's ecological cycles. The lived reality of these people, invisibilised until very recently, stands in contrast with the world of progress, whose 'achievement' is a system which asphyxiates all that is alive and has generated a landscape replete with many different forms of violence.

As such, we should not be surprised to find ourselves in 'the epoch of survival'. We are passing through a crossroads in which the future of the human species is being defined.[1] Traditional visions of progress and development are incapable of offering ways out of this crisis. Moreover, it is precisely these visions that are, in fact, directly responsible for the complex and grave crises which currently afflict humanity.[2]

Faced with this scenario, throughout much of the world different social sectors have undertaken to recover existing alternatives, as well as proposing new ones, aimed at transcending the dominant concepts of modernity.[3] Above all, indigenous peoples from the Amazon and Andean regions of Latin America are showing great determination in reaffirming their origins and, in some cases, are even striving to strengthen their ancestral practices. In this way, they seek to project their past onto the future.

This reaffirmation of indigenous alternatives coincides with debates about post-development. The list of authors questioning the visions, theories, policies, and practices of conventional development is growing daily. In addition to Wolfgang Sachs' now classic contribution from 1992,[4] other reference points worth mentioning include Arturo Escobar, Enrique Leff, Gustavo Esteva, Eduardo Gudynas and Vandana Shiva, as well as many others. As such, there is no shortage of people attempting to build bridges between the diverse shores of human experience. Such bridges enable us to strengthen our efforts at constructing other worlds, worlds in which all existing living beings on the planet can enjoy a dignified life. In this context, Living Well stands out as 'the most attractive alternative to capitalist modernity'.[5]

The shipwreck of development

Slowly, but surely, the promise of development, nourished by notions of progress that emerged with modernity, is losing its grip on society. Let us recall how, in the fourth point of his Inaugural Address on 20 January 1949, US President Harry Truman gave the world a social goal to aspire to: development, as encapsulated in the phrase the 'American Way of Life'. And, now, finally, this extraordinarily powerful illusion is being dispelled.

Consequently, Truman called on the world to overcome what he saw as the opposite of development, namely underdevelopment. According to Truman, underdevelopment existed in large swathes of the planet. In order to set about this task, his proposed yardstick for comparing levels of development was the 'development' of the big industrialised countries. Guided by this, the campaign to develop the world rapidly became the broadest and most sustained campaign ever seen in human history. First and foremost, development was conceived as a state-centric process, in which the market was, and still is, assigned a far from negligible role as the main institution responsible for organising the economy (and also society itself).[6]

Right from the outset, this crusade was criticised. Since then the limitations of development have become increasingly clear, especially in recent years. However, despite all this, the crusade for development continues unabated today. A broad spectrum of different approaches to development now exists, ranging from the most economistic versions which equate development with gross domestic product (GDP) growth, to the most complex versions, human-scale or sustainable development. This is just the tip of the iceberg. However, as disenchantment with development spreads throughout the world, a post-development landscape is also taking shape, rooted in the growing strength of alternative proposals and discussions. Unceta summarises these debates clearly, by locating them within the contributions of Living Well.[7]

The basis of the current critique of the concept of development is interesting. On the one hand, the concept rules and regiments the lives of a large part of humanity. Yet, perversely, despite the fact that development is so strongly yearned for, it has become a fantasy that is impossible to achieve.

Furthermore, it is now clear that even those countries considered to be developed also appear to be prisoners to progress. There are unmistakable signs of serious contradictions, conflicts and difficulties emerging in the USA, Europe and Japan. These include, amongst other things, the growing gulf between the rich and the poor, dissatisfaction even amongst those sectors of society which have benefitted from accumulating large amounts material wealth, and the inability to solve the urgent unemployment crisis using the traditional tools available. Meanwhile, in parallel, the destruction of Nature[8] continues unabated. What is more, even countries, such as China, often seen as recent 'success stories' of development, have, in the last few years, also embarked along the same path. It is as if the emerging shipwreck has been hardwired into their development.

We can conclude from this that the world is in the midst of a generalised 'bad development',[9] which is even afflicting those countries considered to be developed. Yet, as Tortosa explains, the problem involves much more than this:

> The contemporary world system serves to promote 'bad development'. The reasons for this are obvious. It is a system based in efficiency as a means to maximize results, reduce costs and achieve endless accumulation of capital … In a world in which 'anything goes', the problem does not lie with the rules of the game, but rather with the game itself. In other words, the world system is badly developed not through some malfunctioning of the system, but precisely because of the system's own internal logic and its normal functioning. Thus, it is this systemic logic that we must devote our attention towards.[10]

It is clear that this 'bad development' does not afflict all countries equally. It is much more evident in the peripheral countries than in the capitalist core. A complex situation exists in which the world's impoverished countries remain dependent on the logic of the accumulation of transnational capital, an accumulation process centred around an increasingly violent and insatiable extractivism.[11]

All of this goes to explain why we are witnessing an ever-greater flourishing of alternative conceptions in many different parts of the world, including in those parts of the world where society has achieved the highest living standards. Interestingly, and of profound importance, many of these alternative proposals originate from traditionally marginalised and exploited social sectors. It is the indigenous peoples who, in adverse conditions, are striving to uphold their ancestral values, experiences and practices.[12]

These are the concerns taken up in this article.

On the meaning of Living Well

Most approaches to conventional development, including many of the critical currents, have emerged from western knowledge systems associated with so-called modernity. In contrast to this, we are drawn to the fact that the alternative visions of Living Well are more profoundly transformative, in that they actually escape the limits of the dominant capitalist civilisation, a system that is based in anthropocentrism and utilitarianism. This article pays special attention to visions held by the peoples of Abya-Yala, the continent which, since the arrival of the European Conquistadors, has been known as America.[13]

The most well-known terms for Living Well are the phrases used in Ecuador, *Buen Vivir*, and in Bolivia, *Vivir Bien*.[14] Equivalent concepts can be found in South America's traditionally marginalised, but not extinct, indigenous languages. Amongst other terms, these include: *sumak kawsay* (in Quechua), *suma qamaña* (in Aymara), *ñande reko* or *tekó porã* (in Guarani), *pénker pujústin* (in Shuar) and *shiir waras* (in Ashuar). Other indigenous peoples also have similar notions. In Chile, the Mapuche have *kyme mogen*; in Panama, the Kuna have *balu wala*; and, in Nicaragua, the Miskitus have *laman laka*. This latter concept is also shared by Mayan traditions in Guatemala and in Chiapas, Mexico.

Such approaches are not only to be found in Latin America. Similar approaches and proposals also exist in the values, experiences and, above all, existing practices in different periods and different regions of Mother Earth. These varied approaches go by different names and have different characteristics in different parts of the world and amongst different cultures. In many respects, they are similar to the indigenous practices in South America, while in other respects they may differ. In Africa, *Ubuntu* stands out as one such practice. *Ubuntu* refers to a sense of community[15] in which a person is a person only by virtue of the existence of other people and other living beings.[16] Also of interest is the Indian concept of *Swaraj* which refers to radical ecological democracy.[17]

These proposals gained political momentum at the turn of the millennium, and in some countries, they came to take centre stage in national debates. Their impact was especially strong in Bolivia and Ecuador. Both of these countries, whose national states were oligarchic and of colonial origin, were in a moment of deep crisis and experienced intense revolts throughout the neoliberal era. This was due to the organisational strength of the indigenous movements, in alliance with other popular forces.

The indigenous world has still not managed to banish the processes of conquest and colonisation, processes which have lingered well into today's republican era. Yet, despite this, what distinguished this eruption of indigenous movements was the sheer vigour with which they stepped forward as political subjects and standard bearers of their own worldview or *Weltanschauung*. This is what lies behind the emergence and political power of Living Well as a new paradigm.

As Living Well, with its vision of living in harmony with Nature, emerged as a concept, a parallel process was also underway. The accumulated criticisms levelled against development gained maturity, and ecological alternatives began to grow in strength. These two parallel processes resonated well with each other. However, the convergence between these two processes presents both an opportunity and a threat. On the one hand, the current moment offers good possibilities for developing, in a horizontal and respectful way, new ways of understanding the world and imagining alternatives. On the other hand, traditional readings of modernity may, once again, give rise to new schemes for appropriating, subordinating and usurping these indigenous visions. This would indeed be unfortunate.

Of great contemporary relevance, all these counter-visions are also, in different ways, deeply rooted in history. This is especially true of the indigenous outlooks. Thus, Living Well represents philosophical visions of indigenous peoples which cannot be compared to western philosophies. They are living philosophies and practices, relying neither on professional philosophers nor on theories. Above all, they are based on communal experiences, collective memories and a multiplicity of daily life practices. As daily breathed experiences they stand apart from frigid concepts.

An important aspect of Living Well, a political discourse par excellence, is that it does not consist of completely finished proposals that are no longer open to discussion. The concept does not emerge from academic reflections, or from proposals elaborated by any political party. Rather, Living Well emerges from a Millenarian Andean Amazon context or similar contexts which herald other rationalities and other forms of understanding the world. Importantly, it simultaneously combines both thought and emotion.[18,19] This makes it extremely difficult, if not impossible, to understand the concept of Living Well using the theoretical instruments of modernity.

These cosmovisions are bound to specific territories and arise from non-capitalist communitarian roots that are in harmony with Nature. They offer a distinct way of understanding the world compared to the western epistemology. Viewed this way, Living Well is suggestive of transformation on a civilisational scale, based on moving away from anthropocentrism and towards biocentrism. In fact, Living Well is best understood as the interweaving of multiple harmonious relations, none of which has a single centre. It is not an individualist approach but a communal one. Neither one-dimensional nor mono-cultural, it is based in plurality and diversity. Above all, understanding Living Well requires a deep process of intellectual decolonisation of our understanding of political, social and economic issues, as well as, of course, in the cultural sphere.[20]

It is important to stress that when we talk about Living Well in Ecuador and Bolivia we are in fact thinking in the plural. In other words, we imagine many different Living Wells coexisting, rather than a single and homogeneous Living Well. Such a single and homogeneous version of Living Well would in any case be impossible to crystallise. In contrast to what occurred with the concept of 'development' in the mid-twentieth century, Living Well should not take the form of a single global command defining what society should look like.

Although we will continue to refer to Living Well in the singular throughout this text, we shall not lose sight of the plurality that the term does in fact encapsulate. This is important, as this conception of multiple coexisting Living Wells opens the door to paths which, on the one hand, need to be imagined in order to be constructed, and, on the other hand, are in fact already a reality. The major potential of these visions and experiences lies in the fact that they are simultaneously about both reconstruction and construction. However, this is not all that they offer. As Enrique Leff has noted, Living Well not only offers the possibility of collectively imagining other forms of organising life, but also affords different ways of understanding the world.[21] These twin aspects are what give the concept its great potential.

As such, Living Well is a lived experience that is profoundly subversive of the future. It would be wrong to suggest that it is merely in an invitation to go backwards in time in order to reconnect with an idyllic world that no longer exists for anyone who is not a part of it.

However, in order for Living Well to live up to its transformative potential, efforts should be made to avoid it becoming a kind of religion with its own catechisms, manuals, ministries and political commissars.[22]

Of fundamental importance is the fact that indigenous knowledge has no concept that is analogous to the idea of development. There is no notion of a linear life process based on a state of before and after. In other words, the dichotomy between underdevelopment and development, a dichotomy through which people and countries must pass in order to achieve well-being just as occurred in the western world, does not exist. Neither do the concepts of wealth and poverty exist, as determined by the accumulation of material goods or the lack thereof. And, of course, another distinguishing factor is that indigenous knowledge sees human beings as just one more actor in Nature and not as its 'crown'.

Living Well draws great inspiration from harmony, based on a way of living in which humanity as a species is in harmony with itself, and in which individuals live harmoniously in community. And, from this, another basic premise comes, namely that communities are also harmonious with each other, all the way up to peoples and nations. And, in turn, all individuals and communities must live in harmony with Nature.

This conception of life, in which relationality plays an overarching role, suggests an endless flow of complex interactions and exchanges. Living Well is premised on giving and receiving, in an ongoing process of reciprocities, complementarities and solidarities. In other words, it takes the form of an ethical perspective which must govern human life. At its heart is the need to care for one's self and for other living beings while striving for balance that enables life to flow. And, in this inspiring world of harmonies and balance, life itself is the supreme consideration. Thus, Living Well can also be understood as a political confrontation in which the reproduction of life is prioritised over the reproduction of capital.

Thus, the essence of the debates around Living Well encompasses a holistic approach to understanding life in community as a complementary relationship with Pacha Mama (Mother Earth). These two elements, community and Nature, are the fundamentals on which Living Well is built. However, this is not all. The spiritual world of the indigenous cultures is also an essential aspect of Living Well, its *sumac kawsay*. Having said this, to the extent that different understandings of Living Well do exist, it is also necessary to avoid it becoming a homogenising concept that ends up restricting the visions and understandings of other people.

This cosmovision simultaneously draws on both the history and the present of indigenous peoples. Living Well is, above all, rooted in the principle of historical continuity of these communities. The past and the future merge into a present in which these transformative alternatives are constructed and reconstructed. As such, Living Well in the present is as much an option for the future as it is recognition of the past. Without idealising it, it is nonetheless vital to understand that, in broad terms, the indigenous community has a collective project for the future, based on continuity from its own past. These Amazonian and Andean utopias are encapsulated in diverse ways – through discourse, political projects, social and cultural practices, and also economic ones. Herein lies one of Living Well's strongest potentials – the ability to draw on the experiences of people who have known, since time immemorial, how to live a dignified and harmonious existence. And, while we must not idealise indigenous reality, this is the fundamental task at hand.

The indigenous world exists as it is: a world which has been the victim of conquest and colonialism. And, even in the current era of republics, the long colonial night of domination, exploitation and repression still exerts a tremendous force. Colonial and capitalist influences remain a part of today's reality, increasing their reach in multiple ways throughout the world. As such, this should banish once and for all any romantic notions of indigenous reality that we may have.

Similarly, the notion of indigenous experiences is not exempt from conflicts. For example, discriminatory or dogmatic approaches may arise. There is a danger that this would result from separating a conception of Living Well from that of *sumac kawsay*, rather than just differentiating the two concepts. This is an indication of what Living Well may actually mean in indigenous communities themselves, as they adopt a dogmatic isolationist position. This could have the effect of closing the door on a broad dialogue between different forms of knowledge and wisdoms, a dialogue which humanity is in such dire need of having.

We must complement and broaden our concepts and experiences by incorporating other discourses, proposals and practices from around the world, based on a common spiritual approach to the struggle for a civilisational transformation. Indeed, one of the great challenges of our time is to find a way to instigate and enrich this dialogue of voices at the margins of modernity between those of us who are developing alternative approaches that question the direction of history.

These initiatives for dialogue must be based in the participation of multiple political subjects, all of whom are agents of change in their own respective territories. Any dialogue needs to be rooted in these concrete contexts.

Furthermore, we must be alert to the danger of manipulating the concept of Living Well and perverting its sense and scope, as is occurring in Ecuador and Bolivia. The governments of these countries have emptied the concept of all its content. This is happening despite the fact that this cosmovision, Buen Vivir as it is known in Ecuador and Vivir Bien as it is known in Bolivia, as well as its equivalents in indigenous languages, was incorporated into the constitutions of both the Republic of Ecuador, in 2008, and of the Plurinational State of Bolivia, in 2009. These countries have even referred to *socialism of Living Well*, *community-based socialism* or *bio-socialism*. Nonetheless, despite this rhetoric, the politics of these countries has given rise to a neo-developmentalism based in a rampant extractivism in order to finance processes aimed at modernising capitalism. This is the reality, plain and simple.

Thus, we must not fall into the propaganda 'trap' which the governments of these countries are putting out. They have managed to vampirise the concept of Living Well in order to satiate their hunger for concentrating power and disciplining their societies, turning it into a device for modernising capitalism. In fact, the concept of Living Well has become an aberration of itself.

The utopia of Living Well already exists in the indigenous world

We insist that Living Well, through its garnering of lived experience in resistance to colonialism and its sequels, is already nourishing a way of life in various indigenous communities. This is especially so in those communities which have never been fully absorbed into capitalist modernity, or those which have resolutely remained outside it. However, even in those communities which have 'succumbed' to modernity, it is still possible to find elements of what might be considered Living Well.

Such processes do not just exist in the indigenous world. Even in other spaces not directly linked to the indigenous world, people are constructing communal ways of living in which they can live in harmony with one another and with Nature. As such, we are optimistic that, in the hypothetical event that indigenous communities should cease to exist, people living in other worlds would have learnt from the indigenous ways of living and their values, and would do their utmost to protect them through applying them in other social and cultural realities.

A starting point to better understand Living Well could be a 'philosophical' approach, if we can call it this. Much has been written in this regard, and it is of great importance. We especially recommend work by the Intercultural Amawtay Wasi University.[23, 24]

An understanding of the meaning of the *chakana*, also known as the Andean or sacred cross, provides insight into the meaning of unity in diversity. At the heart of this lies relationality, which entails reciprocity and complementarity, as well as solidarity between life's different elements.

These are, without doubt, the fundamental elements of Living Well. However, it is not easy for those of us who are sons and daughters of modernity to understand. Atawallpa Oviedo Freire, an outstanding scholar of this theme, takes a resolute approach to this. He advocates that the phrase *sumac kawsay* should actually remain untranslated into other languages, lest its meaning becomes distorted from its intended spirit, and the concept loses its transformative potential.

This is no trivial matter. As we noted earlier, on the one hand there is the risk of paving the way for new forms of dogmatisms and purisms, and at the other extreme there is the risk of falling into new fashionable approaches at the behest of government institutions. While we acknowledge Living Well's deep rootedness in indigenous culture, we also see it as an open concept from which it is possible to embark on building other worlds. Such an approach avoids closing the door on a broad and enriching debate and dialogue with those other forms of wisdom and knowledge which also strive to transcend modernity. This is where the debates about post-development and degrowth come in.

For this to happen, it is necessary to adequately appreciate so-called ancestral knowledge, bearing in mind that defining what is actually meant by ancestral knowledge is itself a complex task. This requires bridging different forms of knowledge and wisdoms in a respectful manner, and answering the call to put technology at the service of life instead of capital accumulation.

Working out a way to ensure that technology does not fall prisoner to the designs of capital accumulation, and to ensure that knowledge serves the demands of the community, is vital. It is the crux of the matter.

In this respect, we can learn important lessons from Ubuntu, the most widely used and well-known free software operating system. Ubuntu is based on the idea that users are freely ceded the right to improve on the original design. In this way, the original designer of the operating system can also continue to benefit into the future. The challenge we are faced with is to find ways of exerting human control over technologies rather than the other way around. This approach was recommended by Ivan Illich, an author whose ideas are experiencing a renewed relevance in the context of the debates about degrowth and the search for profoundly transformative alternatives.[25]

Living Well depends on our abilities to make use of systems for developing and appropriating scientific and technological advances that draw on, and are fully respectful of, ancestral knowledge and wisdom. Understanding their histories makes it possible to harness those practices which have endured until now. This approach is especially important given that many of these practices and beliefs have survived centuries of colonisation and marginalisation.

Ancestral knowledge offers us countless lessons and has laid the ground for important advances in science. It is unfortunate, and ironic, that much ancestral wisdom is now patented by multinational corporations and it is these corporations which reap the profits. This is happening, for example, with many plants, and even animals, from the Andes and Amazon regions.

In addition to learning from those cultures and practices that have survived and are alive today, we can also benefit from studying the tragic histories of those cultures which, for a variety of reasons, did not survive. Studying these failures (including their own errors, aggressions towards Nature, or levels of inequality and violence) may also hold clues as to how to construct innovative solutions for today's social and ecological challenges.

From the above reflections, we can conclude that it is necessary to reduce the many different forms of dependency that keep us chained to capital's demands. These include dependencies related to technology, consumption patterns, methods of administration, and our education systems which transmit capital's values, norms and expectations.

To this effect, the impoverished countries must undergo a transformation away from the currently existing mode of accumulation which is based on primary production and exports. This requires exposing the inherent conditions behind this type of dependent economy, in order to design a strategy which allows for benefiting from natural resources in an intelligent way. This is a vital part of a planning process geared towards building post-extractivist economies.

At the political level, Living Well offers a different style and form of government and decision-making, both at the community level and at the level of Ayllu.[26] Living Well is rooted in a horizontal approach to society based on self-governing community-oriented action and self-management.[27] This precludes vertical command structures, and, in particular, individual leadership by enlightened dictators. Broad and participatory discussion processes allow consensus to be built, and subsequently gain the support of the community. Our own democratic approaches and structures have much to learn from these experiences.

A key point is that the solution to these challenges does not lie with the state as it currently exists today. And even less does it lie with the market. We are faced with the task of thinking up another form of state, one which could contribute to the construction of a non-authoritarian society and which is controlled from below. Such a state could be a plurinational one, as proposed by Bolivia and Ecuador's indigenous movements. However, we must admit that not much progress has been made on this in Bolivia, and even less in Ecuador.

These institutions of self-government must take shape at different levels, rooted in the community. A big challenge is how to recover the political dimension in these lived spaces in society.

In social and economic terms, work is a central element of Living Well. Work is understood as a collective institution for constructing society based in mutual assistance in a communal environment. It is distinct from the alienating and exploiting work that occurs under capitalism. Economic liberalism ingenuously proclaims that work should serve individual gain based on the hope that the final result will still be positive for all. In contrast to this, work in Living Well is destined to achieve the common good of the population. One works to satisfy collective needs and community interests, and work may even occur under festive conditions that show affection towards the community.

A number of indigenous forms of economic relations stand out in this regard: *Minka (minga), Ranti-ranti (randi-randi), Uyanza, Uniguilla, Waki, Makikuna*. Many other forms also exist. These are all examples of Living Well's particular forms of economic organisation, based above all in reciprocity, complementarity, interconnectedness and solidarity. These forms and practices of socio-economic organisation have enabled many indigenous communities to confront the oblivion and exclusion which the prevailing colonial system had consigned them to. Furthermore, by stimulating creativity and solidarity, encouraging economic savings tied to social and political demands, and strengthening communal identity, these institutions have helped communities to sustain their own production in extremely adverse conditions. Consequently, these indigenous forms and practices also articulate a strong dimension of cultural and ceremonial ritual that mobilises and builds community unity, as well as serving as spaces for the intermingling of socio-cultural norms.

Needless to say, applying such forms of organising production and consumption to broader, non-communal spaces may give rise to various complications. Attempting to integrate them into conventional micro- or macroeconomic epistemology would appear to be impossible. It may be tempting to use these practices and their cultural logic as a potential way of enriching the productive functioning of any given economy. However, such an approach risks simply adapting Living Well to modernity's prevailing business demands, rather than overcoming these demands. This is what is occurring with 'Green Capitalism', and it is a complete perversion of the concept of Living Well.

In any case, these difficulties highlight the challenge of imagining, and from there constructing, economies rooted in the ideas of relationality, reciprocity, solidarity, interconnectedness and, above all, harmony and balance.

In order to draw some lessons which allow us to attempt to construct the economy of Living Well, we must first appreciate the limitations of the conventional economy. Central to understanding these limitations are the foundational elements of the indigenous cosmovision. Concretely, it is necessary to value and understand the importance of social and ecological justice, which are intimately related, as neither can exist without the other.

Even more urgent than the need to overcome capital's exploitation of Nature is the need to put an end to the exploitation of human beings for capital accumulation. This implies questioning many so-called 'truths', especially the insistence that humanity's problems can only be solved through economic growth.

Dignified life for the community must be achieved in the here and now, and cannot merely be dangled as a promise for tomorrow. If a balance exists in the way in which basic needs are satisfied, there is no need for the economy to grow in order for all the members of the community to have a dignified life. Instead, what is required is an appropriate redistribution of wealth and equitable distribution of incomes between all community members. This both requires, and would result in, ways of living that are entirely different from the runaway consumerism which capitalist globalisation has spread throughout the world.

Another crucial factor lies in the recognition that Living Well cannot limit itself to the rural world. Though scarcely articulated, it is a fact that that some of its basic proposals do originate precisely from these areas. Contemporary cities, characterised by their frenetic and individualising pace, seem very far from offering a life that is both solidary and respectful of the environment. Furthermore, if we accept that, by definition, there is no such thing as a sustainable city, the task of imagining what Living Well means in an urban context becomes even more complicated.

Envisioning Living Well for and from the cities presents the concept with a huge challenge. Nonetheless, no one can deny that many options for taking up this challenge do in fact exist. In Latin America, one important strength that people are drawing on is the fact that many of those who have migrated to cities still maintain close ties with their rural communities of origin. For example, in the city of El Alto in Bolivia, groups of these recently arrived migrants have formed to construct/reconstruct/showcase examples of Living Well.

In cities elsewhere, many interesting practices and proposals also exist. As evidence of this continually growing universe of urban alternatives, we highlight what have become known as 'transition towns'. These are initiatives which seek to bestow the communities themselves with the power to construct a post-petrol economy in the face of climate change. This urban movement for building alternatives is active throughout much of the world, and is developing successful proposals, such as the emerging 'energy transition', or Energiewende as it is known in Germany.[28]

The multi-scale implications of Living Well

Rooted in biocentricism, Living Well serves as a platform for discussing our collective responses to the urgent challenges currently facing humanity. Living Well is a source of strength in confronting the devastating effects of climate change at the planetary level. It also provides a basis for confronting the growing social and economic inequalities which are behind the uncontrollable rise in violence throughout the world. When reflecting on the meaning of embarking on a transition to Living Well, an initial premise is that human beings must take priority over capital, and must live in harmony with Nature. This is basic to ensuring human survival.

The search for these new ways of living implies revitalising political discussion, after years of obfuscation by economistic visions of ends and means. Deification of the economy, and in particular the market, has resulted in the abandonment of many non-economic instruments that are vital for improving living conditions. For example, the belief that market measures can be used to resolve global environmental problems is an error which could cost us very dearly. The application of laws and regulations, even as yet still insufficient, is demonstrably more effective than capitalism's market-based 'laws' of supply and demand.

However, more is needed. We cannot continue to commodify Nature, as this only hastens its rampant exploitation. On the contrary: we need to decommodify it. We must re-establish our connection with Nature, based on a relationship of respect, responsibility and reciprocity, and the basic principle of relationality. Only in this way can Nature's capacity to regenerate itself be safeguarded.

Here the question of common goods is vital. These are goods which belong to, are held in usufruct by, or are consumed by, a relatively large group of individuals or by society as a whole. These may be natural or social systems, tangible or intangible (such as Wikipedia). While differing in their specifics from one another, common goods share the aspect of having been inherited or constructed collectively. However, we must not deceive ourselves. As with other types of goods, common goods may also become the target of pillage and looting.[29]

In order to effectively benefit from and defend common goods, it is necessary to locate our political discussions within an agenda that is broad and participatory. This requires identifying and defining the common character of each good in question. Existing conditions for disposing of common goods directly, immediately and without commercial or other kinds of mediation must be protected. Existing common goods must not be privatised, and nor must those which have not yet been created. There is a need to design, experiment with and produce a technological and juridical framework that is conducive to creativity and innovation in the production of common goods. It is also necessary to foster free and open access to common intellectual goods.

These words reek of utopia. Yes. This is exactly what we are dealing with. We have no other option than to write all possible scenarios of a utopia that as yet remains to be constructed – a utopia which implies a critique of reality from the principles encapsulated by Living Well; a possible utopia which, on the one hand, is a project of solidary and sustainable life in the here and now, and on the other hand points us in the direction of what ought to be in the future. It represents an alternative option that is collectively imagined, politically conquered and constructed, and implemented through democratic actions, at each step along the way, and wherever this may be. We must be to true to our goal of overcoming the misery of modernisation. And, as the German journalist Thomas Pampuch has so aptly put it, we must do this in a way that does not merely imply the modernisation of misery.[30]

The multiple complexities of contemporary life cannot be explained with uni-causal explanations. Consequently, the resolution of these problems demands a multi-disciplinary approach.

To the extent that society actively takes up the proposals generated by Living Well, especially at the community level, these experiences have the potential to catapult themselves to the forefront of debates that are underway throughout the world. They can even serve as a catalyst for constructively confronting the growing alienation of a large majority of the world's inhabitants. Respectfully taking up these indigenous visions will greatly enrich post-developmentalist debates.

While it is extremely difficult to take up the challenge of constructing Living Well in societies immersed in the whirlwind of capitalism, especially its large cities, we are nonetheless convinced that many options do exist to begin constructing this utopia. This can happen in many different places, including in industrialised countries and in the cities themselves.

Let us avoid taking states as our starting point. Similarly, we must recognise the market for the totalising institution that it is. A genuine democratisation of power demands social participation and control from the grassroots of society, both in the countryside and in the cities, in neighbourhoods and in communities. Social movements have a vital role to play in this, as do those recently established political parties that are rooted in, and resonate with, their respective societies.

Despite our optimism in the potential for the collective pursuit of different alternatives, above all at the community level, we would be ill advised to downplay the very real global challenges we are faced with. For example, a solution needs to be found to the current intolerable international economic situation, and its social, ecological and economic problems. Although beyond the scope of this chapter, a broad consensus exists as to the need to disarm the international financial market's speculative structures. This includes the question of capital flight, as so-called 'dirty money', such as money linked to wars and terrorism, escapes to fiscal paradises. Many financial institutions serve as tools for large states, or institutions controlled by a small number of powerful states, to exert political pressure and impose (typically unsustainable) conditions on weaker states. External debt has been, and continues to be, used in this way, having been transformed into a tool of political domination.

We must question the very existence of such institutions. (Acosta and Cajas Guijarro include some interesting global proposals on these themes.)[31]

Thus, Living Well urges us to construct a life of self-sufficiency and self-management. On the one hand, this is between humans living in community in such a way as to strengthen the local and that which belongs to the community directly. And, on the other hand, the task is to safeguard Nature's power to regenerate itself. Individual states can support the renewal of local, national and regional decision-making spaces, which in turn can provide the basis for constructing democratic spaces at the global level. Such a process will generate new territorial and conceptual maps.

This is, to say the least, a monumental challenge for humanity.[32]

A brief reflection on reinventing the future

We are tasked with embarking on a transition process, guided by utopian perspectives in which humans live in harmony with Nature, and starting from the thousands of diverse alternative practices which already exist throughout the world. Many of these already existing processes are non-capitalist and are rich in potential. In this process, Living Well closely resonates with degrowth and post-extractivism.[33]

We sit before a 'great transformation'. The driving force of such a transformation will be concrete practices, not theories alone. This includes the diverse range of possible globally oriented actions. The Yasuní-ITT initiative to leave crude oil in the subsoil in the Ecuadorean Amazon was, and still is, a great example of the kind of global action that can arise from civil society in a small country such as Ecuador.[34] And, Living Well has many lessons to offer these multiple efforts.

A crucial aspect of this is the need to challenge the concept of Progress itself. The notion of Progress, understood as a uni-directional global institution based on a productivist path and a mechanistic vision of economic growth, has failed. Our goal is not to replicate the supposedly successful examples of the developed countries. On the one hand this is simply not possible, and, on the other hand, they are not actually success stories.

The most important contribution that Living Well can make, at both national and international levels, is stimulating dialogue. Of particular significance in this respect is the contribution it can make to a collective process aimed at bridging different forms of ancestral and modern forms of knowledge and wisdom. There is no better means of achieving this than through frank and respectful debate. Such a debate is already well underway in many parts of the world.

This poses the challenge of how to overcome existing differences. We consider that Modernity and capitalism are indeed the apogee of civilisations based in capital's domination of both human beings and Nature, and that these different transformative alternatives have the potential to come together in Living Well.

A key element of this coming together of different alternative visions will be in ensuring that respectful and constructive relations exist between those with different understandings of Living Well. On the one hand, there are those who barricade themselves behind a concept of Living Well based on ancestral authenticity, and, on the other, there are those who seek to transform the concept into an open one, albeit one which is rooted in recuperating the fundamental tenets of indigenous peoples' millenarian cultures. On one shore lies the reconstruction of a concept drawn from ancestral knowledge, and which may yearn overly towards the past. And, on the other shore (yet along the same road), the same concept exists and is also going through a process of reconstruction – and even construction. However, on this shore, the gaze is set to the future. There is much potential for coming together, should those who currently yearn for the past begin to look more to the future (and, indeed, the present) and should those who currently gaze towards the future adopt a less sanctimonious view of the past.

We reiterate that Living Well, with its roots in the Andean and Amazonean indigenous world, is by no means the only proposal for transformative alternatives. Many others exist. The historical task before us lies in bringing together these multiple efforts at constructing communal life. Examples of this include the Zapatistas, as well as the multiplicity of feminist, peasant and ecological struggles.[35] There is also great possibility for convergence with the budding 'degrowth' movement. Many other examples also exist.

Our task is far from easy. Overcoming dominant visions and constructing new ways of living will take time. It requires constructing along the way, through a process of unlearning, relearning, and learning to learn all at once. It also demands a strong resolve, will and humility.

We repeat our conviction that Living Well is a concept that is in ongoing construction and reproduction. It is not a static concept and even less is it a backwards-looking one. Essentially, Living Well is a central element of what can be understood as 'the philosophy of life' for many indigenous societies which have only been partially incorporated into modernity. And, from this perspective, despite the fact that historically these communities have been marginalised, Living Well has the potential to assert itself as a globally impacting proposal.

In conclusion, Living Well understands community as the conjuncture in which living beings, both past and future generations, come together in harmony – a harmony which also includes Mother Earth. In other words, Living Well takes as its starting point the preservation of life, based on the broad understanding that life includes both the environment and our grandchildren. Human beings are not isolated individuals, as we form part of both a social and a natural community. It is these communities, peoples, nations and countries that must relate harmoniously to one another and to nature.

This twin reencountering, the bringing together of Nature and community, challenges us to take a step towards constructing new forms of civilisation centred around two intimately related goals: Human Rights and the Rights of Nature.

Disclosure statement

No potential conflict of interest was reported by the author.

Acknowledgements

The author is grateful to Atawallpa Oviedo Freire for his comments on an earlier version of this text, and to Kolya Abramsky for the translation.

Notes

1. Giraldo, "Utopias en la era de la supervivencia,"
2. Translator's note: in the Spanish original, 'Humanidad' is written with a capital letter throughout most of the chapter. This has been translated as 'humanity' (with a lower case 'h') in English, as giving it a capital letter has a religious connotation that does not appear to be the intention of the Spanish original.
3. Translator's note: the Spanish original refers to 'Modernidad' with a capital M. This has been translated here and throughout the text as 'modernity' with a lower case 'm'.
4. Sachs, *Development Dictionary*.
5. See above.
6. Harry S. Truman, Inaugural Address, January 20, 1949. Online by Harry S. Truman Presidential Library and Museum. https://trumanlibrary.org/whistlestop/50yr_archive/inagural20jan1949. htm.
7. Unceta, "Desarrollo, postcrecimiento y Buen Vivir."
8. Translator's note: In the Spanish original, 'Naturaleza', with a capital N has been used throughout this text. Here I have left the capital N in the English translation, 'Nature'.
9. Translator's note: the original Spanish is 'maldesarrollo', which is considered something of a standard concept in Spanish. Although no similar standard concept exists in English, the meaning is best understood with a literal translation: 'bad development'.
10. Tortosa, "Maldesarrollo y mal vivir."
11. Acosta, "Las dependencias del extractivismo."
12. Acosta, "Riesgos y amenazas para el Buen Vivir"; "El Buen Vivir Sumak Kawsay"; "Pos-crecimiento y pos-extractivismo"; "Iniciativa Yasuní-ITT"; "Las dependencias del extractivismo."
13. See additional texts by Acosta in Oviedo Freire, http://dspace.ucuenca.edu.ec/ bitstream/123456789/21746/1/pydlos_libro_%20CONSTRUYENDO%20BUEN_VIVIR. pdf; Huanacuni Mamani, "Vivir Bien/Buen Vivir Filosofía"; Giraldo, "Utopias en la era de la supervivencia"; Gudynas, "Buen Vivir: sobre secuestros, domesticaciones, rescates y alternativas"; Esterman, "Ecosofía andina"; Solón, "¿Es posible el Buen Vivir?"; Houtart , "El concepto del sumak kawsay (Buen Vivir)."
14. Translator's note: See note 1.
15. Translator's note: The Spanish original here is 'comunitario'. This is problematic to translate into English, as depending on the sense in which it is used it can mean 'communitarian', 'communal' or 'relating to community', all of which have slightly different meanings. Each use of the word 'comunitario' in the Spanish original has been translated on a case-by-case basis, using what I consider the appropriate English translation in each instance.
16. D'Alisa, Demaria, and Kallis, "Decrecimiento."
17. Kothari, Demaria, and Acosta, "Buen Vivir, Degrowth and Ecological Swaraj."
18. Translator's note: the Spanish original is 'sentipensares'. This is a combined word that includes 'sentir', 'to feel', and 'pensar', to think. These two verbs appear to have been combined to create a noun. It appears to be a hybrid word that the author invented himself. I have attempted to encapsulate this with the less succinct, but hopefully roughly equivalent, phrase 'other rationalities and other forms of understanding the world that simultaneously combine both thought and emotion'.
19. Escobar, "Sentipensar con la tierra."
20. Quijano, "Cuestiones y Horizontes – Antología Esencial."
21. Leff, "Imaginarios sociales y sustentabilidad."

22. Acosta, "Riesgos y amenazas para el Buen Vivir."
23. This university was closed by Rafael Correa's government because it did not conform to the established criteria for higher education and its neo-developmental project to modernise capitalism.
24. Universidad Intercultural Amawtay Wasi, "Aprender en la sabiduría y en el Buen Vivir."
25. Illich , "Obras reunidas."
26. This a term used, in many parts of the Andean and Amazonean region, to describe the wider collection of families related to one another by way of consanguinity and affinity.
27. Translator's note: the Spanish original here is 'autogestión'. There is no ideal translation of this concept into English. The nearest English equivalent is 'self-management'.
28. Müller, "Alemania: La transición energética."
29. See Helfrich, "Wem gehört die Welt? Zur Wiederentdeckung der Gemeingüter"; or Mattei, "Bienes Comunes – Un manifiesto."
30. Pampuch, "Das Elend der Modernisierung."
31. Acosta and Cajas Guijarro, "Instituciones transformadoras para la economía global."
32. Equally, it is necessary to support solutions aimed at achieving world peace. This implies bringing about a massive disarmament process and diverting resources away from arms in order to satisfy humanity's most pressing needs. Were this to happen, it would result in a greatly reduced level of violence globally. Important though this is, it is not, however, in itself enough. As long as we do not re-establish peace with Mother Earth, peace amongst humans will also remain impossible. As such, this demands a reconnection with Nature based on harmony, as is at the heart of Living Well.
33. Acosta and Brand, "Salidas del laberinto capitalista"; and Acosta, "Pos-crecimiento y pos-extractivismo."
34. Acosta, "Iniciativa Yasuní-ITT."
35. Acosta and Machado, "Movimientos comprometidos con la vida."

Bibliography

Acosta, Alberto. *"Riesgos y amenazas para el Buen Vivir,"* en la Revista Ecuador Debate No. 84. CAAP: Quito, 2012. http://repositorio.flacsoandes.edu.ec/bitstream/10469/3514/2/RFLACSO-ED84.pdf.
Acosta, Alberto. *El Buen Vivir Sumak Kawsay, una oportunidad para imaginar otros mundos.* Barcelona: ICARIA, 2013. http://www.icariaeditorial.com/. Other versions also published in French (2014), German (2015), Portuguese (2016), as well as a first version published in Ecuador (2012).
Acosta, Alberto. "Pos-crecimiento y pos-extractivismo: Dos caras de la misma transformación cultural." In *Pos-crecimiento y Buen Vivir. Propuestas globales para la construcción de sociedades equitativas y sustentables*, FES-ILDIS, edited by Gustavo Endara. Quito, 2014. http://www.redeamlat.org/wp-content/uploads/2017/09/11348.pdf
Acosta, Alberto. "Iniciativa Yasuní-ITT – La difícil construcción de la utopía." 2014. Accessed October 19, 2017. https://www.rebelion.org/noticia.php?id=180285
Acosta, Alberto. *Las dependencias del extractivismo – Aporte para un debate incompleto.* Revista Aktuel Marx No. 20, Nuestra América y la Naturaleza. Santiago de Chile: Actuel Marx Intervenciones, 2016. http://www.lom.cl/16e67afa-dea4-4b02-96f3-646ca68b5d71/El-sociometabolismo-del-capital-y-la-depredaci%C3%B3n-de-la-vida-Debates-sobre-el-extractivismo.aspx
Acosta, Alberto and Brand, Ulrich. *Salidas del laberinto capitalista – Decrecimiento y Postextractivismo.* Barcelona: ICARIA, 2017.
Acosta, Alberto and Cajas Guijarro, John. "Instituciones transformadoras para la economía global – Pensando caminos para dejar atrás el capitalismo." In La osadía de lo nuevo – Alternativas de política económica, edited by the Permanent Working Group from the Rosal Luxemburg Foundation, Abya-Yala, 133–197. Quito, 2015. http://www.rosalux.org.ec/attachments/article/875/La%20osad%C3%ADa%20de%20lo%20nuevopdf.pdf.
Acosta, Alberto and Machado, Decio. *"Movimientos comprometidos con la vida. Ambientalismos y conflictos actuales en América Latina,"* en la Revista Colección OSAL, 67–94. Buenos Aires: CLACSO, 2012. http://biblioteca.clacso.edu.ar/clacso/osal/20120927103642/OSAL32.pdf.

D'Alisa, Giacomo, Federico Demaria, and Giorgios Kallis, eds. *Decrecimiento*. Barcelona: Vocabulario para una nueva era, ICARIA, 2015.

Escobar, Arturo. *Sentipensar con la tierra – Nuevas lecturas sobre desarrollo, territorio y diferencia*. Ediciones Unaula: Medellín, 2014.

Esterman, Josef. *"Ecosofía andina – Un paradigma alternativo de convivencia cósmica y de vida plena."* In *Bifurcación del Buen Vivir y el sumak kawsay*, edited by Atawallpa Oviedo Freire. Ediciones SUMAK: Quito, 2014. https://books.google.de/books?id=Vpm_oQEACAAJ&dq=Bifurcaci%C3%B3n+del+Buen+Vivir+y+el+Sumak+Kawsay&hl=de&sa=X&redir_esc=y.

Giraldo, Omar Felipe. *Utopias en la era de la supervivencia – Una interpretación del Buen Vivir*, Editorial México: ITACA, 2014.

Gudynas, Eduardo. *"Buen Vivir: sobre secuestros, domesticaciones, rescates y alternativas."* In *Bifurcación del Buen Vivir y el sumak kawsay*, edited by Atawallpa Oviedo Freire. Ediciones SUMAK: Quito, 2014.

Helfrich, Silke, and Heinrich Böll Foundation. *Commons – Für eine neue Politik jenseits von Markt und Staat, transcript*. Bielefeld: Verlag, 2012.

Houtart, François. *"El concepto del sumak kawsay (Buen Vivir) y su correspondencia con el bien común de la humanidad."* In *Revista Ecuador Debate No. 84*, edited by Hernán Ibarra Crespo. CAAP: Quito, 2011. http://repositorio.flacsoandes.edu.ec/bitstream/10469/3514/2/RFLACSO-ED84.pdf.

Huanacuni Mamani, Fernando. *Vivir Bien/Buen Vivir Filosofía, políticas, estrategias y experiencias regionales, Convenio Andrés Bello, Instituto Internacional de Investigación y CAOI*: La Paz, 2010.

Illich, Iván. *Obras reunidas*. México: Fondo de Cultura Económica, 2015.

Kothari, Ashish, Federico Demaria, and Alberto Acosta. "Buen Vivir, Degrowth and Ecological Swaraj: Alternatives to sustainable development and the Green Economy." Development 57 no. 3/4, 2015. doi:10.1057/dev.2015.24. https://link.springer.com/article/10.1057/dev.2015.24

Leff, Enrique. *"Imaginarios sociales y sustentabilidad." en la revista Cultura y representaciones sociales* 5, no. 9. México: UNAM, 2010. http://www.journals.unam.mx/index.php/crs/article/view/19202/18202.

Mattei, Ugo. *Bienes Comunes – Un manifiesto*. Madrid: Trotta, 2013.

Müller, Tazzio. "Alemania: La transición energética - Combinar escalas y estrategias para el cambio." In ¿Cómo transformar? Instituciones y cambio social en América Latina y Europa, Permanent Working Group of the Rosa Luxemburg Foundation. Miriam Lang, Belén Cevallos y Claudia López, Fundación Rosa Luxemburg, and Oficina de la Región Andina. Quito, 2015. http://www.rosalux.org.ec/attachments/article/880/C%C3%B3mo%20transformarFINAL.pdf.

Pampuch, Thomas. *Das Elend der Modernisierung – Die Modernisierung des Elends: Unterentwicklung und Entwicklungspolitik in Lateinamerika*. Berlin: Institut für Vergleichende Sozialforschung, 1982.

Quijano, Aníbal. *Cuestiones y Horizontes – Antología Esencial – De la dependencia histórica-estructural a la colonialidad/decolonialidad del poder*. CLACSO: Buenos Aires, 2014.

Sachs, Wolfgang. *The Development Dictionary: A Guide to Knowledge as Power*. London: Zed Books, 1992.

Solón, Pablo. *¿Es posible el Buen Vivir?, Reflexiones a Quema Ropa sobre Alternativas Sistémicas*, Fundación Solón: La Paz, 2016.

Tortosa, José María. *Maldesarollo y mal vivir*. Quito: Ediciones Abya-Yala, 2011. https://web.ua.es/es/iudesp/documentos/publicaciones/maldesarrollo-libro.pdf.

Unceta, Koldo. *Desarrollo, postcrecimiento y Buen Vivir – Debates e interrogantes*. Quito: Ediciones Abya-Yala, 2014. http://filosofiadelbuenvivir.com/wp-content/uploads/2015/02/Desarrollo-postcrecimiento-y-Buen-Vivir-2014.pdf.

Universidad Intercultural Amawtay Wasi. *Aprender en la sabiduría y en el Buen Vivir*. Quito, 2004 (Published in three languages: Quechua, Spanish and English).

Reflecting the Post-Development gaze: the degrowth debate in Germany

Daniel Bendix

ABSTRACT
Post-Development has reproduced the 'development gaze' by focusing on interventions and struggles in the South. This paper draws attention to the German version of degrowth, *Postwachstum*, as a possible Post-Development approach in the North. It thus contributes to the Post-Development agenda by including the North as a 'development' problem and by overcoming the view of the North as a homogeneous neo-liberal, capitalist, Eurocentric bloc. The paper examines key *Postwachstum* contributions with regard to their correspondence to insights of and gaps in the Post-Development debate. It argues that *Postwachstum* needs to include a postcolonial perspective on global inequalities and question the 'development'–modernity–coloniality nexus more profoundly in order to provide a valuable contribution to the Post-Development agenda.

Introduction

The Sustainable Development Goals (SDGs) have slightly shifted the focus from the usual suspects – 'less developed' countries in the South – to include Northern countries as objects in need of societal change. The move away from the 'development gaze',[1] ie a perspective on the South as the locus of problems, bears witness to the influence of critiques such as Post-Development. However, the Post-Development debate to date has inadvertently reproduced the development gaze by focusing on how 'development' is applied to and in the South, rather than also reflecting it back to the North. What is more, Post-Development has at times reified 'essentialised accounts of the West and the Rest'[2] by inversing colonial stereotypes to 'an evil West and a noble South'.[3]

This paper counters these pitfalls of Post-Development by bringing to the fore possible Post-Development approaches in the North. Here, the focus is on the degrowth debate in Germany to address the question of how it complements or furthers the Post-Development agenda by 'devis[ing] theories and strategies of how to fight global inequality and achieve a "good life" for all in a non-Eurocentric [...] manner'.[4] The paper does so by including the North as a 'development' problem and by destabilising the view of the North as a homogeneous neo-liberal, capitalist, Eurocentric bloc. Germany's debate on degrowth – referred to as *Postwachstum* (post-growth) in German – is peculiar if compared to the French and Spanish context.[5] A particular focus on Germany is timely as it is Europe's economically and politically most powerful nation and a leading actor in international debates and treaties on 'development'.

Degrowth is commonly presented as a radical Northern internal critique in its call for socio-ecological transformation, its demands for a less consumptive, sufficiency oriented, sustainable lifestyle, and its advocacy of local communities and social movements as degrowth agents.[6] It has not been institutionalised politically to any considerable extent, but civil society and social movements experiment with various alternative practices.[7] Discussions on the relation between Southern critiques of development and Northern critiques of growth have been ongoing, particularly at the International Degrowth Conferences. In this context, Latouche[8] and Martínez-Alier[9] have made valuable contributions. In addition, Illich's various publications have been a frequent point of reference for degrowth thought. However, academic endeavours to bring degrowth and Post-Development together are still rare.[10] Escobar has focused on the specific degrowth positions of the Research & Degrowth group in Barcelona to juxtapose the philosophical and ontological roots of Post-Development and degrowth as 'transition discourses'. Kothari et al. regard degrowth as an approach 'emerging from within the "belly of the beast" (capitalist or industrialized countries)' that 'break[s] from dominant logic' and 'differ[s] sharply from today's notion of development'.[11] Ziai has explored some contributions of German *Postwachstum* and suggests understanding 'degrowth as a specifically European [Post-Development] concept: secular, science-based and oblivious to the problems of universalism'.[12] This paper builds on these analyses to further explore the contributions of the specifically German degrowth debate over *Postwachstum* as put forward by leading intellectuals to investigate its correspondence to insights of and gaps in the Post-Development debate. The paper concentrates on the inspirational and founding texts and thus leaves aside more recent scholarly work on *Postwachstum* as presented at the International Degrowth Conference in Leipzig or published online on websites and blogs.

The contributions are analysed in order to discern the different and maybe contradictory proposals under the umbrella of *Postwachstum*, and to ascertain their (in)compatibility with the Post-Development agenda. I argue that the German *Postwachstum* debate offers a valuable shift in the 'development' perspective through its focus on economic, ecological and social problems in the North, but that it at times lacks sensitivity to global interconnectedness and hierarchies, that its rejection of the Western development path is only partial, and that it does not sufficiently take into account the function of colonial difference for legitimising inequalities and exploitation. This paper suggests that for German *Postwachstum* to become a valuable Northern Post-Development approach, it should seek inspiration from the ecofeminist contribution to take a postcolonial, *longue durée* perspective on the global dominance of the North and to depart from a fundamental critique of the Western 'development'–modernity–coloniality nexus.

Lessons from and gaps in the Post-Development debate

The critique of development reached unprecedented levels with Post-Development approaches that fundamentally questioned the project of 'development' since the early 1990s.[13] Avoiding the common concerns about failures, defects and deficits of 'development' interventions in the South, this perspective challenged dominant notions of socio-economic change by pointing to the destructive effects of 'modernisation' and 'development aid', and the restriction of a good life to socio-economic indicators. Here, Post-Development's aim was to 'displace [development] from its centrality in the representations about conditions in Asia, Africa, and Latin America'.[14]

More recent studies have extended Post-Development's early focus on the post-Second World War era, highlighted the longer trajectory of development thought and practice, and thus brought to the fore various dimensions of the persistence of discourses and practices from the colonial era in contemporary 'development' thinking and interventions. Such Post-Development work has explored the continuation of colonial-era relationships between so-called donor and recipient countries,[15] the impact of racialisation,[16] identity formations of 'development' professionals,[17] the establishment of power relations,[18] and the reproduction of colonial power in development policy."[19] Post-Development thus poses the crucial question of how Western discourses and practices of 'modernity' and 'development' keep the world bifurcated into 'traditional' and 'modern', or in need of intervention and prone to intervene. It is thus concerned with what decolonial scholars have criticised as the operation of 'colonial difference'.[20] In this paper, such a focus is transferred to the degrowth debate in Germany.

Post-Development authors have been accused of reactionary romanticism by uncritically celebrating the 'traditional' as well as local resistance and by disregarding those in the so-called developing world who desire 'development' in the form of capitalist, Eurocentric socio-economic change.[21] Their romanticism was allegedly nurtured by armchair scholarship with no connection to people's day-to-day struggles.[22] This paper follows the more optimistic work of Post-Development that empirically explores people's livelihood practices and on this basis suggests that 'alternatives to development' are indeed a concrete possibility.[23] It thus focuses on the perspectives of a particular stream of thought (*Postwachstum*), which is connected to concrete practices, to enquire to what extent it rejects or embraces dominant notions of 'development'.

Post-Development has criticised 'development' for its shapelessness as it may assume a variety of meanings and can be filled with any content as long as it is couched in terms of the public good.[24] Yet denominators of what is commonly understood by the concept of 'development' can be discerned[25] and entail the assumption that history and socio-economic change take place in a linear, progressive manner, that North and South are at different stages of a single universal time, and that the North is the culmination of 'development.'"[26] This study addresses the question whether and, if yes, in what way such notions of linear, teleological, universal socio-economic change are invoked or rejected in *Postwachstum*.

The idea of 'many people in the global North [that] development … happens in the South'[27] implies that the South has to change and that the North provides the models to be followed. However, with the nascent realisation of the limits to capitalist growth by Northern scientific and political elites comes the partial recognition of the Post-Development perspective that 'the priority should not be Third World development, … but First World "de-development".'[28] Interestingly, Post-Development critiques have inadvertently reproduced the 'development gaze' by primarily criticising how ideas and practices of 'development' operate in the South, thereby disregarding the 'centre' and resistance against 'development' in the North. The few works of Post-Development that mention 'over(-)development'[29] do not tackle the question in depth, but merely point out the necessity to delve into this issue:

> A crucial first step, then, in building any anti-racist perspective on development is to include a concern with wealth creation and 'overdevelopment' (eg in Europe and North America) more prominently in our conceptions.[30]

This paper attempts to contribute to this by exploring how degrowth criticises 'development' in the North and how it may enhance the Post-Development agenda.

While Post-Development work criticises development studies and the practice of development for 'notions of difference, between here and there, now and then, us and them, developed and developing',[31] it at times reifies this colonial separation of the world by inversing the stereotypes. Thus, 'the world [is] divided into an evil West and a noble South'.[32] This not only disregards the diversity of interests and struggles in the South, but also does not do justice to those in the North. Ideas and practices of 'development' are not restricted to the Global South, and the North can thus be explored with a similar perspective.[33] The North has also never been a monolithic bloc: Struggles against capitalist expropriation, racism and colonialism, and for global solidarity, have marked this region as well.[34] This study builds on these insights by exploring *Postwachstum* as contributing to Post-Development in the North. Even though the case for turning the gaze towards activities in the North has been made,[35] this has to date not included a systematic examination of potential Post-Development ideas in the North.

Before delving into the *Postwachstum* debate, the following section sketches the history of degrowth and *Postwachstum*, and highlights the influences of Post-Development on degrowth to date.

Degrowth in Europe and *Postwachstum* in Germany

The critique of growth in the West has a long history, dating back to proponents of classical political economy. The term 'degrowth' itself was first introduced by Gorz in 1972 in its French version *décroissance*.[36] In the same year, the Club of Rome published its influential report *The Limits to Growth* that warned of the detrimental ecological effects of continuous economic growth. The interest in critiques of growth diminished with the end of the oil crisis and the beginning of neo-liberalism until the 1990s.[37]

The debate then re-emerged in France, and the degrowth phase since the turn of the millennium was primarily occupied with critiquing the dominant understanding of sustainable development. Degrowth may be understood as a variant of the sustainability concept heralded by the Brundtland Report 1987 and the Rio Earth Summit 1992 – the difference being that it stresses the oligarchic nature of the economic model and the necessity of sufficiency. The idea of degrowth has been adapted differently in various European countries.[38] The first international degrowth conference, entitled 'Economic De-growth for Ecological Sustainability and Social Equity', happened in Paris in 2004. Since then, several more conferences have taken place across Europe. For the German context, the 2014 International Degrowth Conference in Leipzig, with about 3000 participants, was particularly relevant for anchoring the ideas in the German public imaginary.

The inception of degrowth in Spain was *inter alia* influenced by debates in the South[39] and the French *décroissance* intellectual Latouche regards Post-Development as one of the origins of Degrowth.[40] In this perspective, contraction of capital in the Global North and reduction of dominance vis-à-vis the Global South are necessary for flourishing in the South.

For the Research & Degrowth context, the global perspective is a given as well and Post-Development is commonly cited as one of the principal intellectual influences.[41] According to Demaria et al., degrowth means a 'redistributive downscaling of production and consumption in industrialised countries as a means to achieve environmental sustainability, social justice and well-being' and 'implies an equitable redistribution of wealth … across the Global North and South'.[42] As will be shown, the influence of Post-Development thinking on degrowth is less evident in the German intellectual context. However, with the debates at and since the International Degrowth Conference in Leipzig in 2014[43] and stronger exchange with the Spanish Research & Degrowth circle, Post-Development and postcolonial perspectives that stress the imperial dimension of growth or capitalism in Germany see more and more reception,[44] particularly in degrowth activist circles.[45]

The agendas and political affiliations of the major *Postwachstum* thinkers in Germany are diverse. As part of the self-reflection of and by the German degrowth movement, Schmelzer has proposed a useful categorisation into five distinct positions.[46] Conservative degrowth ideas[47] believe Northern societies have lived beyond their means, call for social transformation, and advocate for a reduction of the welfare state, a strengthening of patriarchal family models, and extended individual responsibility. This position is categorised as *Postwachstum* by Schmelzer since it is convinced of the inevitability of economic contraction, but not as advocating a project of social-ecological transformation and therefore not as part of the degrowth movement. Liberal or social-reformist positions[48] are concerned with the sole focus and dependence on growth of 'modern' societies. They do not promote structural transformation of capitalism, but rather focus on ecological reforms such as internalisation of until now externalised ecological costs. Sufficiency-oriented positions[49] call for a radical reduction of industrial, globalised production and consumption and see the solution in less external supply and localisation. The anti-capitalist current[50] understands the multiple crises (social, economic, ecological, democratic) as rooted in capitalism and its relations of ownership and domination. Last but not least, the ecofeminist position[51] considers capitalism's distinction between the productive and reproductive sphere and thus its disregard for the material basis of life as fundamental for exploitation not only of nature but also of women and people in the Global South.

The contribution of *Postwachstum* to the Post-Development agenda

The following exploration of *Postwachstum* in light of the lessons from and gaps in the Post-Development debate focuses on these five lines of thought: first, the sufficiency-oriented position exemplified by the economist Paech, because it is the most prominent and widely discussed degrowth position in Germany. Second, the conservative position impersonated by Miegel is analysed because its influence is peculiar to the German context.[52] Moreover, the liberal position is looked at because has a strong foothold amongst environmental non-governmental organizations (NGOs). The anti-capitalist position is scrutinised because it is quite influential for degrowth activist circles. Last but not least, the ecofeminist position as exemplified by Bennholdt-Thomsen's book *Geld oder Leben* (*Money or Life*) is examined since it is increasingly considered by degrowth scholars and activists who previously have been charged with gender-blindness.

Wealth creation, 'overdevelopment' and global connectedness

Postwachstum's obvious contribution to the Post-Development agenda seems to be that it addresses the detrimental effects of (economic) growth in the early industrialised countries in Europe and North America. Here, the works under scrutiny have as their starting point the global ecological crisis as well as the financial and economic crisis of 2008. They concur that these are the result of a 'comprehensive aberration of society',[53] but have different perspectives on what and who is responsible and on how it should be addressed. For *Postwachstum* to serve as a complement to Post-Development, it is crucial how its proponents understand the effects of growth and how the South is included in the theoretical reflections.

First of all, they differ in their perspectives on why one should be concerned about the negative aspects of the West's growth orientation. The conservative position places emphasis on the detrimental effects of growth on the fabric of Western societies – characterised as 'fragile',[54] 'stranded',[55] and 'unable to cope'[56] – but also pays attention to the destruction of nature: 'Just like the Western economic patterns and ways of life existentially endanger environment and nature, they also threaten the stability of the social fabric'.[57] Paech's *Liberation from Excess*[58] also rejects growth and what is widely considered progress as ecologically and culturally devastating. It places emphasis on the exploitative character of the North's growth orientation vis-à-vis the Global South as it regularly mentions the fact that consumer societies externalise the costs of their consumption and production to the periphery.[59] Seidl and Zahrnt, in line with the common understanding of 'sustainable development', see the consumption of resources in industrialised countries as problematic for 'future generations and people in developing and emerging countries'.[60] Schmelzer and Passadakis depart from anti-globalisation movements and are motivated by 'global social [and ecological] inequality and injustice'.[61] Bennholdt-Thomsen is concerned about the widening of the gap between the rich and the poor both globally and nationally, and about the dynamics, such that the profit-maximisation of some people threatens the basic livelihoods of many others.[62] Her perspective furthermore entails that current economic globalisation is a continuation of colonial economic policy based on the exploitation of nature and people's labour in the South, and of women more generally[63] – what ecofeminists have termed the 'colonies of the white man'.[64]

The solutions put forward for the diagnosed 'aberration' show commonalities, but also important differences. All approaches agree that Western modes of production and consumption cannot be upheld. Miegel regards the downsizing of the welfare state in the North as an inevitable reaction to a shrinking economy, but also mentions that since the early industrialised countries have sufficient material goods, they should now 'queue behind' so that the 'economically weak of this world' can satisfy their needs.[65] How this should be undertaken is not spelt out. Here, Schmelzer and Passadakis are slightly more explicit. They demand 'to fight prosperity' and call for 'redistribution of income and capital' to the South – also as a means to settle the climate debt of the North.[66] Furthermore, they see 'de-globalisation' as a way for the countries of the South to increase their scope of action with regards to trade.[67] For Paech, the general solutions are sufficiency and subsistence in the North.[68] He also advocates for de-globalisation, but mainly for ecological reasons and with a focus on what de-globalisation does for the re-localised people in the North.[69] He does not consider the historical debt of the North vis-à-vis the South. The ecofeminist perspective is in line with Paech's focus on subsistence, but sees such an orientation as useful for both the North and the South as well as for their relation.[70] Furthermore, it highlights the spiritual, empowering dimension of 'feeling connected to the natural environment' by reducing the dependence on money and wage labour.[71]

Redistribution does not play a role for Bennholdt-Thomsen or for Paech, Miegel or Seidl and Zahrnt. Miegel even believes that 'the wealthy countries since long support the poorer ones economically'.[72] He obviously refers to official development assistance (ODA) and does not take into account that ODA stands at less than a third of the annual debt payments flowing from the South to the North.[73] In Seidl and Zahrnt's edited volume, the interests and stakes of people in the Global South are hardly taken into account. The only essay in this book that refers to the South in a meaningful way is the contribution on consumption.[74] In Røpke's view, increasing consumption in the North takes away resources for better living standards in the South. Growth is pushed by increasing consumption for which cheap fossil fuels as well as global inequalities, which allow for an exploitation of workers in the South, are key.

As became evident, interdependencies between North and South do not play a major role for the conservative, liberal, and sufficiency perspectives in *Postwachstum*, but are key to the ecofeminist and anti-capitalist[75] positions. What is more, and this is true for all but the ecofeminist proponents of *Postwachstum*, is the lack of a longer historical perspective. The interventions mainly put the last 200 years and industrialisation centre stage. This most likely has to do with the principal concern being ecological destruction and climate change. The South is thus only seen as affected by 'growth' and 'progress' insofar as ecological and climate change hit it, which are understood as due to the extensive use of fossil fuel in the West. However, and recognised by ecofeminist thought, ideas of progress as well as expansive, exploitative relations to people and nature have a longer trajectory in the West and are inextricably connected to the 500 years of colonial expansion.[76] This is well exemplified by the following quote from a person enslaved in Barbados in 1667: 'The Devil was in the Englishman that he makes everything work; he makes the Negro work, the Horse work, the Ass work, the Wood work, the Water work and the Winde work'.[77]

Without the wealth accumulated through the exploitation of the Americas and the enslavement of millions of Africans, European and US-American industrialisation would not have taken place.[78] Lacking this perspective, authors such as Paech offer little sensitivity for the fact that reducing industrial capacity and being able to think about sufficiency and de-globalisation is based on a long history of exploitation. What is more, the *Postwachstum* contributions under scrutiny here do evidence little understanding of imperial politics for safeguarding the access to resources in the South and for defending the West's prosperity.[79] Here, *Postwachstum* could hark back to the ecological critique of the 1990s in Germany. According to Spehr,[80] for example, the instruments of domination of the so-called industrialised countries have to be reduced for socio-ecological transformation to happen in North and South. This includes pushing back the global economic sector (ie reducing the capacity for economic intervention in the South) as well as inhibiting the North's capacity for military interventions in the South.

Linear, teleological, universal socio-economic change

This section deals with the question whether dominant notions of 'development' are embraced or rejected in *Postwachstum* – and whether they propose new blueprints or advocate pluriversality. Here, again, the different perspectives are rather diverse and only partially provide helpful contributions to the Post-Development agenda.

The anti-capitalist position intends to go beyond the critique of growth to advance 'globalization-critical demands' with its concept of a 'solidarity post-growth economy'.[81] The authors understand the 'growth paradigm' as a 'fundamental hegemonic project of capitalist development'[82] and aim at an economy 'that assures global social rights for everybody'.[83] It is supposed to be orientated towards 'that which is necessary for the good life rather than towards profit and growth rates; cooperation instead of competition; the (re)productive instead of the division between (male) production and (female) reproduction; [...]; and de-centrality, glocalization, and de-globalization'.[84]

This approach can thus be understood as in line with the Post-Development agenda in displacing a specific notion of capitalist, patriarchal, globalised development from the centre of social imaginaries and practices.

The ecofeminist contribution to the recent *Postwachstum* debate is straightforward in its rejection of the Western development path in which human activity beyond money-making and exchange value is rendered useless. Bennholdt-Thomsen criticises 'the ideology of developed and underdeveloped economies and societies',[85] because the 'subsequent judgements regarding other ways of life directly connect to the debates of the Conquista' on whether the colonised people should be considered human or not.[86]

In contrast to Schmelzer and Passadakis' as well as Bennholdt-Thomsen's rather fundamental critique of the Western development path, the South appears as quasi-naturally following whatever the West does, in Seidl and Zahrnt's edited volume:

> A turning away from the growth orientation on our part would influence the economic policy of these countries, because our economic development shapes development ideas in these countries.[87]

These authors seem to not question the classic 'development gaze', taking up the modernisation perspective that 'people in developing and emerging countries' lag behind and attempt to catch up.[88]

Miegel's work adheres to the idea of linear, teleological 'development' with the West as its culmination.[89] The West is understood as merely having gone too far and only in need of change now. He refers to the South as 'underdeveloped countries'[90] and contrasts the problematic patterns of production and consumption in the West with the lifestyle of 'close-to-nature peoples'.[91] According to him, 'people of earlier times had a fine feeling' for not 'transgressing natural boundaries', something that 'close-to-nature peoples show ... until today most directly'.[92] Miegel thus evidences the idea that people, societies, and world regions inhabit different yet continuous temporal spaces, as well as different cultural development stages.[93]

The Post-Development debate brought to the fore the oppressive nature of universalist positions, even when coming from an anti-development position.[94] Here, Schmelzer and Passadakis refrain from positing new universalisms beyond demanding 'universalist egalitarianism'.[95] Paech's and Miegel's *Postwachstum* proposals, even though the former allegedly rejects 'the fairy tale of progress', however, come across as new blueprints. For instance, Paech proposes a solution for growth-orientation in a universalist manner: 'The only responsible organizational principle for societies and lifestyles in the 21st century is called reduction – understood as liberation from that excess that not only blocks our life but renders our existence so vulnerable'.[96]

This position obviously sees ideas of a desirable path of socio-economic change in a universal manner. This is incongruent with the Post-Development position of pluriversality, also within the North.[97] Non-Western versions of development or alternatives to development are not considered in any of the degrowth contributions as inspiring for the North.

Miegel's idea for the future is also not a world where many worlds fit:

> Plan A according to which the peoples of the early industrialised countries have proceeded, shows more and more weaknesses. Its bearing elements are: progress, growth, wealth creation. It functioned well on this basis for a long time. But this time is coming to an end. Therefore, a Plan B needs to be devised now [for the peoples of the early industrialised countries and the rest of humanity] … .[98]

This quote on the one hand again evidences that 'progress' and 'growth' are not seen as problematic per se – for example, because of their implication in colonial violence such as the trade with enslaved Africans. On the other, it clearly indicates a (Eurocentric) perspective of universalism. He sees the need to envision the next comprehensive plan for everybody.

All in all, the critique and rejection of the West's development path is only partial in *Postwachstum*: While Bennholdt-Thomsen is clear in her critique of Western modernity and economic 'progress' since the outset of colonisation, and Schmelzer and Passadakis 'question the economic development path that was taken through the industrial revolution in the second half of the 19th century,'[99] Miegel does not – as just mentioned – find fault with industrialisation per se, but regards it as no longer a viable development path. What the degrowth contributions – except for the ecofeminist one – have in common is that they do not take into account the long history of colonialism, and stick to the 'myth of industrialization'.[100] Departing from the idea that the West 'developed' because of particular cultural traits and that this was an intra-European affair, they thus adhere to the narrative that a number of countries independently developed or industrialised between 1750 and 1950. Here, world-system or dependency theorists such as Wallerstein seem a useful correction by proposing to rather understand this societal change as 'the story of the secular expansion of the world-economy as a whole' and that 'a dozen or two came to enclose the principal fruits of the expansion and development of the capitalist world-economy' that already began in the sixteenth century.[101]

Colonial difference

The major contribution of the degrowth debate is that it principally shifts the focus to the North and sees regions commonly deemed developed as in need of transformation and intervention. This is an obvious de- and reflection of the 'development gaze'. The crucial question, however, remains how Global North – or those whose lifestyles are seen as in need to de-grow – and South are characterised and portrayed in this endeavour. The third aspect of this paper is thus how *Postwachstum* understands differences between the Global North and South and whether this reifies inequalities.

The contributions concur in mentioning the South as particularly affected by climate change and ecological destruction. It emerges as the innocent victims of the North's or the global consumer class' obsession with economic growth and consumption. In the anti-capitalist narrative, the Global South additionally appears as inhabiting agency and capable of relevant knowledge production for the North: This perspective aligns with anti-globalisation movements, references the Asian NGO Focus on the Global South's idea of deglobalisation,[102] and also mentions 'postcolonial and Post-Development theory' as sources of inspiration.[103] In Bennholdt-Thomsen's contribution, the South mainly appears negatively affected by the growth economy's tendency to appropriate all forms of subsistence economy. While the agency of people in the South does not come out in this book, her and her ecofeminist peers' earlier publications evidence acute awareness of the autonomous knowledge and practices of particularly women peasants in the South.[104] In Paech's book, the Global South does not play an active role, but merely enters the stage as a sink for the pollution of the North. By deliberately focusing on the North only, the sufficiency position lacks a global perspective. This *inter alia* leads Paech to propose unilateral actions on the side of the wealthy: to just refrain from the dominant lifestyle.[105] He does not mention possible negotiation processes with, or inspirations from, the South. He proposes a 'cushioning of negative growth'[106] through social welfare, but only thinks of the people in the North; not of the effects for people in the South who might also need 'cushioning' regarding possible harmful effects of reduction in the North.[107]

Miegel brings up non-Western worlds rather prominently in comparison with most of the other *Postwachstum* contributions under scrutiny here. This, however, should be interpreted as motivated by 'renewing' the West and 'saving' it from cultural annihilation, rather than by concern for social-ecological transformation to the advantage of the marginalised in the South and North. In his tale of the end of growth orientation, the South appears to be a mass of billions of people longing for material prosperity and leaving their 'dismal living conditions'[108] or as a mass of people dying, starving and forced to migrate due to climate change.[109] On the one hand, people in the Global South are thus presented as the destitute, passive Other 'coming for us' and desiring Western 'development'. On the other hand, however, the South appears fundamentally different due to a different relation to nature. Above, I already mentioned Miegel's occupation with 'close-to-nature peoples'. While this is a continuation of the colonial depiction of 'primitive people', it could also be interpreted as an appreciation of a respectful, sustainable human–nature relationship. 'Other cultures and close-to-nature peoples'[110] are here constructed as culturally distinct on the basis of their relation to nature. This homogenising and culturalist recognition of difference is in line with Miegel's focus on cultural renewal in the West and his emphasis on spiritual and non-material values rather than redistribution or social-ecological transformation.

It is thus not true that '[c]ultural differences between the West and the Rest (Hall) are nowhere being addressed in the degrowth texts'.[111] However, the human–nature relation is itself naturalised by Miegel and not presented as social. It is similar to the exoticisation criticised by Kiely[112] in some Post-Development work. Interestingly, Miegel mentions that he does not regard the 'peoples of the early industrialised countries' as 'able to act swiftly and efficiently due their generation-long-imprint'.[113] This, however, does not lead him to look for the agency or epistemologies of people from the South to deal with the crises in the North.[114] In contradiction with this 'the West and the Rest' view, Miegel's tends to universalise the Western experience of enlightenment and capitalism. For him, 'man' has a 'natural urge for expansion' and 'has overcome natural constraints with the help of his culture'.[115] This includes for him the exploitation of oil and coal.[116] At the same time, 'man' has thus 'lost his footing in nature'.[117] This not only universalises the human experience on a global scale, but also universalises Western societies.

In contrast to all the other contributions, the ecofeminist work confronts the issue of colonial difference head-on. Bennholdt-Thomsen characterises 'our social system' of industrialisation and growth as founded on a 'disregard for women's work', 'disrespect for nature', and 'colonialist pillage'.[118] Moreover, she diagnoses a 'collective neurotic fear of scarcity' that stabilises the ignorance of subsistence processes.[119] This view of Western modernity is underlined by Mies through her thesis that 'what we call "European civilisation"' is based on 'external as well as internal … colonial relations' as the 'hidden deep structure'.[120] The binary divide between Western patriarchal capitalism and the freedom of a life of subsistence, for which the ecofeminist positions at the time have been criticised, is still present, and also explicitly upheld when Bennholdt-Thomsen mentions the exploitation of the labour of 'primitive people' (*Naturvölker*) in colonial times.[121] At the same time, she points out that sufficiency oriented non-Western societies have been constructed as uncivilised in order to expand and universalise the capitalist economic structures.[122]

Conclusion

Postwachstum's obvious contribution to the Post-Development agenda is that its focus on Western wealth creation re-centres the North as the problem for global economic, ecological and social transformation. However, except for the ecofeminist perspective it lacks a longer historical perspective. Here, it could hark back to postcolonial and world-system approaches which bring to the fore that Europe's historical development and present formation cannot be understood without taking into account colonial conquest.[123] For this, focusing on the industrial revolution as an intra-European affair is counterproductive. *Postwachstum* seems in need of destabilising and un-learning myths of Northern supremacy by turning its gaze towards the history and present of the coloniality–modernity–development nexus.

Postwachstum is not entirely critical of the Western development path. Here as well, the subsistence position needs to be exempted, and the anti-capitalist perspective is also an exception, even though this strand lacks the longer postcolonial perspective just mentioned. While the economic growth aspect is evidently the focus, *Postwachstum* does not always connect this to a rejection of the idea of linear, teleological progress. What is more, it does not do away with the colonial dichotomy of 'modern' versus 'traditional' – even if it at times appreciates the 'traditional' in the South as more respectful to nature. Even the ecofeminist contribution does not entirely escape such colonial difference. However, it is the only *Postwachstum* position that takes non-Western worldviews seriously, and does not neglect them as useful sources for societal change in the North.

Postwachstum understands 'modernity' as primarily capitalist and economical, but does not pay enough attention to the question of how colonial difference legitimises the model of prosperity and exploitative consumption and production in the North. Most of the contributions scrutinised here are not really able to enhance our understanding of the connection between colonial difference and 'overdevelopment', or how the South has been portrayed as closer to nature in order to legitimise its exploitation. Here, a reconsideration of ecofeminist thought since the 1980s may be recommended, and could be complemented by more recent decolonial perspectives on human–nature hierarchies.[124] This is in line with Brand's observation that, in order to carve out the requirements for social-ecological transformation in solidarity with oppressed people in the North and South, the crucial degrowth issues of production and consumption need to be understood 'as capitalist, patriarchal, racialised or postcolonial social conditions'.[125]

To fully grasp the state and potential of degrowth as a Post-Development agenda for the North, it would be useful to compare the German debate to those in other Northern contexts. As mentioned above, the French and Spanish degrowth debates seem closer to Post-Development thought. In addition, it would be necessary to take a closer look at, for instance, the German degrowth practices. The initiatives assembled at the Degrowth Conference and meeting and at the Summer Schools seem open to reflecting on the North's colonial legacy and to questioning Northern epistemologies. What is more, *Postwachstum* could not only look more towards the South for epistemological and practical inspiration, but also devote more energy to forging alliances with other struggles in Germany such as the refugees' movement that is concerned with global inequalities and criticises Germany's colonial present.

Disclosure statement

No potential conflict of interest was reported by the author.

Acknowledgements

I would like to thank Aram Ziai and the reviewers for their helpful advice. This work was supported by the DFG Research Group 'Landnahme, Acceleration, Activation. Dynamic(s) and (de-)stabilisation of modern growth societies' at Friedrich Schiller University Jena.

Notes

1. Escobar, *Encountering Development*, 155.
2. Corbridge, "Beneath the Pavement," 144.
3. Kiely, "The Last Refuge," 38.
4. Ziai, "Post-Development," 849.
5. Muraca, *Gut leben*, 33–6.
6. Demaria et al., "What Is Degrowth?"
7. D'Alisa, Demaria, and Kallis, *Degrowth*, pt. 3.
8. Latouche, *Survivre au Développement; Entre Mondialisation et Décroissance*.
9. Martinez Alier, *Environmentalism of the Poor*.
10. Escobar, "Degrowth, Postdevelopment, and Transitions"; Ziai, "Post-Development Concepts?"; Kothari, Demaria, and Acosta, "Buen"; Fees, Lauth, and Weichelt, "Der Globale Süden"; Thiele, "Post-Development Discourse."

11. Kothari et al., "Buen Vivir, Degrowth and Ecological Swaraj," 366.

12. Ziai, "Post-Development Concepts?," 150.

13. Sachs, *Development Dictionary*; Ferguson, "Anti-Politics Machine"; Escobar, *Encountering Development*.

14. Escobar, "Degrowth, Postdevelopment, and Transitions," 4.

15. Biccum, "Development and The 'New' Imperialism?"; Noxolo, "Claims."

16. White, "Thinking Race"; Kothari, "'Race' in Development."

17. Eriksson Baaz, *Paternalism of Partnership*; Heron, *Desire for Development*.

18. Crush, *Power of Development*; Cooke and Kothari, *Participation*.

19. Wainwright, *Decolonizing Development*; Bendix, "Curbing Population Growth."

20. Dussel, *Invention of the Americas*; Quijano, "Coloniality of Power."

21. Corbridge, "Beneath the Pavement"; Kiely, "Last Refuge."

22. McGregor, "New Possibilities?", 1693.

23. Gibson-Graham, "Surplus Possibilities."

24. Sachs, *Development Dictionary*.

25. Ziai, "Post-Development."

26. Dussel, *Invention of the Americas*; Kothari, "History, Time and Temporality"; Kebede, "African Development"; Quijano, "Coloniality of Power."

27. Chari and Corbridge, *Development Reader*, 1.

28. Bennett, "Under-Development, Over-Development, Post-Development," 983.

29. Power, "Anti-Racism"; Bennett, "Under-Development, Over-Development, Post-Development."

30. Power, "Anti-Racism," 36–7.

31. White, "Thinking Race," 413.

32. Kiely, "Last Refuge," 38.

33. Cowen and Shenton, "Invention of Development."

34. Linebaugh and Rediker, The Many-Headed Hydra; Federici, *Caliban and the Witch*.

35. Habermann and Ziai, "Development, Internationalism and Social Movements."

36. D'Alisa, Demaria, and Kallis, "Introduction," 1.

37. Ibid., 2.

38. Muraca, *Gut leben*, chap. II.

39. Escobar, "Degrowth, Postdevelopment, and Transitions," 4.

40. Latouche, *Farewell to Growth*, 56–7.

41. Demaria et al., "What is Degrowth?," 192–3.

42. Ibid., 209.

43. http://www.degrowth.de/en/conferences/

44. Fees, Lauth, and Weichelt, "Der Globale Süden," 52.

45. http://www.degrowth.de/en/summer-school-2016/

46. Schmelzer, "Spielarten der Wachstumskritik," 118.

47. Miegel, *Exit*.

48. Seidl and Zahrnt, *Postwachstumsgesellschaft*.

49. Paech, *Befreiung vom Überfluss*.

50. Schmelzer and Passadakis, *Postwachstum*.

51. Bennholdt-Thomsen, *Geld oder Leben*.

52. Muraca, *Gut leben*, 35.

53. Miegel, *Exit*, 15.

54. Ibid., 134.

55. Ibid., 145.

56. Ibid., 149.

57. Ibid., 134.

58. Paech, *Befreiung vom Überfluss*.

59. Ibid., 39, 46, 49, 53, 61.

60. Seidl and Zahrnt, *Postwachstumsgesellschaft*, 9.

61. Schmelzer and Passadakis, *Postwachstum*, 11.

62. Bennholdt-Thomsen, *Geld oder Leben*, 10, 20.

63. Ibid., 26.

64. Mies, "Notwendigkeit, Europa zu entkolonisieren," 32.
65. Miegel, *Exit*, 228.
66. Schmelzer and Passadakis, *Postwachstum*, 84.
67. Ibid., 87.
68. Paech, *Befreiung vom Überfluss*, 114.
69. Ibid., 116.
70. Bennholdt-Thomsen, *Geld oder Leben*, 74.
71. Ibid., 37.
72. Miegel, *Exit*, 40.
73. Ellmers, *Developing Country Debt*, 3.
74. Røpke, "Konsum."
75. Schmelzer and Passadakis, *Postwachstum*, 84.
76. Quijano, "Coloniality of Power"; Bernstein, "Colonialism, Capitalism, Development."
77. Anon., *Great Newes*, 6–7.
78. Galeano, *The Open Veins of Latin America*; Wallerstein, *Unthinking Social Science*.
79. This estimation is based on the major publications analysed here. Within the internationally connected German degrowth movement, the anti-capitalist position has developed further and the North–South dialogue has also intensified. The former can be recognised in the contributions at the Leipzig Conference 2014 and at the Degrowth Summer Schools of 2015 and 2016. The latter is *inter alia* evident in the wide discussion of Acosta's and Gudynas' work on *Buen Vivir* as well as Ashish Kothari's on radical ecological democracy.
80. *Die Ökofalle*.
81. *Postwachstum*, 67.
82. Ibid., 20.
83. Ibid., 67.
84. Ibid.
85. Bennholdt-Thomsen, *Geld oder Leben*, 32.
86. Ibid., 33.
87. Seidl and Zahrnt, *Postwachstumsgesellschaft*, 18, fn. 1.
88. Ibid., 9.
89. Cf. Kebede, "African Development."
90. Miegel, *Exit*, 100.
91. Ibid., 45.
92. Ibid.
93. Cf. Dussel, *Invention of the Americas*.
94. Ziai, "Ambivalence of Post-Development."
95. Schmelzer and Passadakis, *Postwachstum*, 90.
96. *Befreiung vom Überfluss*, 11.
97. Kebede, "African Development."
98. Miegel, *Exit*, 96.
99. Schmelzer and Passadakis, *Postwachstum*, 73.
100. Wallerstein, *Unthinking Social Science*.
101. Ibid., 118.
102. Schmelzer and Passadakis, *Postwachstum*, 78.
103. Ibid., 68.
104. eg Bennholdt-Thomsen and Mies, *Eine Kuh für Hillary*.
105. *Befreiung vom Überfluss*, 145.
106. Ibid.
107. Cf. Fees, Lauth, and Weichelt, "Der Globale Süden," 15–6, 39.
108. Miegel, *Exit*, 187.
109. Ibid., 29, 100.
110. Ibid., 193.
111. Ziai, "Post-Development Concepts?," 149–50.
112. "Last Refuge."

113. Miegel, *Exit*, 99.
114. Cf. Santos, *Epistemologies of the South*.
115. Miegel, *Exit*, 43.
116. Ibid., 44.
117. Ibid.
118. Bennholdt-Thomsen, *Geld oder Leben*, 13, 24–6.
119. Ibid., 26.
120. Mies, "Notwendigkeit, Europa zu entkolonisieren," 21.
121. Bennholdt-Thomsen, *Geld oder Leben*, 26.
122. Ibid., 27–35.
123. Dussel, *Invention of the Americas*; Quijano, "Coloniality of Power."
124. Casas, "Transcending the Coloniality of Development."
125. Brand, "Degrowth und Post-Extraktivismus," 34.

Bibliography

Anon. *Great Newes from the Barbadoes, Or, A True and Faithful Account of the Grand Conspiracy of the Negroes against the English and the Happy Discovery of the Same with the Number of Those That Were Burned Alive, Beheaded, and Otherwise Executed for Their Horrid Crimes: With a Short Discription of That Plantation*. London: L. Curtis, 1676.

Bendix, Daniel. "From Fighting Underpopulation to Curbing Population Growth: Tracing Colonial Power in German Development Interventions in Tanzania." *Postcolonial Studies* 18, no. 4 (6 September 2016): 1–18. doi:10.1080/13688790.2016.1228137.

Bennett, Cary. "Supporting the Posts in Development Discourse: Under-development, Over-development, Post-Development." *Sociology Compass* 6, no. 12 (2012): 974–986.

Bennholdt-Thomsen, Veronika. *Geld oder Leben: Was uns wirklich reich macht* [Money or Life: What Makes us Really Rich]. München: oekom, 2010.

Bennholdt-Thomsen, Veronika, and Maria Mies, eds. *Eine Kuh Für Hillary. Die Subsistenzperspektive* [A Cow for Hillary. The Subsistence Perspective]. München: Frauenoffensive, 1997.

Bernstein, Henry. "Colonialism, Capitalism, Development." In *Poverty and Development into the 21st Century*, edited by Tim Allen and Alan Thomas, 241–270. Oxford: Oxford University Press, 2000.

Biccum, April. "Development and the 'New' Imperialism: A Reinvention of Colonial Discourse in DFID Promotional Literature." *Third World Quarterly* 26, no. 6 (2005): 1005–1020.

Brand, Ulrich. "Degrowth und Post-Extraktivismus: Zwei Seiten einer Medaille? [Degrowth and Post-Extractivism: Two Sides of the Same Coin?]" Working Paper der DFG-KollegforscherInnengruppe Postwachstumsgesellschaften, no. 5 (2015).

Brigg, Morgan. "Empowering NGOs: The Microcredit Movement through Foucault's Notion of Dispositif." *Alternatives: Global, Local, Political* 26, no. 3 (2001): 233–258.

Casas, Tanya. "Transcending the Coloniality of Development: Moving Beyond Human/Nature Hierarchies." *American Behavioral Scientist* 58, no. 1 (1 January 2014): 30–52. doi: 10.1177/0002764213495030.

Chari, Sharad, and Stuart Corbridge, eds. *The Development Reader*. London: Routledge, 2008.

Cooke, Bill, and Uma Kothari, eds. *Participation: The New Tyranny?* London-New York: Zed Books, 2001.

Corbridge, Stuart. "'Beneath the Pavement Only Soil': The Poverty of Post-development". *The Journal of Development Studies* 34, no. 6 (1 August 1998): 138–148. doi:10.1080/00220389808422549.

Cowen, Michael, and Robert Shenton. "The Invention of Development." In *The Power of Development*, edited by Jonathan Crush, 27–43. London: Routledge, 1995.

Crush, Jonathan, ed. *Power of Development*. London: Routledge, 1995.

D'Alisa, Giacomo, Federico Demaria, and Giorgos Kallis, eds. *Degrowth: A Vocabulary for a New Era*. London: Routledge, 2014.

D'Alisa, Giacomo, Federico Demaria, and Giorgos Kallis, eds. "Introduction." In *Degrowth: A Vocabulary for a New Era*, edited by Giacomo D'Alisa, Federico Demaria, and Giorgos Kallis, 1–17. London: Routledge, 2014.

Demaria, Federico, Francois Schneider, Filka Sekulova, and Joan Martínez-Alier. "What is Degrowth? From an Activist Slogan to a Social Movement." *Environmental Values* 22, no. 2 (1 April 2013): 191–215. doi: 10.3197/096327113X13581561725194.

Dussel, Enrique. *The Invention of the Americas. Eclipse of 'the Other' and the Myth of Modernity*. New York: Continuum, 1995. http://bibliotecavirtual.clacso.org.ar/ar/libros/dussel/1492in/1492 in.html.

Ellmers, Bodo. *The Evolving Nature of Developing Country Debt and Solutions for Change*. Brussels: Eurodad, 2016. http://www.eurodad.org/developing-country-debt-solutions.

Eriksson Baaz, Maria. *The Paternalism of Partnership. A Postcolonial Reading of Development Politics*. London-New York: Zed Books, 2005.

Escobar, Arturo. "Degrowth, Postdevelopment, and Transitions: A Preliminary Conversation." *Sustainability Science* 10, no. 3 (2015): 451–462. doi:10.1007/s11625-015-0297-5.

Escobar, Arturo. *Encountering Development. The Making and Unmaking of the Third World*. Princeton: Princeton University Press, 1994.

Federici, Silvia. *Caliban and the Witch: Women, the Body and Primitive Accumulation*. New York: Autonomedia, 2004.

Fees, Dorothee, Katja Lauth, and Clara Luisa Weichelt. *Der Globale Süden in der Deutschen Postwachstumsdebatte*. Marburg: Phillipps-Universität Marburg, 2015.

Ferguson, James. "The Anti-Politics Machine. 'Development' and Bureaucratic Power in Lesotho." *The Ecologist* 24, no. 5 (1994): 176–181.

Galeano, Eduardo. *Open Veins of Latin America: Five Centuries of the Pillage of a Continent*. New York: Monthly Review Press, 1997.

Gibson-Graham, J.k. 'Surplus Possibilities: Postdevelopment and Community Economies'. *Singapore Journal of Tropical Geography* 26, no. 1 (1 March 2005): 4–26. doi:10.1111/j.0129-7619.2005.00198.x.

Habermann, Friederike, and Aram Ziai. "Development, Internationalism and Social Movements. A View from the North." In *Exploring Post-Development. Theory and Practice, Problems and Perspectives*, edited by Aram Ziai, 212–227. London - New York: Routledge, 2007.

Heron, Barbara. *Desire for Development. Whiteness, Gender, and the Helping Imperative*. Waterloo: Wilfrid Laurier University Press, 2007.

Kebede, Messay. "African Development and the Primacy of Mental Decolonization." *African Development* 19, no. 1 (2004): 107–129.

Kiely, Ray. "The Last Refuge of the Noble Savage? A Critical Assessment of Post-Development Theory 11(1):30-55." *European Journal of Development Research* 11, no. 1 (1999): 30–55.

Kothari, Ashish, Federico Demaria, and Alberto Acosta. "Buen Vivir, Degrowth and Ecological Swaraj: Alternatives to Sustainable Development and the Green Economy." *Development* 57, no. 3 (1 December 2014): 362–375. doi:10.1057/dev.2015.24.

Kothari, Uma. "An Agenda for Thinking about 'Race' in Development." *Progress in Development Studies* 6, no. 1 (2006): 9–23.

Kothari, Uma. "Commentary: History, Time and Temporality in Development Discourse." In *History, Historians and Development Policy. A Necessary Dialogue*, edited by Christopher Bayly, Vijayendra Rao, Simon Szreter, and Michael Woolcock, 65–70. Manchester-New York: Manchester University Press, 2011.

Latouche, Serge. *Entre Mondialisation et Décroissance : L'autre Afrique* [Between Globalization and Degrowth: The Other Africa]. La Bauche: À plus d'un titre, 2007.

Latouche, Serge. *Farewell to Growth*. London: Polity Press, 2009.

Latouche, Serge. *Survivre au Développement. De la Décolonisation de l'Imaginaire Économique À la Construction d'une Société Alternative* [Surviving Development. From the Decolonization of the Economic Imaginary to the Construction of an Alternative Society]. Paris: Mille et une nuits, 2004.

Linebaugh, Peter, and Marcus Rediker. *The Many-Headed Hydra: The Hidden History of the Revolutionary Atlantic*. London-New York: Verso, 2000.

Martínez-Alier, Joan. *The Environmentalism of the Poor. A Study of Ecological Conflicts and Valuation*. Northhampton, MA: Edward Elgar, 2003.

McGregor, Andrew. "New Possibilities? Shifts in Post-Development Theory and Practice." *Geography Compass* 3, no. 5 (2009): 1688–1702. doi:10.1111/j.1749-8198.2009.00260.x.

Miegel, Meinhard. *Exit: Wohlstand ohne Wachstum* [Exit: Prosperity without Growth]. Berlin: List, 2010.

Mies, Maria. 'Über die Notwendigkeit, Europa zu entkolonisieren' [On the Necessity to Decolonise Europe]. In *Subsistenz und Widerstand. Alternativen zur Globalisierung* [Subsistence and Resistance. Alternatives to Globalization], edited by Claudia von Werlhof and Veronika Bennholdt-Thomsen, 19–40. Wien: Promedia, 2003.

Muraca, Barbara. *Gut leben. Eine Gesellschaft jenseits des Wachstums* [Living Well. A Society beyond Growth]. Berlin: Wagenbach, 2014.

Noxolo, Patricia. "Claims: A Postcolonial Geographical Critique of 'Partnership' in Britain's Development Discourse." *Singapore Journal of Tropical Geography* 27, no. 3 (2006): 254–269.

Paech, Niko. *Befreiung vom Überfluss: Auf dem Weg in die Postwachstumsökonomie* [Liberation from Excess: The Road to a Post-Growth Economy]. Stuttgart: oekom, 2012.

Power, Marcus. "Anti-Racism, Deconstruction and 'Overdevelopment.'" *Progress in Development Studies* 6, no. 1 (2006): 25–39.

Quijano, Anibal. "Coloniality of Power, Eurocentrism, and Latin America." *Nepantla: Views from South* 1, no. 3 (2000): 533–580.

Røpke, Inge. "Konsum: Der Kern des Wachstumsmotors [Consumption: The Core of the Growth Engine]." In *Postwachstumsgesellschaft: Neue Konzepte für die Zukunft* [Post-Growth Society: Concepts for the Future], edited by Irmi Seidl and Angelika Zahrnt, 103–115. Marburg: Metropolis, 2010.

Sachs, Wolfgang. *The Development Dictionary. A Guide to Knowledge as Power.* London-New Jersey: Zed Books, 1992.

Santos, Boaventura de Sousa. *Another Knowledge Is Possible: Beyond Northern Epistemologies.* London-New York: Verso, 2008.

Santos, Boaventura de Sousa. *Epistemologies of the South: Justice Against Epistemicide.* Boulder: Paradigm, 2014.

Schmelzer, Matthias. "Spielarten Der Wachstumskritik. Degrowth, Klimagerechtigkeit, Subsistenz - Eine Einführung in Die Begriffe Und Ansätze Der Postwachstumsbewegung [Varieties of Growth Critique. Degrowth, Climate Justice, Subsistence - An Introduction to the Terminology and Approaches of the Post-Growth Movement]." In *Atlas der Globalisierung. Weniger wird mehr,* edited by Barbara Bauer, Dorothee d'Aprile, Katharina Döbler, Nlels Kadritzke, Stephan Lessenich, and Steffen Liebig, 116–121. Berlin: Le Monde diplomatique - Kolleg Postwachstumsgesellschaften, 2015.

Schmelzer, Matthias, and Alexis Passadakis. *Postwachstum. Krise, Ökologische Grenzen und soziale Rechte.* Hamburg: VSA, 2011.

Seidl, Irmi, and Angelika Zahrnt. *Postwachstumsgesellschaft: Neue Konzepte für die Zukunft* [Post-Growth Society: New Concepts for the Future]. Marburg: Metropolis, 2010.

Spehr, Christoph. *Die Ökofalle. Nachhaltigkeit Und Krise. Wien, Promedia* [The Ecotrap. Sustainability and Crisis]. Wien: Promedia, 1996.

Thiele, Lasse. "Post-Development Discourse: Lessons for the Degrowth Movement." 2015. http://www.degrowth.de/en/2015/07/post-development-discourse-lessons-for-the-degrowth-movement-part-1/

Wainwright, Joel. *Decolonizing Development. Colonial Power and the Maya. Antipode Book Series.* Oxford: Blackwell, 2008.

Wallerstein, Immanuel. *Unthinking Social Science. The Limits of Nineteenth-Century Paradigms.* Cambridge: Polity Press, 1991.

White, Sarah. "Thinking Race, Thinking Development." *Third World Quarterly* 23, no. 3 (2002): 407–419.

Ziai, Aram. 'Post-Development Concepts? Buen Vivir, Ubuntu and Degrowth'. In *Epistemologies of the South: South-South, South-North and North-South Global Learnings. Other Economies,* edited by Boaventura De Sousa Santos and Theresa Cunha, 143–154. Coimbra: CES, 2015.

Ziai, Aram. "Post-Development: Premature Burials and Haunting Ghosts." *Development and Change* 46, no. 4 (1 July 2015): 833–854. doi:10.1111/dech.12177.

Ziai, Aram. "The Ambivalence of Post-development: Between Reactionary Populism and Radical Democracy." *Third World Quarterly* 25, no. 6 (2004): 1045–1060. doi:10.1080/0143659042000256887.

Fossil-fuelled development and the legacy of Post-Development theory in twenty-first century Africa

Stefan Andreasson iD

ABSTRACT
This article examines the legacy of Post-Development theory, in particular its relevance and applicability to debates about Africa's future. It scrutinises Post-Development theory, and its claims about the end of development, through the prisms of Africa's continued pursuit of development and its political economy of energy. It considers the impact of these aspects of Africa's developmental efforts on the ability of Post-Development theory to remain relevant in light of recent developments. Revisiting basic claims of Post-Development theory provides insights into the enduring disconnect and incommensurability between Africa's twenty-first century socio-economic trajectories and the core assumptions of Post-Development theory.

The last 40 years can be called the age of development. This epoch is coming to an end. The time is ripe to write its obituary.[1]

We have got to be so impatient with moving Africa forward relentlessly – we have no choice. In 2025, there is absolutely no reason why Africa should not be totally lit up with the power it needs to industrialise.[2]

Introduction

This article examines the legacy of Post-Development theory, in particular its relevance and applicability to debates about Africa's future. Post-colonial Africa's marginal position in the global economy and international system of states,[3] combined with the propensity of ortho-dox development scholars to graft an essentially Western modernisation trajectory onto blueprints for socio-economic development in Africa,[4] ought to have made the continent a fertile target for heterodox scholars considering alternatives forms of development and even alternatives to development. As pointed out by Matthews in one of the key contributions to Post-Development theory in Africa, 'many of the factors that led to the disillusionment of Post-Development theorists are prominent in Africa'.[5] Nevertheless she also makes it clear that 'Post-Development has had little to say about Africa'.[6] Indeed, it is not clear whether Post-Development theory and attendant societal critiques of development that proliferated

---

iD http://orcid.org/0000-0002-8443-7271

in the last few decades of the twentieth century have had any lasting effect on how development is pursued in twenty-first century Africa.

To evaluate this question of Post-Development theory's legacy and its relevance to contemporary Africa, the article examines what lessons can be drawn by scrutinising Post-Development theory, and its claims about the end of development, through the prisms of Africa's pursuit of development and its political economy of energy. It considers the impact of these aspects of Africa's continued developmental efforts on the ability of Post-Development theory to provide insights into recent developments, such as the ideational and normative ramifications of pursuing socio-economic development by means of an intensifying exploitation of Africa's fossil fuels in the current context of an increasing emphasis globally on renewable sources of energy and a transition to a low carbon economy. Revisiting basic claims of Post-Development theory provides insights into the enduring disconnect and incommensurability between Africa's twenty-first century socio-economic trajectories and the core assumptions of Post-Development theory.

Development, exhausted and rejuvenated

The body of scholarship referred to as Post-Development theory constitutes the most fundamental critique and, for some of its adherents, total rejection of the modern notion of development as it emerged and became concretised in various policies and projects in the decades following World War II.[7] Ziai identifies two main strands of Post-Development theory: sceptical and neo-populist. Neo-populism constitutes a more sweeping critique that is essentially 'anti-development' and prone to romanticise tradition and community. The sceptical approach entails a more nuanced criticism commensurate with the emergence of a 'radical democratic' approach to development studies, wherein criticism of development recognises the political and economic power structures within which any fruitful debate on radical alternatives to the status quo must be located.[8] The 'neo-populist' strand corresponds largely to what Simon describes as 'anti-development'.[9] While the developments and trajectories identified in this article can more straightforwardly contribute to a refutation of the core claims of anti-development, they pose, as recently argued by Matthews,[10] serious questions for more nuanced versions of Post-Development theory too.

The opening declaration of Sachs's *Development Dictionary* in 1992 asserted that the era of development, predicated on modernisation by means of deepening the structures of capitalism including global economic integration, had proven itself unable to deliver the growing populations of the formerly colonised world from exploitation, poverty and related hardships.[11] There had been, echoing Heilbroner's memorable phrase, no 'great ascent' of Empire's downtrodden,[12] but rather what Pritchett a few decades later described as 'divergence, big time' between Global North and South.[13] Nowhere, it seemed, was that failure more pronounced than in Africa. The colonial history of Africa was one in which the continent's many misfortunes (oftentimes external in origin) have been combined and utilised by imperial rulers and scholars alike to produce a view of the continent as essentially inadequate, a place of systemic failure in terms of its ability to engage with and partake in the modern world.[14]

Despite rhetorical shifts in the post-colonial era, the core aspects of this Western view on Africa persisted and seemed also vindicated by empirical evidence. In sharp contrast to Africa's developmental potential as identified in the influential 1981 World Bank report,

Accelerated Development in Sub-Saharan Africa,[15] the 1980s saw the entrenchment and deepening of economic crises, violent conflicts and human suffering across the continent – indeed a 'Lost Decade'.[16] Africa's developmental failures were documented in seminal works dissecting what Sandbrook described as the continent's 'economic stagnation',[17] and van de Walle as its 'permanent crisis'.[18] An even more damning verdict emerged from Easterly and Levine's influential study: 'Africa's economic history since 1960 fits the classical definition of tragedy: potential unfulfilled, with disastrous consequences'.[19] Given the litany of failures, Africans were presumably yearning for alternatives to what was generally referred to by its critics as the modern development project, whether in its capitalist, socialist or Third Way guise.

Sachs and his colleagues identified the end of WWII and the emergence of the Cold War, and of the United States as the pre-eminent global power, as the beginning of the Era of Development,[20] as would subsequently Rist in his *History of Development*.[21] But while Sachs, and many Post-Development theorists with him, believed that, by the 1990s, this era has come to an end, we can still observe development's lodestar – the modern, industrialised and technologically advanced market state – shining bright across the firmament of the Southern skies. The primary difference today is that the notion of development is less Western-centric.[22]

A range of developmental models, all squarely embedded in the overarching context of modernisation, are now on offer and thus competing with the Washington Consensus[23]; a model that has also been reconsidered and revised.[24] New offerings range from that of Chinese state capitalism, constituting the most significant competitor with the Western model, to various others as exemplified by the diverse examples of the BRICs (Brazil, Russia, India and China),[25] and perhaps even in some extreme hybrid form the rapid and petroleum-fuelled modernisation of the Gulf states and their increasingly prominent role in global economic affairs.[26] This diversity of approaches to development is a reminder of Simon's caution, that references in the anti- and post-development literature to a single or homogeneous 'development project ... is unhelpful, as there neither was nor is such a monolithic or singular construction, even during the heyday of modernization in the 1960s and early 1970s'.[27]

Persistent pursuit of development

If there is a waning of the West in terms of its influence globally, this does not mean the end of development. The strategic framework of the African Union's 2001 New Partnership for Africa's Development (NEPAD), which constitutes the key pan-African statement of the continent's ambitions for the twenty-first century, focuses squarely on the goal of sustained development by means of economic growth and poverty reduction.[28] There is in NEPAD's declaration no substantial deviation from the key assumptions that have underpinned the Era of Development. It constitutes, according to Owusu's charting of Africa's developmental policy journey from the Dependency-inspired Lagos Plan to NEPAD, an 'endorsement of neoliberalism'.[29]

> What is needed is a commitment on the part of governments, the private sector and other institutions of civil society, to genuine integration of all nations into the global economy and body politic. This requires the recognition of global interdependence with regard to production and demand, the environmental base that sustains the planet, cross-border migration, a global financial architecture that rewards good socio-economic management, and global governance

that recognises partnership among all peoples. We hold that it is within the capacity of the international community to create fair and just conditions in which Africa can participate effectively in the global economy and body politic.[30]

While then South African president Thabo Mbeki enveloped these developmental and policy-specific aspirations in his broader vision for an 'African Renaissance', based on African values including the humanist notion of *Ubuntu*, one framework was not intended to replace the other. Rather, the values embodied in the African Renaissance, some of which align with Post-Development notions of valuing the local and respecting traditional systems of knowing and doing, would on this account facilitate the arrival of modernity albeit in African guise.[31] What Africans want, according to this vision, is integration into the global economy on fair terms, not to reject mainstream development in order to seek radically different alternatives. It may be criticised as a very top-down and statesman-led approach to pursuing development, as opposed to one generated from the bottom up via civil society movements. But it is nevertheless the approach that has largely driven developmental policy across the continent, including in countries like South Africa where, according to Brooks, participatory democracy is 'largely considered to have failed'.[32] This even though the African Union's *Common African Position (CAP) on the Post-2015 Development Agenda* affords civil society a prominent place in the declaration of its 'participatory approach'.[33]

In her recent re-examination of Post-Development theory in Africa, Matthews provides several illustration of a persistent 'desirability of development' across the continent.[34] It is a continent exemplified by the aspirations of 'modern man', who embraces rather than rejects the basic components of development and which therefore casts doubt on the more strident of Post-Development theory's assumptions about 'what people want' in developing regions (i.e., the supposed rejection of pursuing greater economic growth and material affluence in favour of non-material and non-economic measures of well-being). Matthews identifies the high-profile case of 'service delivery protests' in South Africa as an example. These protests, very much driven by grassroots agency, are directed against the state's failure to deliver basic conditions associated with development – from access to flushing toilets to decent housing and jobs – and not against the notion of development itself.[35] Critically, she argues that Post-Development theorists have failed to understand the degree to which conventional notions of development became vested with notions of justice and redress: the very desirability of development which is by some development critics all too easily dismissed simply as a matter of African minds still being colonised.[36] Having access to basic material necessities goes to the heart of human dignity, and the lack of such access remains a daily reminder of a previous colonial condition that gave rise to the current inequality in access in the first place.

That such commitments to development are evident across the Global South does not necessarily mean that Post-Development theory amounts to a failed intellectual project. But it does tell us something important about the resilience of development defined as modernisation, and about the challenges with which twenty-first century Post-Development theorists must contend: emerging and complex forms of modernity that retain and reanimate tradition in ways not easily accommodated by Post-Development theory,[37] as well as resilient popular support, including in traditional communities, for orthodox manifestations of development[38] Truly an elusive yet formidable hydra to be confronted by the Post-Development sceptic.

Thus Sachs's assertion that '[t]he idea of development stands like a ruin in the intellectual landscape' is hardly the view of development suggested by Africa's twenty-first century trajectory.[39] Nor does his claim, that the idea of development has become 'outdated' and that, 'above all, the hopes and desires which made the idea fly, are now exhausted', seem plausible today.[40] This is perhaps the most exaggerated statement in Sachs's and his fellow theorists' obituary for the Era of Development when judging it from the perspective of social and political developments in Africa today. The track record of development actors, including governments, development agencies and the 'NGO industry', has certainly been criticised.[41] But the notion of a project that is exhausted seems an assertion too far.

A rather troubling conceptualisation of development is inherent in this particular account. There seems to be something aloof, even dismissive, inherent in the idea that development has, in Sachs's words, merely 'eliminated innumerable varieties of being human and have turned the world into a place deprived of adventure and surprise'.[42] There are presumably some forms of 'adventure and surprise' that those who are coping with dire poverty might conceivably want to trade for comfort and predictability. In this sense, Post-Development becomes susceptible to what Corbridge referred to as 'wobbly romanticism' ('only the rich get lonely, only the poor live hospitably and harmoniously') and 'implausible politics' ('we can all live like the Mahatma, or would want to').[43] We may be concerned about some manifestations and consequences of modernity in materially wealthy societies, but it was not only life outside society that, in Hobbes' vivid characterisation, was 'nasty, brutish and short'. That remains for many an apt description of life below the poverty line today.

Africa Rising, and falling

In contrast to the expectations embodied in the *Development Dictionary* and corresponding critiques of development, the twenty-first century saw the emergence of a rather more promising socio-economic trajectory of sustained economic growth across most of Africa, even if the World Bank points out that Africa's economic diversification was rather modest and vulnerability to swings in commodity prices remained high.[44] From this new trajectory emerged the widely heralded notion of Africa Rising: an idea and a bold representation of a vigorous Africa, not merely another policy or blueprint. It emphasised Africa's economic growth and increasing foreign direct investment,[45] as well as the region's favourable demographics and increasing purchasing power of its emerging middle class.[46] EY's report, *Africa 2030 – Realising the Possibilities*, was representative of the new global consensus on Africa's current trajectory:

> Despite any lingering scepticism, the evidence of the continent's clear progress over the past decade is irrefutable. The reality is that a diverse range of African countries have now experienced consistent and robust growth for over a decade – certainly the longest period of sustained growth since most countries attained independence in the early 1960s.[47]

Africa was no longer an outlier, a developmental failure. Instead the continent had begun to contribute to global economic growth and would become the locus of investment and opportunity as other, more saturated, regions of the Global South offered less impressive returns on capital. Demographers and corporations alike described an African Century that would make the world take note. This more positive analysis of the continent's economic and developmental potential and, crucially, its need to industrialise is emphasised in a wide range of international and regional declarations and policy frameworks, such as the 2016

G20 summit in Hangzhou, the Sixth Tokyo International Conference on African Development held in Nairobi that same year, the African Union's *Agenda 2063* and the United Nations General Assembly resolution proclaiming the period 2016–2025 as the 'Third Industrial Development Decade for Africa'. Summarising the relevance of these frameworks and the imperative of African industrialisation, Li Yong, Director General of the United Nations Industrial Development Organisation (UNIDO), asserts that, '[m]y numerous meetings with African leaders and visits to dozens of countries … have convinced me that Africa is committed to industrialization'.[48]

Then again, seemingly all good things come to an end. The claim about an exhaustion of the development project could be considered vindicated following the abrupt decline of the trajectory underpinning the notion of Africa Rising, beginning with the oil price crash and the end of the commodities super-cycle from around 2014 onwards. Combined with a failure to turn sustained economic growth into significant diversification of national economies, the sharp loss of export earnings for Africa's many commodity-dependent economies, and in particular the oil-exporting ones, has become a serious threat to the continent's overall economic progress.[49] Thus another false start, another vindication of 'Afro-pessimism', and the tortuous trajectory of post-colonial Africa's economic woes reasserting itself yet again.[50] Dismissing the idea of Africa Rising as lacking in substance, Taylor argues that we are instead witnessing a case of 'dependency redux' as the economic foundations of this success story are in fact much weaker than assumed:

> [T]he story of 'Africa Rising' is just that, a story, where growth-for-growth's sake replaces development and the agenda of industrialisation and moving Africa up the global production chain has been discarded. Instead, Africa's current 'comparative advantage' as a primary commodity exporter is reinforced, even whilst such dynamics reproduce underdevelopment. This is celebrated as 'progress'.[51]

This, then, are two tales of Africa: rising and falling. The question is whether Africa's post-colonial crises can ever be transcended by means of orthodox development, or whether this promise is bound to remain what Rahnema insisted was merely a 'deceitful mirage'?[52] Pursuing development seems, however, the course that most African countries will choose to stay. Young argues that Africa's post-colonial state has been consigned to history, as of the 1990s 'eviscerated' by the combined forces of economic decline and market reform.[53] Africans have ever since been forging their own identities and shaping their own goals, the colonial shadow ever receding. Those goals, however, remain remarkably well aligned with exogenous models of development on offer from the West and the rising powers of the Global South. The global system is in transition, but in some ways it also remains more stable and resilient than anticipated in terms of asymmetrical relations between its more and less powerful actors. African states and related actors remain marginalised in the international system, but also determined to improve their situation within that system as currently constituted rather than seeking to radically depart from it.[54] The political economy of energy is one area that can provide useful insights into this determination.

Fossil-fuelled development

The question of energy, how to obtain it and how to use it, is inextricably intertwined with the notion of modernisation and development. That is, to develop is to exploit, to produce and to consume. In order to do all of these things energy is (along with finance/credit) one of the indispensable ingredients of sustaining and reproducing the modern world: what Di Muzio aptly describes as our 'petro-market civilisation'.[55] In their introduction to *Energy, Capitalism and World Order*, Di Muzio and Ovadia explain how the harnessing of fossil fuels make possible the emergence of modern, industrial civilisation.[56] Previously, in the 'age of efflorescences'[57]:

> civilizations were more immediately tied to the rhythms of plant photosynthesis and the power of wind, water, animals and unfree labour … what we would today call 'economic growth' could flourish from time to time but was never sustained.[58]

In *Carbon Democracy*, Mitchell takes this argument further to show that twentieth-century modern democracy, via the power of organised labour, grows out of the coal-based fossil fuel economy.[59] Fossil fuel-based energy has been the ultimate enabler of modernity, and no other endeavour symbolises the desire for development more than does the craving for energy. There is, furthermore, a strong correlation between energy usage and mainstream indicators of improvements in living circumstances, such as the UN's Human Development Index (HDI).[60]

In this context, then, the fact that there has emerged a big and very costly gap between demand and supply of energy in Africa becomes particularly relevant. McDonald demonstrates that:

> Africa is the most under-supplied region in the world when it comes to electricity, but its economies are utterly dependent on it. This contradiction is explained in part by the enormous inequalities in electricity access, with mining and industry receiving abundant supplies of cheap power whilst more than 80 percent of the continent's residents remain off the power grid.[61]

Kessides estimates that 25 of 48 countries in Sub-Saharan Africa are experiencing 'crippling' shortages of electricity and regular blackouts, resulting in a loss of 2.1% of the region's GDP.[62] Mohammed, Mustafa and Bashir argue that 'access to modern energy is considered one of the foremost factors contributing to the disparity between developed and developing nations'.[63] This, according to McDonald, is the inevitable outcome of what he terms 'electric capitalism'.[64] Electricity is 'an integral part of all capitalist activity', and since (especially southern) African economies are very electricity-intensive, with ambitious plans to massively increase electricity-generation capacity, the development of electricity markets, and energy markets generally, becomes a particularly useful way to understand broader dynamics of 'capitalist accumulation and crisis' on the continent.[65] The path-dependent nature of South Africa's energy-intensive and dependent economy, and the difficulties in producing concrete alternatives to it given its strong anchoring in the power structures of the state, has been outlined by Fine and Rustomjee in their seminal contribution on South Africa's 'Minerals-Energy-Complex', and more recently in analyses by Baker and colleagues and Scholvin.[66]

Africa's energy gap is greater than in any other developing region, and closing it has now become one of the key goals for African governments and the organisations in Africa and abroad that co-operate with them to pursue economic development. As the President of the African Development Bank, Akinwumi Adesina, described the situation to delegates of the Bank's annual meeting in Lusaka in May 2016:

> Children learn in the dark. Businesses operate in the dark. Surgeries are done in the dark. The greatest hindrance to Africa's growth and development is lack of electricity. It is unacceptable that 138 years after Thomas Edison developed the light bulb, hundreds of millions of people cannot have access to electricity to simply light up the bulb in Africa.[67]

In addition to the human and economic costs of inadequate access to safe and reliable sources of energy, the energy gap stands as a modern-day indicator that indicts Africa's failure to develop. Whether economists and development scholars labour under a 'tyranny of GDP' that restricts and limits the ways in which we are able to understand what it means to develop and how we choose to measure progress,[68] few argue with the significance of not being able to switch on the lights and have them stay on. The quest for access to energy goes to the very heart of the desire to transcend a debilitating state of affairs in which people die from pulmonary disease when, in the absence of power plants delivering reliable supplies of energy, they have to burn wood, dung and coal; where children cannot study after dark as electrical lighting is not available; and where their parents cannot afford their children's education as the lack of energy stands as a key impediment to job-creating economic growth.

In this context, intensifying efforts by African governments and energy companies in collaboration with international energy companies to exploit the continent's energy resources, and in particular its oil and natural gas deposits,[69] are a testament to the enduring determination by governments and businesses to achieve development by means of modernisation. The primary goal across Africa's energy-rich states today is not how to phase out the reliance on fossil fuels but how to more effectively exploit them, even if in combination with developing renewable options. As noted by Collier, the era of natural resource exploitation is nowhere near its end across the relatively underexplored and underdeveloped countries of the Global South.[70]

Thus the political, economic and technocratic questions about bridging Africa's energy gap revolve primarily around how to fully embrace and constructively exploit Africa's resource wealth while at the same time avoiding the 'resource curse' that has afflicted Africa's oil producing countries in particular.[71] This, combined with a trajectory of increasing resource exploitation in the pursuit of economic growth and development, is as good an indicator as any of the lasting triumph of the Era of Development and the drive for modernisation. On all of these accounts, the African trajectory runs counter to the expectations of an exhausted development project as outlined in the first edition of Sachs's *Development Dictionary* and by Post-Development theory more generally.

Turning development 'green'

It is by now also recognised that African countries will be among the ones most severely affected by climate change, which of course their own drives to industrialise and develop on the back of fossil fuels are contributing to. Consequently there are movements afoot across Africa whereby environmental groups, sometimes in collaboration with governments, push for a 'greener' future and are contributing to a reconfiguring the African state in the process.[72] A transition to renewable sources of energy is also modestly under way and might increase to contribute two-thirds of the growth in demand for power by 2020.[73] International agreements such as the one reached in Paris in 2015 will also have some impact in nudging African countries in the direction of low-carbon alternatives. Munang and Mgendi argue that the Paris Agreement on climate change presents 'a unique opportunity ... to realise the dream of an environmentally sustainable and economically flourishing continent'.[74]

Others are however decidedly less optimistic. With an insider's view of the negotiations that produced the Paris Agreement, Dimitrov argues that it:

favors developed countries of the North, who won most of the key battles … [whereas it] is least fair to the African Group and other Least Developed Countries. It does not include references to their special circumstances, is weak on international dimensions for adaptation policy, and precludes any future claims for liability and compensation.[75]

Even allowing for a move towards a 'greening' of African economies, the core aims of orthodox development – notably the pursuit of economic growth and increasing market shares – remain in place. Considering the development of an ostensibly 'green economy' in South Africa, the continent's leader in renewable energy investments, Death argues that it is the decidedly liberal and market-driven discourse of 'green growth' that is being prioritised by South Africa's government: 'rather than a focus on limits and scarcity … the emphasis is on new markets, new services, and new forms of consumption'.[76] This growth model stands in stark contrast to other 'discourses' including what he terms a 'Green revolution', which entails a radical reconfiguration of economic activity to align with post-developmental concepts such as 'ecological virtues' and 'limits to growth', and 'Green transformation', which entails an 'explicit focus on social justice, equity and redistribution' where growth is a means rather than an end.[77]

> It is through focusing on South Africa's 'brand' as a rising power, with a youthful and energetic population and a rich natural environment, and the country as the economic and political 'gateway to Africa', rather than its environmental and social contradictions, that South Africa can be positioned as a global leader on the green economy.[78]

China has emerged as a key contributor to rapidly increasing investments in renewables across the African continent (albeit from a very low base), especially in solar power and in particular in South Africa.[79] Shen and Power explain that Chinese energy companies have been 'pushed' into African markets 'by the need to deal with over-production, excess capacity and over-investment' at home.[80] In this case too, the main aim is to capture new markets and, by extension, offering alternative paths to socio-economic development. The goal of increasing and sustaining economic growth, industrialisation and technological diversification – in a sense, to modernise – remains the same, even if it should ideally be accomplished with lower-carbon or non-carbon sources of energy. Environmental sustainability is not the main goal. Illustrating this point, Schmitz argues that even where key actors among the rising powers of the Global South support policies relevant to climate change mitigation, such as China's extensive involvement in renewable energy investments in Africa:

> [they] are not primarily concerned with environmental or climate issues. Their prime concerns are securing energy for the nation or particular regions, fostering new green industries and making them competitive, creating jobs and incomes in these industries or laying the foundation for increasing public revenue. Mitigating climate change is not irrelevant, but it tends to be a co-benefit rather than a driver.[81]

Thus, the central role of the political economy of energy, including its new manifestations in renewable sources of energy and the 'green economy', in shaping twenty-first century Africa's developmental trajectories is a key manifestation of the enduring legacy of the Era of Development. The emerging drive for alternatives to fossil fuels and achieving a low-carbon transition – granting that they should be successful (which remains highly uncertain) – is manifestly not an attempt to find and offer alternatives to development as has been a primary ambition of the scholarly community of Post-Development theorists. Rather it is a move towards entrenching modernity across African societies by alternative means.

Conclusion: the legacy of Post-Development?

In the end we are, not surprisingly, left with a plethora of questions. While there is no scope to answer them all here, they are nevertheless worth acknowledging when considering the continued relevance of Post-Development theory for Africa and the Global South more generally. Just as Marx was long on the failings of capitalism but short on the nature of socialism, Post-Development theory is good at generating questions about development, but less prolific when it comes to identifying alternatives thereto. This is not necessarily a problem in itself, but it does mean that concluding thoughts on the legacy of Post-Development theory are inevitably going to be characterised by a degree of tentativeness.

What *is* the legacy of Post-Development theory, in Africa and across the Global South? Do the critiques of development as initially put forth by Sachs and colleagues stand vindicated? Do they have a future as meaningful, and effective, scholarly critiques of orthodox development thinking and practice? Can it be argued that, irrespective of whether concrete alternatives *to* development have been produced, Post-Development has nevertheless achieved a crucial intervention in the debates about development, thus forcing a change in the dominant development discourse by making it less replete with simplistic and taken-for-granted assumptions? As noted by Escobar, one of the most prominent contributors to these debates, the discourses themselves really do matter.[82]

Or is it, alternatively, the case that Post-Development has had its moment in the sun (or at least the seminar room), only to be eclipsed by subsequent economic developments and by an irrepressible belief in, and attraction to, development-as-modernisation and its attendant promise of a better life across the Global South? Therefore, is the best way to understand what drives popular politics and societal change across the Global South today merely a case of Rostow's fifth and final stage of development, the 'Age of high mass consumption', finally achieving the status of universal dogma?[83] Does the Post-Development ambition to move beyond the modernist development discourse, by arguing for alternatives to development (but failing to identify them), constitute what Storey characterised as a Pontius Pilate politics,[84] whereby intellectuals wash their hands of the seemingly intractable problems of exploitation, poverty and human suffering that still afflict far too many people across the world – what in Kiely's and Corbridge's vivid dismissals of Post-Development amounts to a detached and even insidious form of Ivory Tower romanticising of the Noble Savage and of global poverty?[85] It is not an entirely straightforward judgment to make.

What seems clear is that, for at least the middle classes and more secure working classes of the Global South that have escaped the historical misery of the *lumpenproletariat* and modern day 'precariat', decades of economic globalisation have coincided with significant improvements in living circumstances. The problem is that those benefits have not been distributed evenly. The so-called Elephant Curve illustrates clearly who are the winners (middle and working classes across the Global South, and the very wealthy in the Western world), and losers (the very poorest across the Global South and the working and middle classes of the West) in a world of increasing economic globalisation.[86] It is therefore difficult to accept assertions such as those made by Andrews and Bawa, that globalisation is 'inherently bad for the poor'.[87] The existence of substantial numbers of winners, even among many losers, is furthermore significant because it makes a comprehensive, coherent and sustained challenge to the status quo on development that Post-Development theory aspires to that much more difficult and therefore unlikely.

What do these developments entail for the legacy and continued relevance of Post-Development theory? It is evident that orthodox development strategies have produced significant winners across the Global South, if less so in Africa. This is the case even if development as conventionally understood and pursued will never become a panacea for all of the world's poor – neither perfect positive-sum game, nor inevitably zero-sum. To the extent that these beneficiaries of development gain a more prominent voice in public discourses and national politics across the world, including in Africa (even though the continent remains home to so many of those who have not yet benefitted), we can expect that the ideational influence and normative power of development by means of economic growth and modernisation will remain an attractive proposal.

There are those who may find little hope in what is on offer and may therefore give up on development, considering it the ultimate pretence and diversion in an unsustainable world. But the idea and promise of development retains for a vast majority of the world's population the potency it has acquired since the Enlightenment and industrial revolution. Indeed, Matthews begins her recent analysis of the relevance of Post-Development theory to Africa by acknowledging that Sachs, in the preface to the new edition of his *Development Dictionary*, now recognises that the Global South has become 'the staunchest defender of development'.[88] Indeed, he has come to recognise the extent to which the idea of development has 'been charged with hopes for redress and self-affirmation'.[89] This intertwining of the idea of development with desires for justice and improvement across the Global South is in line with the argument pursued throughout this article. To offer something more appealing and attractive than what has manifestly become a primary pursuit of societies worldwide in the Era of Development remains the challenge for development's detractors.

Disclosure statement

No potential conflict of interest was reported by the author.

Notes

1. Sachs, *The Development Dictionary*, 1.
2. Adesina, "Speech Delivered by President Akinwumi Adesina."
3. Andreasson, "Elusive Agency."

4. Andreasson, "Orientalism and African Development Studies."
5. Matthews, "Post-Development Theory," 377.
6. Ibid., 374.
7. Nederveen Pieterse, "After Post-Development"; Rist, *History of Development*; Simon, "Development Reconsidered"; Ziai, *Exploring Post-Development*.
8. Ziai, "The Ambivalence of Post-Development"; see also Andreasson, *Africa's Development Impasse*, ch. 3.
9. Simon, "Development Reconsidered."
10. Matthews, "Colonised Minds?"
11. Sachs, *Development Dictionary*.
12. Heilbroner, *The Great Ascent*.
13. Pritchett, "Divergence, Big Time."
14. Andreasson, "Orientalism and African Development Studies."
15. World Bank, *Accelerated Development*.
16. Michaels, "Retreat from Africa."
17. Sandbrook, *Politics of Africa's Economic Stagnation*.
18. van de Walle, *African Economies and Politics*.
19. Easterly and Levine, "Africa's Growth Tragedy," 1203.
20. Sachs, *Development Dictionary*, 1.
21. Rist, *History of Development*.
22. Bremmer, "End of the Free Market."
23. Sheppard and Leitner, "*Quo Vadis* Neoliberalism?"
24. Rodrik, "Goodbye Washington Consensus."
25. Leftwich, "Bringing Politics Back In"; Nederveen Pieterse, "Global Rebalancing"; Stephen, "Rising Powers."
26. Coates Ulrichsen, "The GCC States."
27. Simon, "Development Reconsidered," 186.
28. Kanbur, "The New Partnership for Africa's Development."
29. Owusu, "Pragmatism and the Gradual Shift," 1656.
30. African Union, *New Partnership for Africa's Development*, 8.
31. Andreasson, *Africa's Development Impasse*; Vale and Maseko, "South Africa and the African Renaissance."
32. Brooks, "Mass Movement and Public Policy," 106.
33. African Union, *Common African Position*.
34. Matthews, "Colonised Minds?"
35. Ibid., 3–4.
36. Ibid.
37. Gyekye, *Tradition and Modernity*; Therborn, "Entangled Modernities."
38. De Vries, "Don't Compromise Your Desire."
39. Sachs, *Development Dictionary*, 1.
40. Sachs, *Development Dictionary*, 1.
41. Easterly, "The Cartel of Good Intentions."
42. Sachs, *Development Dictionary*, 4.
43. Corbridge, "Beneath the Pavement, Only Soil."
44. World Bank, *Africa's Pulse*, 9.
45. Bush and Harrison, "New African Development?"
46. Samba Sylla, "From a Marginalised to an Emerging Africa?"
47. EY Africa, *Africa 2030*, 3.
48. Yong, "Africa's Decade of Industrialization."
49. Taylor, "Dependency Redux."
50. Rieff, "In Defense of Afro-Pessimism."
51. Taylor, "Dependency Redux," 22.
52. Rahnema, "Introduction," x.
53. Young, "End of the Post-Colonial State."

54. Andreasson, "Elusive Agency."
55. Di Muzio, "Capitalising a Future Unsustainable."
56. Di Muzio and Ovadia, *Energy, Capitalism and World Order*.
57. Di Muzio, *Carbon Capitalism*.
58. Di Muzio and Ovadia, *Energy, Capitalism and World Order*, 6.
59. Mitchell, *Carbon Democracy*.
60. Martínez and Ebenhack, "Understanding the Role of Energy Consumption."
61. McDonald, *Electric Capitalism*, xv.
62. Kessides, "Powering Africa's Sustainable Development," S58.
63. Mohammed, Mustafa, and Bashir, "Status of Renewable Energy Consumption," 453.
64. McDonald, *Electric Capitalism*, xv.
65. Ibid.
66. Baker, Newell, and Phillips, "The Political Economy of Energy Transitions"; Fine and Rustomjee, *The Political Economy of South Africa*; Scholvin, "South Africa's Energy Policy."
67. Adesina, "Speech Delivered by President Akinwumi Adesina."
68. Morse and Bell, "Sustainable Development Indicators," 225.
69. Andreasson, "Competition for Energy Resources in Sub-Saharan Africa."
70. Collier, *The Plundered Planet*.
71. Ross, "Political Economy of the Resource Curse"; Ross, *The Oil Curse*.
72. Death, *The Green State in Africa*.
73. Linklaters, *Renewable Energy in Africa*, 6.
74. Munang and Mgendi, "The Paris Climate Deal and Africa."
75. Dimitrov, "The Paris Agreement on Climate Change," 8.
76. Death, "The Green Economy in South Africa," 8.
77. Ibid., 6–7.
78. Ibid., 2.
79. Shen and Power, "Africa and the Export of China's Clean Energy."
80. Ibid., 12.
81. Schmitz, "Who Drives Climate-Relevant Policies?" 1–2.
82. Escobar, "Making and Unmaking of the Third World."
83. Rostow, *Stages of Economic Growth*.
84. Storey, "Post-Development Theory."
85. Kiely, "Last Refuge of the Noble Savage"; Corbridge, "Beneath the Pavement, Only Soil."
86. Milanovic, *Global Inequality*.
87. Andrews and Bawa, "A Post-Development Hoax?" 926.
88. Sachs, quoted in Matthews, "Colonised Minds?" 1.
89. Ibid., 5.

Bibliography

Adesina, Akinwumi. "Speech Delivered by President Akinwumi Adesina at the Opening Session of the Annual Meetings of the African Development Bank Group." Lusaka, Zambia, May 24, 2016. Accessed October 20, 2016. http://www.afdb.org/en/news-and-events/article/speech-delivered-by-president-akinwumi-adesina-at-the-opening-session-of-the-annual-meetings-of-the-african-development-bank-group-lusaka-zambia-may-24-2016-15717/

African Union. *The New Partnership for Africa's Development (NEPAD)*. Abuja: NEPAD, 2001. Accessed October 20, 2016. http://www.nepad.org/resource/new-partnership-africas-development

African Union. *Common African Position (CAP) on the Post-2015 Development Agenda*. Addis Ababa: African Union. Accessed February 7, 2016. http://www.who.int/pmnch/development_agenda.pdf?ua=1

Andreasson, Stefan. "Orientalism and African Development Studies: The 'Reductive Repetition' Motif in Theories of African Underdevelopment." *Third World Quarterly* 26, no. 6 (2005): 971–986.

Andreasson, Stefan. *Africa's Development Impasse: Rethinking the Political Economy of Transformation*. London: Zed Books, 2010.

Andreasson, Stefan. "American and British Strategies in the Competition for Energy Resources in Sub-Saharan Africa." In *A New Scramble for Africa: The Rush for Energy Resources in Sub-Saharan Africa*, edited by Sören Scholvin, 13–31. Farnham: Ashgate, 2015.

Andreasson, Stefan. "Elusive Agency: Africa's Persistently Peripheral Role in International Relations." In *African Agency in International Politics*, edited by William Brown and Sophie Harman, 143–157. London: Routledge, 2013.

Andrews, Nathan, and Sylvia Bawa. "A Post-Development Hoax? (Re)-Examining the past, Present and Future of Development Studies." *Third World Quarterly* 35, no. 6 (2014): 922–938.

Baker, Lucy, Peter Newell, and Jon Phillips. "The Political Economy of Energy Transitions: The Case of South Africa." *New Political Economy* 19, no. 6 (2014): 791–818.

Bremmer, Ian. "The End of the Free Market: Who Wins the War between States and Corporations?" *European View* 9, no. 2 (2010): 249–252.

Brooks, Heidi. "The Mass Movement and Public Policy: Discourses of Participatory Democracy in Post-1994 South Africa." *Journal of Modern African Studies* 55, no. 1 (2017): 105–127.

Bush, Ray, and Graham Harrison. "New African Development?" *Review of African Political Economy* 41, no. sup1 (2014): S1–S6.

Coates Ulrichsen, Kristian. "The GCC States and the Shifting Balance of Global Power." CIRS Occasional Papers, Washington: Georgetown University. Accessed October 20, 2016. https://repository.library.georgetown.edu/bitstream/handle/10822/558292/CIRSOccasionalPaper6KristianCoates™Ulrichsen2010.pdf

Collier, Paul. *The Plundered Planet: Why We Must – And How We Can – Manage Nature for Global Prosperity*. Oxford: Oxford University Press, 2010.

Corbridge, Stuart. "'Beneath the Pavement Only Soil': The Poverty of Post-Development." *Journal of Development Studies* 34, no. 6 (1998): 138–148.

De Vries, Peter. "Don't Compromise Your Desire for Development! A Lacanian/Deleuzian Rethinking of the Anti-Politics Machine." *Third World Quarterly* 28, no. 1 (2007): 25–43.

Death, Carl. *The Green State in Africa*. New Haven, CT: Yale University Press, 2016.

Di Muzio, Tim. "Capitalizing a Future Unsustainable: Finance, Energy and the Fate of Market Civilization." *Review of International Political Economy* 19, no. 3 (2012): 363–388.

Di Muzio, Tim. *Carbon Capitalism: Energy, Social Reproduction and World Order*. London: Rowman and Littlefield International, 2015.

Di Muzio, Tim, and Jesse Salah Ovadia. *Energy, Capitalism and World Order: Toward a New Agenda in International Political Economy*. Basingstoke: Palgrave Macmillan, 2016.

Dimitrov, Radoslav S. "The Paris Agreement on Climate Change: Behind Closed Doors." *Global Environmental Politics* 16, no. 3 (2016): 1–11.

Easterly, William. "The Cartel of Good Intentions: The Problem of Bureaucracy in Foreign Aid." *The Journal of Policy Reform* 5, no. 4 (2002): 223–250.

Easterly, William, and Ross Levine. "Africa's Growth Tragedy: Policies and Ethnic Divisions." *Quarterly Journal of Economics* 112, no. 4. (1997): 1203-1250.

Escobar, Arturo. "The Making and Unmaking of the Third World through Development." In *The Post-Development Reader*, edited by Majid Rahnema and Victoria Bawtree, 85–93. London: Zed Books, 1997.

EY Africa. *Africa 2030 – Realizing the Possibilities*. EYAfrica, 2014. Accessed October 22, 2016. http://emergingmarkets.ey.com/wp-content/uploads/downloads/2014/10/187.-EY-Africa-2030-realizing-the-possibilities.pdf

Fine, Ben, and Zavareh Rustomjee. *The Political Economy of South Africa: From Minerals-Energy Complex to Industrialization*. London: Hurst, 1996.

Gyekye, Kwame. *Tradition and Modernity: Philosophical Reflections on the African Experience*. Oxford: Oxford University Press, 1997.

Heilbroner, Robert L. *The Great Ascent: The Struggle for Economic Development in Our Time*. New York: Harper & Row, 1963.

Kanbur, Ravi. "The New Partnership for Africa's Development (NEPAD): an Initial Commentary." Working Paper 2002-01. Ithaca: Department of Applied Economics and Management, Cornell University. Accessed October 21, 2016. http://ageconsearch.umn.edu/bitstream/127267/2/Cornell_Dyson_wp0201.pdf

Kessides, Ioannis N. "Powering Africa's Sustainable Development: The Potential Role of Nuclear Energy." *Energy Policy* 74, sup. 1 (2014): S57-S70.

Kiely, Ray. "The Last Refuge of the Noble Savage? A Critical Assessment of Post-Development Theory." *The European Journal of Development Research* 11, no. 1 (1999): 30–55.

Leftwich, Adrian. "Bringing Politics Back in: Towards a Model of the Developmental State." *The Journal of Development Studies* 31, no. 3 (1995): 400–427.

Linklaters. *Renewable Energy in Africa: Trending Rapidly towards Cost-Competitiveness with Fossil Fuels.* London: Linklaters, 2016. Accessed October 24, 2016. http://linklaters.com/Insights/Thought-Leadership/Renewables-Africa/Pages/Index.aspx

Martínez, Daniel M., and Ben W. Ebenhack. "Understanding the Role of Energy Consumption in Human Development through the Use of Saturation Phenomena." *Energy Policy* 36, no. 4 (2008): 1430–1435.

Matthews, Sally. "Post-Development Theory and the Question of Alternatives: A View from Africa." *Third World Quarterly* 25, no. 2 (2004): 373–384.

Matthews, Sally. "Colonised Minds? Post-Development Theory and the Desirability of Development in Africa." *Third World Quarterly* (2017). doi:10.1080/01436597.2017.1279540.

McDonald, David A., ed. *Electric Capitalism: Recolonising Africa on the Power Grid.* London: Earthscan, 2009.

Michaels, Marguerite. "Retreat from Africa." *Foreign Affairs* 72, no. 1 (1992-93): 93–108.

Milanovic, Branko. *Global Inequality: A New Approach for the Age of Globalization.* Cambridge, MA: Harvard University Press, 2016.

Mitchell, Timothy. *Carbon Democracy: Political Power in the Age of Oil.* New York: Verso, 2011.

Mohammed, Y. S., M. W. Mustafa, and N. Bashir. "Status of Renewable Energy Consumption and Developmental Challenges in Sub-Sahara Africa." *Renewable and Sustainable Energy Reviews* 27 (2013): 453–463.

Morse, Stephen, and Simon Bell. "Sustainable Development Indicators: The Tyranny of Methodology Revisited." *Consilience: The Journal of Sustainable Development* 6, no. 1 (2011): 222–239.

Munang, and Mgendi. 2016. "The Paris Climate Deal and Africa." *UN Africa Renewal.* April. Accessed October 24, 2016. http://www.un.org/africarenewal/magazine/april-2016/paris-climate-deal-and-africa

Nederveen Pieterse, Jan. "After Post-Development." *Third World Quarterly* 21, no. 2 (2000): 175–191.

Nederveen Pieterse, Jan. "Global Rebalancing: Crisis and the East-South Turn." *Development and Change* 42, no. 1 (2011): 22–48.

Owusu, Francis. "Pragmatism and the Gradual Shift from Dependency to Neoliberalism: The World Bank, African Leaders and Development Policy in Africa." *World Development* 31, no. 10 (2003): 1655–1672.

Pritchett, Lant. "Divergence, Big Time." *The Journal of Economic Perspectives* 11, no. 3 (1997): 3–17.

Rahnema, Majid. "Introduction." In *The Post-Development Reader,* edited by Majid Rahnema and Victoria Bawtree, ix–xix. London: Zed Books, 1997.

Rieff, David. "In Defense of Afro-Pessimism." *World Policy Journal* 15, no. 4 (1998/99): 10-22.

Rist, Gilbert. *The History of Development: From Western Origins to Global Faith.* London: Zed Books, 2002.

Rodrik, Dani. "Goodbye Washington Consensus, Hello Washington Confustion? A Review of the World Bank's *Economic Reform in the 1990s: Learning from a Decade of Reform.*" *Journal of Economic Literature* 44, no. 4 (2006): 973–987.

Ross, Michael L. "The Political Economy of the Resource Curse." *World Politics* 51, no. 2 (1999): 297–322.

Ross, Michael L. *The Oil Curse: How Petroleum Wealth Shapes the Development of Nations.* Princeton: Princeton University Press, 2012.

Rostow, Walt W. *The Stages of Economic Growth: A Non-Communist Manifesto.* Cambridge: Cambridge University Press, 1971.

Sachs, Wolfgang, ed. *The Development Dictionary: A Guide to Knowledge as Power.* London: Zed Books, 1992.

Samba Sylla, Ndongo. "From a Marginalised to an Emerging Africa? A Critical Analysis." *Review of African Political Economy* 41, no. sup1 (2014): S7–S25.

Sandbrook, Richard. *The Politics of Africa's Economic Stagnation.* Cambridge: Cambridge University Press, 1985.

Schmitz, Hubert. "Who Drives Climate-Relevant Policies in the Rising Powers?" *Third World Quarterly* (forthcoming).

Scholvin, Sören. "South Africa's Energy Policy: Constrained by Nature and Path Dependency." *Journal of Southern African Studies* 40, no. 1 (2014): 185–202.

Shen, Wei, and Marcus Power. "Africa and the Export of China's Clean Energy Revolution." *Third World Quarterly* 38, no. 3 (2017): 678–697.

Sheppard, Eric, and Helga Leitner. "*Quo Vadis* Neoliberalism? The Remaking of Global Capitalist Governance after the Washington Consensus." *Geoforum* 41, no. 2 (2010): 185–194.

Simon, David. "Development Reconsidered: New Directions in Development Thinking." *Geografiska Annaler: Series B, Human Geography* 79B, no. 4 (1997): 183–201.

Stephen, Matthew D. "Rising Powers, Global Capitalism and Liberal Global Governance: A Historical Materialist Account of the BRICs Challenge." *European Journal of International Relations* 20, no. 4 (2014): 912–938.

Storey, Andy. "Post-Development Theory: Romanticism and Pontius Pilate Politics." *Development* 43, no. 4 (2000): 40–46.

Taylor, Ian. "Dependency Redux: Why Africa is Not Rising." *Review of African Political Economy* 43, no. 147 (2016): 8–25.

Therborn, Göran. "Entangled Modernities." *European Journal of Social Theory* 6, no. 3 (2003): 293–305.

Vale, Peter, and Sipho Maseko. "South Africa and the African Renaissance." *International Affairs* 74, no. 2 (1998): 271–287.

Van de Walle, Nicholas. *African Economies and the Politics of Permanent Crisis, 1979-1999*. Cambridge: Cambridge University Press, 2001.

World Bank. *Accelerated Development in Sub-Saharan Africa: An Agenda for Action*. Washington, DC: World Bank, 1981.

World Bank. *Africa's Pulse: An Analysis of Issues Shaping Africa's Economic Future*. Vol. 8, October 2013. Accessed October 21, 2016. http://www.worldbank.org/content/dam/Worldbank/document/Africa/Report/Africas-Pulse-brochure_Vol8.pdf

Yong, Li. "Africa's Decade of Industrialization." *Project Syndicate*. Accessed February 6, 2017. https://www.project-syndicate.org/commentary/africa-industrialization-potential-by-li-yong-2017-02

Young, Crawford. "The End of the Post-Colonial State in Africa? Reflections on Changing African Political Dynamics." *African Affairs* 103, no. 410 (2004): 23–49.

Ziai, Aram. "The Ambivalence of Post-Development: Between Reactionary Populism and Radical Democracy." *Third World Quarterly* 25, no. 6 (2004): 1045–1060.

Ziai, Aram, ed. *Exploring Post-Development: Theory and Practice: Problems and Perspectives*. London: Routledge, 2007.

Colonised minds? Post-development theory and the desirability of development in Africa

Sally Matthews

ABSTRACT

While post-development theory is very concerned with the ways in which development has impacted upon the countries of the Global South, there has been relatively little written on post-development theory from an African perspective. This paper identifies some of the ways in which post-development theory fails to adequately understand the African experience of development. In particular, I explore the difficulty that post-development theory confronts when faced with the continued desire on the part of many people in Africa for development. In his introduction to the new edition of *The Development Dictionary*, Wolfgang Sachs discusses this desire, noting that despite development's many failures, many still associate the concept with self-affirmation and redress. He explains this continued desire for development as being indicative of the need for the decolonisation of the imagination. In this paper, I show some of the problems with this explanation and present alternative ways of understanding the persistence of the desire for development in Africa.

In his preface to the new edition of *The Development Dictionary*, Wolfgang Sachs acknowledges that the contributors to this volume did not fully appreciate the desirability of development for those in the South.[1] He says that while development 'was an invention of the West', it was 'not just an imposition on the rest'.[2] Indeed, it is the South that has emerged as 'the staunchest defender of development'.[3] In this paper, I reflect on the continuing appeal of development with a particular focus on Africa. In so doing, I explore my own gradual disillusionment with post-development theory, using this exploration to identify some of the ways in which post-development theory fails to fully grapple with the continuing desire for development. As my own experiences have been rooted in the African context, my discussion reveals some of the ways in which this context raises particular challenges for post-development theory. It is hoped that the exploration of my growing disillusionment with some aspects of post-development theory will bring out clearly some of the ways in which the African context, which has received relatively little attention in post-development theory, prevents us from too easily embracing some of the positions associated with post-development theory.

Post-development theory read in the post-apartheid South African context

I first encountered *The Development Dictionary* and other post-development texts as a graduate student at a South African university in the early 2000s. The mood in South Africa at the time was positive: then-president Thabo Mbeki had proposed that Africa needed an 'African Renaissance' and it was thought, in South Africa at least, that South Africa could play a leading role in igniting a continent-wide revival, through the rediscovery and revitalisation of Africa's historical achievements.[4] Through the reconsideration of these achievements, advocates of an African Renaissance believed that an 'African century' could be forthcoming – one that would be witness to an Africa that was both economically prosperous and authentically African.[5]

It was in this context that I first read *The Development Dictionary*. Consequently, its contributors' view that the Western path to prosperity had failed and that we needed to chart an alternative resonated with me. I was enthusiastic that Africa could play an important role in fleshing out the alternatives to development advocated by post-development theorists. Indeed, I went on to argue for just that in a paper in this journal in which I declared that 'the diversity of world-views and lifestyles in Africa could provide useful insights for those concerned with describing [alternatives to development]'.[6]

Post-development theory and the Senegalese poor

My interest in post-development theory led me to focus my PhD studies on an organisation called Enda Graf Sahel (EGS), based in Dakar, Senegal.[7] I chose to research EGS because it was one of the few African-based organisations that appeared to have some affiliation with post-development theory, having been discussed in *The Post-Development Reader*.[8] Thus I arrived in Dakar in 2005 to explore the extent to which EGS's approach could be considered an example of post-development practice.

EGS's main office is situated in the relatively poor suburb of Grand Yoff. To get there, I typically took a public bus which ran past the Grand Yoff General Hospital and then walked along a road that crossed over what appeared to be an open sewer, past several market stalls and up a few dusty streets. Two particular encounters on that walk have stuck in my memory. The first was with a man with long matted hair and bloodshot eyes who lay for days on the ground outside the hospital, clutching a bottle containing a yellowish liquid. The second involved what I thought at first was a pile of dirty rags lying under one of the market stall tables early one morning before the stalls had opened. Coming closer, I realised that there was a man inside the rags. He had no limbs.

Before arriving in Dakar, I had lived only in the insular comfort of white South African suburbia and, briefly, in Birmingham, England. Viewed from South African suburbia, post-development theorists' disillusionment with development and their concern that with development would come soulless consumerism and a loss of community made sense. Despite being geographically situated in Africa, the suburb in which I grew up was characterised by the lack of warmth and neighbourliness that post-development theorists remark upon in relation to the developed West.[9] But I found my faith in post-development theory faltering in encounters such as those I describe above. Surely, I thought, these men would be well served by a shining, modern hospital? And weren't indoor bathrooms with flushing toilets rather nice, I reflected guiltily. I found myself questioning post-development theory as I saw in front of me not the conviviality and voluntary simplicity that Gustavo Esteva, Madhu Suri Prakash, Majid Rahnema and other post-development theorists attribute to the 'underdeveloped',[10] but rather something a lot more like the abject poverty so many advocates of development seek to eliminate. While it is possible to embrace post-development theory's critique of development while still accepting that abject poverty and destitution exist and ought to be eliminated, the pervasiveness of poverty I witnessed in Dakar (and elsewhere) made the romanticism of some post-development theory more evident to me than it had been before.[11]

My questioning of some aspects of post-development theory was deepened by my interactions with EGS staff members, none of whom advocated a position that fitted comfortably within a post-development framework. Indeed, EGS's executive secretary, Emmanuel Ndione, responded to my first mention of post-development theory with a mixture of amusement and dismissiveness – this despite the inclusion of a piece he co-authored in *The Post-Development Reader*.[12] While EGS staff members certainly questioned many of the tenets of mainstream development theory, they did not reject development as robustly and comprehensively as the post-development theorists I had been reading did. While many of their projects seek to validate and promote marginalised worldviews and practices in a way that resonates with post-development theory,[13] other key projects like skills development and micro-finance initiatives are quite similar to those typically associated with development work.

Post-development theory and South African 'service delivery' protests

My time in Dakar began a process of partial disillusionment with post-development theory which has been intensified by my observation of popular protest in South Africa. One of the most noteworthy features of the current South African political landscape is the so-called 'service delivery' protest.[14] This term is used to refer to protests which result from dissatisfaction with the state's delivery of services such as public housing, water, electricity, sanitation and education. While the protests play out in a range of ways, they typically include the drafting of a memorandum of some sort to be handed over to a local authority, marching and *toyi-toying*,[15] the blockading of roads and the burning of tyres. Some protests also involve the destruction of property, looting, and confrontations with the police, who have sometimes responded brutally.[16]

These protests raise a range of questions, most of which are beyond the scope of this article. But what is of particular relevance to the discussions that follow are the demands made by the protestors. While it must be stressed that these protests vary greatly and that each has its own particular set of demands, there are certain demands that are frequently articulated. Akinboade, Mokwena and Kinfack report that the most frequent issues raised by the protestors interviewed for their research were inadequate housing, the building and maintenance of roads, the building of clinics, the replacement of pit latrines with flushing toilets, and job creation.[17] Similarly, in a study of a municipality experiencing what is described as 'typical' protests, the Centre for Development and Enterprise provides the following list of demands made by protestors:

> a functional toilet system, better lighting, sports facilities, action in respect of unemployment, the allocation of sites for housing, a community hall, the completion of community projects,

another school, land for a cemetery, a clinic, the allocation of land for business projects, and clean, running water ....[18]

Faced with demands like these, it is difficult to deny that these protestors seem to want goods that are typically associated with 'development'. Protestors making demands like these sound very different to Esteva and Prakash's doña Refugio, a Mexican woman who, while squatting next to her cooking fire, tells Esteva and Prakash that she refuses 'the "convenience" of [an upright] stove (which would save her from squatting) along with many of the other "comforts" of modern society' because she finds meaning and purpose in her community's traditional way of life.[19] The orientation of South African protestors is also very different from that of another person held up by Esteva and Prakash – 'Francisco' – who after 10 years spent working in the United States of America decides to return to his home village in rural Mexico. This village has 'neither the electricity nor any of the comforts to which he had become accustomed', but provides him with a sense of home and respect.[20] For Esteva and Prakash, people like doña Refugio and Francisco represent what they see as promising patterns whereby people are rejecting development. They may well be correct that there are, through-out the so-called 'underdeveloped' world, people who are choosing to reject development and embracing and revitalising alternative, indigenous ways of life. However, we need also to be attentive to those who, like so many South African protestors, are very keen to acquire 'modern conveniences' like electricity and flushing toilets, and are willing to mobilise in a range of ways to get them. Furthermore, we need to acknowledge that one can embrace the goods associated with development (such as electricity and piped water) while also rejecting other aspects that might be associated with many development projects (such as privatisation).

Post-development theory and southern African aspirant 'modern men'

Some of the challenges that South African protests raise for post-development theory find resonance in the writings of anthropologist James Ferguson. While Ferguson's first book, *The Anti-Politics Machine*, is often included within the post-development canon,[21] he later distanced himself from post-development theory.[22] Ferguson indicates that he is sympathetic to post-development theorists' concerns about the ethnocentrism at the heart of the idea of development and the human and environmental degradation caused by development, but he cannot share their enthusiasm for the supposed end of development.[23] Rather than being an opportunity for liberation from the imposition of an undesirable Western lifestyle, Ferguson fears that the failure of development to achieve its goals is likely to amount to the betrayal of poor people's hopes for equality and redress.

In addition to his direct commentary on post-development theory,[24] Ferguson's insistence on taking seriously his informants' desire for development is implicitly a critique of post-development theory. In *Expectations of Modernity*, Ferguson writes about a 'Mr Mukande' who had been a mineworker in a Zambian copper mine.[25] On retirement, the decline of the Zambian economy made it difficult for Mukande to afford urban living, and so he was having to consider retiring to a rural village where, he notes sadly, he would have to live like an 'ordinary villager'.[26] Ferguson and Mukande's discussion of this possibility includes the fol-lowing exchange: "'You wouldn't want to live like an ordinary villager?" [Ferguson] asked.

After a long, searching look into [Ferguson's] eyes, [Mukande] replied: "Would *you* like to do that?'".[27]

In his later book *Global Shadows*, Ferguson describes a similar encounter in Lesotho with a 'Mr Lebona'.[28] Lebona informs Ferguson of his intention to build a rectangular 'European-style' house made of cement with a steel roof, rather than a more 'traditional' Sesotho-style house which would typically be round, made of stone and thatched. On hearing Lebona's plans, Ferguson defends Sesotho-style houses which, in his view, are to be admired for being built using locally available materials and for being well suited to the climate. Lebona's response to Ferguson is instructive:

> Mr. Lebona looked amused. His response, which came quickly and forcefully, gave me pause, and still does. Looking me carefully in the eye, he asked, 'What kind of house does your father have, there in America?' (I was at the time young enough to be regarded as a mere 'student', so the use of my father as the point of comparison was logical). 'Is it round?' No, I confessed; it was rectangular. 'Does it have a grass roof?' No, it did not. 'Does it have cattle dung for a floor?' No. And then: 'How many rooms does your father's house have?' Here, I had to stop and think – which Mr. Lebona appeared to find amazing, as rectangular houses in his experience had either two or three rooms. Finally, I mumbled, 'About ten, I think'. After pausing to let this sink in, he said only: 'That is the direction we would like to move in'.[29]

Both Mukande and Lebona insist that their lives and expectations ought to be comparable with those of Ferguson. Why should Mukande be happy to retire to a rural village to live, as he puts it, 'in the Stone Age', if Ferguson would not be?[30] Why should Lebona be satisfied with a modest hut when Ferguson prefers a many-roomed brick house? More generally, we could ask: What happens when post-development theorists' desire to celebrate 'the other-ness of the other'[31] is confronted with 'others' who insist on their sameness with 'us' and assert their right to live as 'we' do?

* * *

The foregoing discussion ranges from the poor of Dakar to South African protestors to would-be 'modern men' in Zambia and Lesotho. What these varying examples all point to is something that Sachs recognises in his preface to the new edition of *The Development Dictionary*: post-development theorists had 'not really appreciated the extent to which the development idea has been charged with hopes for redress and self-affirmation'.[32] The idea that development is a 'ruin in the intellectual landscape' has not really had much traction in the South which, as Sachs acknowledges, has more fervently defended the idea than the North has.[33] How can critics of development make sense of and adequately respond to this unexpected (at least for many post-development theorists) continued commitment to development?

Decolonisation of the imagination?

One possible way to respond is to explain the continued appeal of development as being due to the colonisation of the minds of those who continue to hanker for development. Given post-development theorists' interest in the discursive power of development, it is not surprising that some claim that development involves a colonisation of minds, heart and imaginations. This is evident, for example, in several of the contributions to *The Post-Development Reader*. In a contribution entitled 'Colonization of the Mind', Ashis Nandy suggests that development is a kind of second colonialism which colonises minds rather than lands. Consequently, 'The West is now everywhere; within the West and outside; in structures and in minds'.[34] Similarly, James Petras's contribution talks about 'cultural terrorism' which entails 'preying on the psychological weaknesses and deep anxieties of vulnerable Third World peoples' making them abandon their old ways and reorient themselves towards the capitalist market and state.[35] Rahnema too presents us with the idea of cultural colonialism using a metaphor whereby he compares development to the AIDS virus, saying that its power lies in its 'internalisation by the host' and that it 'penetrates into people's minds'. In a similar manner to these contributors to *The Post-Development Reader*, Sachs' preface to the new edition of *The Development Dictionary* refers to mental colonisation in attempting to explain development's lasting appeal. Sachs argues that those in the South have compromised their 'right to cultural self-identity' through embracing development and that what is now needed is a 'decolonization of the imagination'.[36]

The claim that development brings with it a whole mind-set and way of seeing the world is one of the most important contributions post-development theory has made to critiques of development. By highlighting that development does not simply entail a set of pro-grammes to address poverty, post-development theorists demonstrate that development can be understood as a new variant of Western hegemony rather than as a way to escape it. However, I have some concerns about the way in which this interest in the discursive power of development has led some post-development theorists to prescribe a 'decoloni-sation of the imagination' in response to people's reluctance to give up the idea of develop-ment. It is to these concerns that I now turn.

The first concern relates to the understanding of colonisation that informs this call for decolonisation. As Aram Ziai points out, some post-development texts present us with sup-posed passive 'victims of development' who have development imposed upon them.[37] The image such texts call to mind is that of a zombie controlled by alien ideas – indeed, one text even uses the term 'victims of zombification' to refer to those who have embraced Western schooling.[38] Similarly, Rahnema compares development to a virus which infiltrates a 'cell' (presumably a person in some 'Third World' country), 'strips off its protective shell and takes up permanent residence'.[39] Consequently, the development victims''motives of subsistence and their sense of belonging to the community' are replaced with a desire for economic gain and individual freedom.[40] This kind of account paints a picture of frugal, community-loving subsistence farmers whose brains are taken captive by an alien force which changes them into nasty, selfish, money-loving ghouls. But careful empirical accounts of the way develop-ment is received on the ground reveal more agency on the part of these supposed 'victims' of development. For example, in his study of development interventions in Zimbabwe, Donald Moore argues that the 'disciplinary effects of development confront not docile bodies but the situated cultural practices and sedimented histories of people and place'.[41] Rather than being an omnipotent force which infiltrates and perverts all it encounters, Moore argues that development is a set of contested ideas and practices which are continually 'refracted, reworked, and sometimes subverted in particular localities'.[42] To see development in this way need not mean denying that the ideas associated with development are powerful and potentially damaging, but it does entail guarding against viewing those who apparently embrace aspects of development as misguided victims with little agency at all.

A second concern with calls for decolonisation of the imagination relates to the possible anti-democratic implications of this call. Ziai argues that some strands of post-development theory are characterised by 'reactionary populism' which conceives of culture as static and therefore regards almost any cultural change as unhealthy.[43] Those who take on 'foreign' ways can then be dismissed as inauthentic or untrustworthy. Consider, for example, Rahnema who says that even if the majority of a community openly express a desire for development, this desire ought not to be trusted.[44] Rather than going along with the views of the majority, Rahnema suggests that we should follow the example of 'vernacular societies' who are apparently not 'blinkered by the myth of equality' and therefore entrust the good of the community to 'the wisest, the most virtuous'.[45] If one believes, as Rahnema appears to, that all those who favour development are victims of mental colonisation, then it becomes all too easy to dismiss their desires.

A third concern relates to the way in which this idea of decolonisation of the imagination may be premised upon a fairly static conception of culture and cultural authenticity which does not give adequate attention to the way in which the lives of many in the contemporary South bear little resemblance to those of their ancestors, whose way of living has been destroyed and cannot easily be revived. I can best illustrate this with a rather scatological example which contrasts the lives of Esteva and Prakash's 'social majorities' with those of contemporary urban Africans.[46] Esteva and Prakash present us with a somewhat romantic image of the sanitary practices of women in the Punjab. We are told that these women experience great conviviality as 'they defecate together in the soft darkness yet-to-be dawn'. Lacking 'modern' sewerage systems, these rural women relieve themselves in the fields surrounding their village, using this time together to share gossip and create close bonds. Reading this image, I could not help but think of South Africa's recent bout of 'poo protests' whereby angry protestors empty buckets of excrement to draw attention to their lack of adequate sanitary provision.[47] Such protestors typically live in tightly populated urban areas and cannot possibly relieve themselves in the manner Esteva and Prakash describe. Rather, what they would like is clean, functioning toilets and sewerage systems that remove their waste. As much as we might want to respectfully uphold age-old sanitary practices that worked in their context, we must also acknowledge that people's contexts have changed as have their cultural practices, and that it is quite plausible and understandable that many in the Global South long not for quiet, communal defecation in a beautiful pasture, but for a clean, hygienic bathroom close at hand.

A final concern relates to the awkwardness that arises when someone living in a place like Berlin (the place from which Sachs writes his call for a decolonisation of the imagination)[48] appeals to those in the South to forgo their desire for the goods and services that those in places like Berlin enjoy. When Western-based post-development theorists suggest that those who long for 'skyscrapers and shopping malls'[49] or who choose to 'discard comfortable, traditional loose-fitting clothes for ill-fitting unsuitable tight blue jeans'[50] are victims of mental colonisation, they surely open themselves up to being called hypocrites. After all, they have easy access to shopping malls and, no doubt, have been known to wear jeans while also perhaps having the privilege of travelling to places without skyscrapers and sampling the foods, clothing and cultural artefacts of other cultures. While it is true that there are Westerners who embrace alternative, more frugal and sustainable lifestyles, this is for the most part a *choice* such people have made (rather than had foisted upon them), and those without this choice might well resent being encouraged to reject the modern conveniences that they have never even been able to access in the first place.

In a related discussion, Ferguson touches on Western anthropologists' discomfort on meeting people in 'the field' who seemingly want to be like them.[51] What is a Western anthropologist with 'well-schooled anticolonial convictions' to do when meeting 'an object of alterity who refuses to be other'?[52] To respond to such an 'other' by simply affirming their desire to take on the practices and lifestyles of those in the West is to pay inadequate attention to the context of global white supremacy and Western hegemony in which these desires take form. But to dismiss such desires as evidence of mental colonisation leaves such anthropologists in the 'awkward role of either condemning or pitying their informants'.[53] The assumption on the part of Western advocates of development that all the world would like to model themselves on the West is rightfully revealed by post-development theorists to be premised upon Western arrogance and to have resulted in a range of oppressive interventions in the rest of the world. However, for those in the West to dismiss any apparent desire for development as evidence of mental colonisation entails assuming they know what is best for non-Western 'others' and prescribing, once again, to such 'others' how they ought to live. The problem described here might be alleviated somewhat when the advocate for mental decolonisation is not Western, but even then if such an advocate has gained access to the benefits of development only to turn around and argue that others ought not to want them, similar problems arise as once again a relatively privileged person with access to particular goods is proclaiming that access to such goods ought not to be desired by others.

Towards a way forward

I have shown above that responding to development's ongoing desirability by calling for a decolonisation of the imagination is not without its problems. However, the concerns outlined above need not lead us to reject post-development theorists' critique of development altogether. In trying to navigate a way forward, I will return to the three cases I discussed earlier to see where attentiveness to the marginalised in Dakar, to South African protestors, and to Ferguson's aspirant southern African 'modern men' might take us.

As I indicate above, Enda Graf Sahel (EGS) has occasionally been cited as an example of post-development practice,[54] but the reality on the ground is somewhat more complex. In common with post-development theorists, EGS staff members reject many of the tenets of mainstream development. Years of working closely with the relatively marginalised in Dakar have led them to discard some of the ideas they had learnt while studying at university and to be more attentive to the preferences of the communities with which they work.[55] However, adopting the communities' own priorities (an approach surely aligned with the general thrust of post-development theory) has led EGS to engage in some programmes that are very compatible with mainstream development – skills development initiatives, for example. EGS's experiences confirm Moore's view that when encountering the many initiatives that are associated with development, people are likely to reject some while welcoming others.[56] Development has, as post-development theorists recognise, come to refer to a very broad range of things. But surely, then, recognition that development's many meanings make it an 'amoeba-like concept'[57] ought to lead not to the outright rejection of anything going by the name of development, but rather to the picking apart of development, taking what is useful and discarding what is not. Two examples are helpful here. One is existing discussion within post-development theory about tools and technology – see for example Ivan Illich's attempts to distinguish between convivial and non-convivial tools.[58] Another is the example discussed by Moore in which people living in Kaerezi, Zimbabwe, embrace some aspects of development (such as a diesel-powered maize grinding mill) while vehemently rejecting others (such as resettlement into grid-like residential complexes).[59] In both these examples an attempt is made to distinguish between aspects of development rather than to embrace or reject it.

In addition to trying to distinguish carefully between different aspects of development, we ought also to distinguish between different aspects of the post-development critique of development. Just as we might want to resist rejecting development in its entirety, the above critique of aspects of post-development theory ought not to lead to the rejection of the entire post-development critique of development. We ought to acknowledge that there is no coherent, single post-development theory, but rather a range of different and related critiques of development. Here we can draw on existing attempts to differentiate between more and less empowering 'strands' of post-development theory, such as David Simon's distinction between anti- and post-development and Aram Ziai's distinction between those post-development thinkers who lean towards reactionary populism and those who embrace radical democracy.[60]

As we move forward, building on some aspects of post-development theory while reject-ing others, we must be mindful of the complexity of people's apparent desire for develop-ment. To bring out some of these complexities, I want to turn to a debate about the meaning of South African 'service delivery' protests. The South African media has routinely labelled protests this way, suggesting that people protest because they lack a particular service (such as water or sanitation) and that they protest in order to pressure officials to provide them with the desired service. However, critics of this labelling argue that talk of 'service delivery' is too simplistic and obscures the more complicated motivations for such protests. According to Richard Pithouse, the 'service delivery myth' presents people as 'consumers or beneficiaries who just need to be plugged into the grid of serviced life by a benevolent state'.[61] This approach obscures the fact that these protests often represent 'rebellion against service delivery as it is currently practiced rather than a demand for it to be speeded up'.[62] For example, there have been instances where people living in informal settlements resist being relocated to state housing because the housing on offer is distant from employment oppor-tunities or family and friends. Shauna Mottiar argues that protestors' demands are less about 'delivering already determined services' and more about agitating for greater democracy and for meaningful recognition of their citizenship.[63]

What these commentaries suggest is that people's desire for 'development' is tangled up with their desire for equality, dignity and redress. While people surely do want water and electricity for their own sake, protests about service delivery are also about what access to water, electricity, adequate sanitation and the like represent. As David Hemson and Kwame Owusu-Ampomah argue, in South Africa the delivery of services like water and electricity is associated with a sense of redress for past injustices.[64] The 'service delivery' protests that ensue when these services are not delivered (or are delivered in unacceptable ways) are a manifestation of the anger and betrayal many South Africans feel when treated dismissively, even contemptuously, by state officials. The denial of such services is experienced by many as a refusal to recognise the humanity of those being denied. This point is brought out nicely in recent comments by opposition politician Julius Malema. With reference to the conditions in the mainly rural provinces he had been visiting, Malema asks 'What kind of dignity is this, without a flushing toilet?' and adds 'Whites, all of them, have flushing toilets, even the hobos'.[65] These comments make clear the way in which the provision of a service – in this case a flushing toilet – is tied to broader questions of racial inequality, redress and dignity.

Similar questions are explored in Ferguson's wrestling with the meaning of Lebona's decision to build a 'European-style' house.[66] Careful consideration of this choice leads Ferguson to conclude that Lebona and others like him are not victims of mental colonisation who mindlessly copy everything they associate with the West, but that such choices are indicative of an insistence on 'common membership in a global society'.[67] Choices like that made by Lebona entail 'a declaration of comparability, an aspiration to membership and inclusion in the world'.[68]

In some ways Ferguson's interpretation of Lebona's actions is grist for the mill of advocates of mental decolonisation as it appears that Lebona associates 'European-style' things with dignity and success. Similarly, Malema's comments on flushing toilets suggest that part of the desirability of flushing toilets is their association with whiteness in a context of persistent racial inequality. We might therefore argue, along with Sachs, that what the idea of development has done is to frame people's desire for equality and recognition 'in terms of the civilizational model of the powerful nations'.[69] This can lead us right back to the call for the decolonisation of the imagination that I critiqued earlier.

Perhaps the best way forward is to acknowledge that those who talk of the colonisation of the mind are correct in highlighting the psycho-social effects of development, but to also heed the concerns I raised earlier in relation to calls for the decolonisation of the imagination. Calling for the decolonisation of the minds of those in the South is not the only possible way to respond to the entanglement of people's desire for dignity, equality and redress with their desire for development. Rather than insisting that those who desire development ought to decolonise their minds, perhaps our attention ought rather to be focused on other ways of loosening the association between dignity and the lifestyle of those in the industrialised West. As long as the powerful live in 'European-style' houses with flushing toilets, it ought to be regarded as utterly unsurprising that the disempowered might desire such houses and forms of sanitation. Instead of focusing on getting those in the South to decolonise their minds so that they reject development, we might push those in the North to recognise the catastrophic environmental implications of continued economic growth in the North and the need for redress and redistribution to address global inequality. Here, some trends in post-development theory, such as the focus on 'degrowth' economics, are promising in that they involve shifting focus towards the Global North.[70]

Finally, and to close, however we choose to build on post-development theory, we must emphasise the importance of being attentive to the range of experiences of those in the South. We must acknowledge both the desires of doña Refugio who seeks to preserve long-standing traditions and to live an avowedly non-Western way of life and those of Mr Mukande who would like a materially comfortable, urban retirement of the kind so many post-development theorists might themselves one day enjoy.

Disclosure statement

No potential conflict of interest was reported by the authors.

Acknowledgements

This article has been strengthened considerably in response to careful comments on an earlier draft from Pedro Tabensky, Aram Ziai and two anonymous reviewers.

Notes

1. Sachs, *Development Dictionary*, viii. Sachs favours the term 'the South' over alternatives like 'the Third World' or 'the developing world'. While there are problems with each term, for consistency I will follow Sachs in using 'the South'.
2. Ibid., viii.
3. Ibid., viii.
4. Mbeki, "African Renaissance."
5. Mbeki, "Arab Reawakening," xv.
6. Matthews, "View from Africa."
7. More on Enda Graf Sahel can be found on their website www.endagrafsahel.org.
8. N'Dione et al., "Reinventing the Present," 364–76. Note that Emmanuel Ndione's name is usually spelt 'Ndione', but I have used here the spelling used in *The Post-Development Reader*. Elsewhere I will spell his name 'Ndione'.
9. See, for example, Latouche, *In the Wake of the Affluent Society*, 11–3.
10. See Esteva and Prakash, *Grassroots Postmodernism*; and Rahnema, *Post-Development Reader*.
11. For critiques of the way in which some post-development theorists romanticise poverty, see Kiely, "Last Refuge."
12. N'Dione et al., "Reinventing the Present."
13. An example here is an EGS project to promote the *Noon* language and culture – see discussion in Matthews, "Responding to Poverty," 73–4.
14. For general discussions of the role of such protests in contemporary South Africa, see Alexander, "Rebellion of the Poor"; and Lodge and Mottiar, "Protest in South Africa."
15. To *toyi-toyi* is to dance in a way that expresses protest or dissatisfaction. *Toyi-toying* has long been a feature of protest action in southern Africa.
16. See Bond and Mottiar, "Movements, Protests and a Massacre."
17. Akinboade et al., "Protest for Improved Delivery," 20.
18. Centre for Development and Enterprise, "Voices of Anger," 14.
19. Esteva and Prakash, *Grassroots Postmodernism*, 57.
20. Ibid., 81.
21. Ferguson, *Anti-Politics Machine*. For examples of instances where this book (or parts of it) are considered to be part of post-development literature, see Rahnema and Bawtree, *Post-Development Reader* (which includes an extract from Ferguson's book) as well as Ziai, "The Ambivalence of Post-Development," 1046.
22. See in particular Ferguson, *Expectations of Modernity*, 245–54.
23. Ibid.
24. Ibid.
25. Ferguson, *Expectations of Modernity*, 152–8 and 229. Mukande is a pseudonym. Note that throughout the book, Ferguson refers to his male respondents using the title 'Mr'. I have retained it only on the first usage, but after that will use surnames only as with all other people mentioned in the paper.
26. Ibid., 153.
27. Ibid., 229.

28. Ferguson, *Global Shadows*, 18–9.
29. Ibid., 18.
30. Ferguson, *Expectations of Modernity*, 153.
31. O'Donovan, "Conversing on the Commons," 532.
32. Sachs, *Development Dictionary*, viii.
33. Ibid., xv, viii.
34. Nandy, "Colonization of the Mind," 170.
35. Petras, "New Cultural Domination," 182.
36. Sachs, *The Development Dictionary*, ix.
37. Ziai, "Ambivalence of Post-Development," 1048.
38. Ki-Zerbo et al., "Education as an Instrument," 154.
39. Rahnema, "Another Variety of AIDS," 119.
40. Ibid.
41. Moore, "Crucible of Cultural Politics," 658.
42. Ibid., 655.
43. Ziai, "Ambivalence of Post-Development," 1055.
44. Rahnema, "Afterword," 388–9.
45. Ibid., 388.
46. Esteva and Prakash, *Grassroots Postmodernism*, 96.
47. There have been a range of such protests in South Africa. For an overview see "'Poo protesters' to once again march over township sanitation services' by Shamiela Fisher, available at http://ewn.co.za/2015/10/03/Seskhona-to-once-again-protest-over-poor-township-sanitation-services.
48. Sachs, *Development Dictionary*, ix, xii.
49. Ibid., viii.
50. Petras, "New Cultural Domination," 187.
51. Ferguson, *Global Shadows*, 155–75.
52. Ibid., 156–7.
53. Ibid., 157.
54. In addition to the inclusion in the *Post-Development Reader* of a chapter co-authored by EGS's Emmanuel Ndione, Ndione's writing has also been linked to post-development theory by Serge Latouche – see Latouche, "L'Afrique peut-elle contribuer?"
55. These shifts are discussed in several EGS publications, most notably Ndione et al., *L'Afrique s'invente*.
56. Moore, "Crucible of Cultural Politics," 673.
57. Sachs, *Development Dictionary*, xix.
58. Illich, *Tools for Conviviality*.
59. Moore, "Crucible of Cultural Politics."
60. Simon, "Separated by Common Ground"; and Ziai, "Ambivalence of Post-Development." Note that their ways of distinguishing between different strands of post-development writing are quite different.
61. Pithouse, "Service Delivery Myth."
62. Ibid.
63. Mottiar, "From Popcorn to Occupy," 605–6.
64. Hemson and Owusu-Ampomah, "Better Life for All," 512.
65. Cited in an article for the *Financial Mail* by Sam Mkokeli. Available at http://www.financialmail.co.za/coverstory/2016/06/15/exclusive-inside-the-mind-of-julius-malema.
66. Ferguson, *Global Shadows*, 18–9. Ferguson also reflects on related issues throughout Chapter Six of *Global Shadows*.
67. Ibid., 173.
68. Ibid., 17.
69. Sachs, *Development Dictionary*, vii.
70. See for example Latouche, "World Downscaled."

Bibliography

Akinboade, O. A., M. P. Mokwena, and E. C. Kinfack. "Protesting for Improved Public Service Delivery in South Africa's Sedibeng District." *Social Indicators Research* 119 (2014): 1–23.

Alexander, P. "Rebellion of the Poor: South Africa's Service Delivery Protests – A Preliminary Analysis." *Review of African Political Economy* 37, no. 123 (2010): 25–40.

Apffel Marglin, F., and S. Marglin, eds. *Decolonizing Knowledge: From Development to Dialogue*. Oxford: Clarendon Press, 1996.

Centre for Development and Enterprise. *Voices of Anger: Protest and Conflict in Two Municipalities*. Johannesburg: Centre for Development and Enterprise, 2007.

Esteva, G., and M. S. Prakash. *Grassroots Postmodernism: Remaking the Soil of Cultures*. London and New York: Zed Books, 1998.

Ferguson, J. *The Anti-Politics Machine: "Development," Depoliticization, and Bureaucratic Power in Lesotho*. Minneapolis, MN: University of Minnesota Press, 1994.

Ferguson, J. *Expectations of Modernity: Myths and Meanings of Urban Life on the Zambian Copperbelt*. Berkeley: University of California Press, 1999.

Ferguson, J. *Global Shadows: Africa in the Neoliberal World Order*. Durham and London: Duke University Press, 2006.

Hemson, D., and K. Owusu-Ampomah. "A Better Life for All? Service Delivery and Poverty Alleviation." In *State of the Nation 2004–2005*, edited by J. Daniel, R. Southall, and J. Lutchman, 511–537. Cape Town: HSRC Press, 2005.

Illich, I. *Tools for Conviviality*. London: Calder and Boyars, 1990.

Kiely, R. "The Last Refuge of the Noble Savage? A Critical Assessment of Post-Development Theory." *The European Journal of Development Research* 11, no. 1 (1999): 30–55.

Ki-Zerbo, J. C. Hamidou Kane, J. Archibald, E. Lizop, and M. Rahnema. "Education as an Instrument of Cultural Defoilation: A Multi-Voice Report." In *The Post-Development Reader*, edited by M. Rahnema with V. Bawtree, 152–160. London and New Jersey: Zed Books, 1997.

Latouche, S. *In the Wake of the Affluent Society: An Exploration of Post-Development*. London and New York: Zed Books, 1993.

Latouche, S. 2004. "L'Afrique peut-elle contribuer à resoudre la crise de l'occident?" [Could Africa Help Resolve the Crisis of the West?] Accessed September 15, 2016. http://www.adelinotorres.info/africa/serge_latouche_l_afrique_peut_elle_contribuer.pdf

Latouche, S. 2003. "The World Downscaled." *Le Monde Diplomatique*, December. Accessed September 15, 2016. http://mondediplo.com/2003/12/17growth

Lodge, T., and S. Mottiar. "Protest in South Africa: Motives and Meanings." *Democratization* 23, no. 5 (2016): 819–837.

Matthews, S. "Post-Development Theory and the Question of Alternatives: A View from Africa." *Third World Quarterly* 25, no. 2 (2004): 373–384.

Matthews, S. "Responding to Poverty in the Light of the Post-Development Debate: Some Insights from the NGO Enda Graf Sahel." *Africa Development* XXXI, no. 4 (2006): 64–84.

Mbeki, T. 1998. "The African Renaissance, South Africa and the World." *Speech to the United Nations University*, April 9. Accessed October 3, 2016. http://archive.unu.edu/unupress/mbeki.html

Mbeki, T. "The Arab Reawakening: An African Renaissance Perspective." In *The African Renaissance and the Afro-Arab Spring: A Season of Rebirth?*, edited by C. Villa-Vicencio, E. Doxtader, and E. Moosa, ix–xv. Washington, DC: Georgetown University Press, 1998.

Moore, D. "The Crucible of Cultural Politics: Reworking 'development' in Zimbabwe's Eastern Highlands." *American Ethnologist* 26, no. 3 (1999): 654–689.

Mottiar, S. "From 'Popcorn' to 'Occupy': Protest in Durban, South Africa." *Development and Change* 44, no. 3 (2013): 603–619.

Nandy, A. "Colonization of the Mind." In *The Post-Development Reader*, edited by M. Rahnema with V. Bawtree, 168–178. London and New Jersey: Zed Books, 1997.

Ndione, E. S., P. De Leener, J. P. Perier, M. Ndiaye, and P. Jacolin. *Réinventer le Présent. Quelques Jalons pour l'Action* [Reinventing the Present: Guidelines for Action]. Dakar: Enda Graf Sahel, 1994.

Ndione, E. S., P. De Leener, J. P. Perier, M. Ndiaye, and P. Jacolin. "Reinventing the Present: The Chodak Experience in Senegal." In *The Post-Development Reader*, edited by M. Rahnema with V. Bawtree, 364–376. London and New Jersey: Zed Books, 1997.

O'Donovan, O. "Conversing on the Commons: An Interview with Gustavo Esteva – Part 1." *Community Development Journal* 50, no. 3 (2015): 529–534.

Petras, J. "The New Cultural Domination by the Media." In *The Post-Development Reader*, edited by M. Rahnema with V. Bawtree, 182–189. London and New Jersey: Zed Books, 1997.

Pithouse, R. 2011. "The Service Delivery Myth." Accessed September 10, 2016. http://sacsis.org.za/site/article/610.1

Rahnema, M. "Development and the People's Immune System: The Story of Another Variety of AIDS." In *The Post-Development Reader*, edited by M. Rahnema with V. Bawtree, 111–131. London and New Jersey: Zed Books, 1997.

Rahnema, M. "Afterword. Towards Post-Development: Searching for Signposts, a New Language and New Paradigms." In *The Post-Development Reader*, edited by M. Rahnema with V. Bawtree, 377–404. London and New Jersey: Zed Books, 1997.

Sachs, W. *The Development Dictionary: A Guide to Knowledge as Power*. 2nd ed. London and New York: Zed Books, 2010.

Simon, D. "Separated by Common Ground? Bringing (Post) Development and (Post) Colonialism Together." *The Geographical Journal* 172, no. 1 (2006): 10–21.

Ziai, A. "The Ambivalence of Post-Development: Between Reactionary Populism and Radical Democracy." *Third World Quarterly* 25, no. 6 (2004): 1045–1060.

Cold critique, faint passion, bleak future: Post-Development's surrender to global capitalism

Ilan Kapoor

ABSTRACT

This article carries out a psychoanalytic critique of Post-Development, arguing that the latter's inattention to the unconscious underpinnings of power not only leaves it unable to explain why development discourse persists, but also deprives it of a radical politics, resulting in a surrender to global capitalism. Drawing on the work of Escobar, Ferguson and Esteva, the article valorises Post-Development's important insights on the production of development discourse and its attendant power mechanisms. But using a Lacanian lens, it also probes Post-Development's failure to address how power is mediated at the level of the subject: in maintaining that (capitalist) development is produced discursively in a cold, impersonal way (like an 'anti-politics machine'), Post-Development ignores the fact that such power is only able to take hold, expand and, crucially, persist through unconscious libidinal attachments (e.g. desires, enjoyment). This failure leaves Post-Development with few resources – beyond localised resistance (Escobar, Esteva) or the call for a universal basic income (Ferguson) – to address the structural challenges of global capitalism. Psychoanalytically speaking, such a (Left) position appears to manifest a secret desire that nothing too much must change: Post-Development may well criticise the disciplinary mechanisms of neoliberal development, but ultimately it engages in an unconscious acceptance of capitalism.

Introduction

In *The Anti-Politics Machine*, while making the case for a Foucauldian discourse analysis, James Ferguson declares that 'the most important political effects of a planned intervention may occur *unconsciously*, behind the backs or against the wills of the "planners" who may seem to be running the show'.[1] He proceeds to demonstrate how development interventions in Lesotho have unintended consequences, which end up advancing institutional authority and control. But he stops short of analysing precisely the role of the *unconscious* in such interventions, preferring to stick to his non-psychoanalytic, Foucauldian predispositions.[2]

Similarly, in *Territories of Difference*, Arturo Escobar reflects on Pieter de Vries' psychoanalytic work on the place of desire in development.[3] Escobar readily admits to the Foucauldian weakness of treating development only discursively: when development is seen simply as an apparatus of power, it ends up disavowing people's subjectivity, that is, it fails to acknowledge that 'development is a desiring machine ... not only an apparatus of governmentality'.[4] He goes on to examine how development can be used to cultivate subjects of alternate developments/modernities – an enduring preoccupation of his – but, like Ferguson, he fails to take up the psychoanalytic challenge.

This article treads where Ferguson and Escobar fear to. It carries out a psychoanalytic critique of Post-Development, arguing that the latter's inattention to the unconscious underpinnings of power not only leaves it unable to explain why development discourse persists, but also deprives it of a deviant or radical politics, resulting in a surrender to global capitalism.[5] Drawing mainly on the work of Escobar and Ferguson, but also of Gustavo Esteva, the article valorises Post-Development's important insights on the production of development discourse and its attendant power mechanisms. But using a Lacanian lens, it also probes Post-Development's failure to address how power is mediated at the level of the subject: in maintaining that (capitalist) development is produced discursively in a cold, impersonal way (like an 'anti-politics machine'), Post-Development ignores the fact that such power is only able to take hold, expand and, crucially, persist through unconscious libidinal attachments (e.g. desires, enjoyment). This failure leaves Post-Development with few resources – beyond localised resistance (Escobar, Esteva) or the call for a universal basic income (Ferguson) – to address the structural challenges of global capitalism. Psychoanalytically speaking, such a (Left) position appears to manifest a secret desire that nothing too much must change: Post-Development may well criticise the disciplinary mechanisms of neoliberal development, but ultimately it engages in an unconscious acceptance of capitalism. Thus, to turn Ferguson's above-mentioned words against themselves: the most important political effects of *Post-Development* occur unconsciously, behind the backs or against the intentions of its exponents.

It should be noted that I focus on Escobar, Ferguson and Esteva primarily because they, more than other Post-Development analysts, draw on Foucauldian discourse analysis. As we shall see, Escobar and Ferguson ground their arguments theoretically, taking a more complex view of discursivity.[6] Esteva, on the other hand, is less theoretically inclined, employing what some have called an 'impoverished' notion of discourse[7] and drawing more eclectically on 'post-modernism' and social movement politics, especially the Zapatista movement.[8] Nonetheless, all three analysts share Foucault's predilections towards discursive productivity which, as I hope to demonstrate, ignores to its own peril the important issue of libidinal desire and agency.

Post-Development's Foucauldian underpinnings

One of Post-Development's notable contributions is to have brought discourse analysis to Development Studies. As is now well known, Foucault defines discourse not simply as a collection of words or utterances, but a set of 'practices which systematically form the objects of which they speak'.[9] For him, discourse constructs objects of knowledge, so that statements and socio-institutional practices centred on, say, madness, homosexuality or medicine prescribe what is sayable (and not sayable) about 'mad' people, 'homosexuals' or doctors. Post-development's ingenuity is to have applied such thinking to the field of development. Thus, Escobar sees development discourse as allowing the West to 'manage and control and, in many ways, even create the Third World politically, economically, sociologically and culturally'.[10] For him, as for Ferguson and Esteva,[11] the construction of knowledge systems in development is coterminous with a will to power and domination. As a result, much Post-Development writing is devoted to challenging the epistemological assumptions and categories of development discourse. Escobar and Esteva are critical of the scientific and economistic thinking that dominates development (e.g. its fixation with technological and narrow economic growth-oriented solutions), as well as its Eurocentric and paternalistic assumptions.[12] In response, they express interest in local culture and knowledge systems, with Esteva echoing Foucault by advocating for the 'insurrection of subordinated knowledges'.[13]

An important way in which discourse plays out in development, for Escobar and Ferguson especially, is through 'governmentality'. This is the Foucauldian notion that fuses 'governance' with 'mentality' (or modes of thought) to underline the co-constitution of knowledge and power. Thus, when an institution identifies and defines a 'problem', it is at the same time creating and rationalising the corresponding strategies (and technologies of power) for addressing it.[14] Escobar examines, for example, how the categorisation of the Third World as 'abnormal', 'underdeveloped' or 'illiterate' yields a host of institutional practices – from field work and the collection of dossiers to the establishment of academic disciplines (e.g. Development Studies, Development Economics) and experts (e.g. food specialists, educators, business trainers or anthropologists). He shows that such institutionalisation opens up new sites not only of expertise but also of power: it ends up regulating and disciplining Third World populations (peasants, children, indigenous people, etc.) and producing 'biopolitical' subjects (e.g. neoliberal entrepreneurial subjects).[15]

Similarly, Ferguson demonstrates how the classification of Lesotho as 'aboriginal' or 'agri-cultural' constructs the country as a 'generic "LDC" – a country with all the right deficiencies, the sort that "development" institutions can easily and productively latch on to'.[16] He underlines how knowledge about the country is accordingly simplified and depoliticised, resulting in the aggrandisement of institutional authority, so much so that, even when development projects fail, they help expand bureaucratic power.

These three commentators' discursive analysis therefore cedes to a biting critique of development. Given what they see as the latter's many failings – the way in which development discourse represents the Third World, its use of hierarchic and Eurocentric categorisation, its implied professionalisation and institutionalisation, its biopolitical production of development subjects – they not only question how development is done, but its very framing, indeed our very need for it.[17] No wonder that they seek out, as we shall see later, radical alternatives.

Cold critique, faint passion

The problem, however, is that this is a cold critique, devoid of human passion. Indeed, the Post-Development writers even admit as much. Ferguson sees his Foucauldian analysis as a 'cold-blooded operation', characterising Lesotho's development apparatus as an 'anony-mous ... anti-politics machine'.[18] Likewise, Escobar describes discourse analysis as allowing for the possibility of standing 'detached' from development in order to examine its social and cultural dimensions.[19] Accordingly, both the subject and object of enquiry, the discourse analyst as much as the development worker or bureaucrat, are caught in an inescapable, impersonal power-ridden network. This is certainly Foucault's import when he declares that power does not operate over-and-above the subject, but is a '*machine* in which everyone is caught, those who exercise power as much as those over whom it is exercised ... It becomes a machinery that no one owns'.[20]

Now contrast this viewpoint with the psychoanalytic one. Lacanian psychoanalysis is quite consistent with Foucault's conception of power/knowledge and how these discipline bodies, produce subjects and shape such modern institutions as asylums, prisons, hospitals, schools and indeed psychoanalysis itself. But while Lacan deploys a similar notion of discourse, he stresses not peoples' inescapable anonymity and detachment in the power/knowledge network, but on the contrary their unavoidable libidinal engagement in it. For him, our entry into language (i.e. the infant's separation from the (m)Other) is accompanied by traumatic loss or lack (from a false sense of plenitude). Desire, then, is the psychic remainder that occurs when we enter the symbolic world – an unconscious desire engaged in a futile quest to fill the lack, to regain once again the impossible fullness.[21] The libidinal is thus the complement to discourse, so that power is never impersonal; it is always passionately invested.

Foucault assumes that power produces the body without any mediation, that is, without any process of interiorisation. As Joan Copjec argues, quoting Foucault against himself, in 'Foucault's work the techniques of disciplinary power (of the construction of the subject) are conceived as capable of "materially penetrat[ing] the body in depth without depending even on the mediation of the subject's own representations. If power takes hold on the body, this isn't through its having first to be interiorized into people's consciousness".[22]

True, Foucault does have a notion of 'desire', but for him it is positively produced, not repressed. In his *History of Sexuality*, for example, he argues that European discourses of sexuality arose in the nineteenth century as a result of social practices (medicine, psychoanalysis) which meant that, far from being repressed, sexuality was spoken about a lot.[23] But as Copjec and others point out, such discursive productivism makes social reality 'realtight'.[24] That is, by refusing any type of negation, gap or excess (what Lacan calls the 'Real'), discourse is reduced to the field of its effects without remainder. The problem with Foucault, then, is his refusal of any type of transcendence: his historicist discursivism ends up reducing society to power–knowledge relationships. But because power is always immanent for Foucault, his is a discursivism which can neither account for itself (how does one apprehend power/discourse if one is always within it?) nor explain how social orders persist or can be changed. If there is no gap between the discursive space and its positive content or effect, then Foucault is at pains to explain either his own role as discourse analyst or how the subject becomes an agent of social transformation. (This Lacanian critique, it should be noted, echoes feminist critiques of Foucault, which take him to task for reducing people to docile bodies and objects of power.)[25]

For Lacanians, it is precisely desire that fixes the subject (however precariously and contingently), explaining how we both (mis)perceive power and become libidinally invested in it. And such desire is not discursively produced, as Foucault would have it, but as noted above is an inherent excess (the Real)[26] to any discourse; it is the result of the insubstantial loss that arises the moment we enter language. Discourse therefore simultaneously implies an unconscious gap or leftover. And it is on the basis of such libidinal excess that Lacanians envisage the possibility of agency and social change. Our passions may well bind us to the world (through intense attachments), but their excess may also help us liberate ourselves.

Rejecting development or enjoying it?

What this implies for Post-Development is that it fails to confront the psychic inclinations that support development discourse. This can be seen, in particular, in Escobar and Esteva's black-and-white argumentation: because they depict development discourse as a form of Western domination of Third World subjects, they assume the latter will reject development, ignoring that many may not be psychically inclined. Both analysts have been roundly criticised, as we know, for homogenising development discourse and painting development subjects with too broad a brush.[27] To wit, Escobar calls for 'alternatives to development', presuming that people are either for or against it.[28] And Esteva often portrays development subjects as 'victims', comparing development to an 'unburied corpse', 'doomed to extinction'.[29]

The glitch is that both analysts provide little evidence of any overwhelming disillusionment with, or indeed demise of, development across the global South. In fact, to date the record is just the opposite. Critics of Post-Development point out that many communities have often fought *for* development (e.g. more jobs, even if they are low-paid, and better access to health, education, etc.).[30] Jonathan Rigg contends, for example, that in Southeast Asia many groups have 'climbed aboard the modernisation bandwagon, whether they be for or against it'.[31] Similarly, Ray Kiely submits that peasant communities are far from disinterested in accumulation, with many already well integrated into the global capitalist agricultural sector.[32] And on the consumer front, development subjects – whether rural farming communities or urban transnational classes – often appear to be yearning for consumer goods. Thus, while Esteva asserts that 'people at the grassroots [in the global South] … are learning to simply say "no" to Coke',[33] precisely the contrary is true. If anything, it is people in the global North who are saying 'No' and those in the South 'Yes': carbonated drink consumption has been steadily declining in North America and Western Europe over the last two decades, with for example a 25% drop in the US between 1998 and 2014. In contrast, soft drink consumption in Mexico (precisely where Esteva grounds his work) has been steadily increasing, with per capita consumption currently one of the highest in the world.[34]

I want to suggest that it is because Escobar and Esteva's Foucauldianism does not explicate how power is libidinally mediated at the level of the subject that it fails to grapple with why people so often acquiesce to development discourse and neoliberal capitalism. The two analysts miss that development subjects may actually desire – nay even *enjoy* – development. To be sure, enjoyment (*jouissance*) in the Lacanian lexicon denotes not simply pleasure, but overwhelming or excessive (unconscious) gratification, so much so that, despite knowing better, the subject may make irrational or counter-productive choices.[35] Think of the way in which nationalists so enjoy the nation that they may scapegoat and vilify 'outsiders', or extreme freedivers enjoy danger so they put their lives at risk. In the same vein, it appears that development subjects (and many of us, for that matter) not only like what development has on offer, but (unconsciously) *love* it: given their above-noted record of embracing development, they are evidently seduced by development's fantasies of wealth, technology and progress and thrilled by iPhones, cars and soda. More pertinent is that even those subjects who may have doubts about development (on account of, say, its social inequities or negative environmental effects), may nonetheless buy into it. This is what Žižek terms 'fetishistic disavowal': one knows something is bad or wrong, but one desires it anyway (because one is so libidinally captivated by it).[36] The upshot is that by ignoring people's psychic inclinations, the proponents of Post-Development underestimate the hold and charms of development discourse.

Post-development may not be wrong in desiring an 'alternative to development', but it errs in believing that people can be easily diverted from the mainstream. By neglecting the subject's unconscious desires, it is unable to explain why development discourse endures or indeed how people can be so invested in it. By the same token, it fails to appreciate the complex libidinal economy at work in development: for example, those who buy wholesale into development, those who buy into it reluctantly (fetishistic disavowal) and those who manage to come to terms with their unconscious desires and direct them elsewhere (what Lacan calls 'traversing the fantasy').[37] It is the latter who may perhaps be able to work towards an 'alternative to development', but the important point is that reaching such an alternative requires working through a complex economy of desire. In other words, radical transformation in development requires more than changing the discourse or the power/knowledge frame as Foucault, Escobar and Esteva would have it; it requires, critically, also attending to people's libidinal attachments.[38]

Bureaucratic power: a question of intent or enjoyment?

Let us not forget Ferguson's neglect of the libidinal as well, evident in his approach to governmentality. He repeatedly emphasises the Foucauldian point that power circulates, so that the expansion of state power in Lesotho is 'subjectless', the result of 'unintended', 'unforeseen' and 'unlikely' state bureaucratic interventions.[39] According to him:

> the outcomes of planned social interventions can end up coming together into powerful constellations of control that were never intended and in some cases never recognized … [It is this] unauthored resultant constellation that I call 'the anti-politics machine'.[40]

Yet again, in following Foucault, Ferguson ignores how power is mediated subjectively. Reading him one gets the unmistakable impression that the development bureaucrat is a quasi-robotic body on (and through) which power is written and exercised. This seems vague and unpersuasive, in my view. It not only erases any meaningful subjectivity on the part of bureaucrats, but appears to allow them to avoid any responsibility by portraying their decision-making process as faceless and somehow disinterested (or at least dispassionate).

Ferguson fails to recognise the important role of unconscious desire and enjoyment (*jouissance*) in bureaucratic politics: for instance, the ways in which development administrators/workers may obtain a certain reassurance and stability from following and applying bureaucratic procedures and rules; enjoy disbursing (state) funds for 'good' causes and programmes; or get a kick out of the prestige (and in the development context, benevolence) of their bureaucratic position and the discretionary power that comes with it. There may even be, as others and I have argued elsewhere,[41] a sadomasochistic dimension to bureaucratic *jouissance*, especially across the global North–South divide: for example, relishing one's position of privilege relative to the Third World 'poor' (i.e. enjoying inequality); or deriving an (unspeakable) satisfaction from siting a toxic environmental project far away from 'us', for instance in a 'remote' area where indigenous people live (i.e. enjoying environmental racism or 'NIMBY'). Here, one luxuriates not despite the recklessness of one's decisions or positioning, but *because* of it.

Ferguson looks off the mark, then, when he insists that institutional decisions are subjectless or unintended. They may not be consciously intentional, but they are unconsciously invested and interested on the part of bureaucratic subjects. In other words, there is no such thing as 'pure' lack of intention of the subjects of which he speaks. By reducing the bureaucratic space to the power–knowledge relationships within it, he misses the disavowed desires, dirty secrets and tainted unspoken enjoyments that affect bureaucrats' choices and strategies.

No wonder that development bureaucracies engage in what Ferguson calls expanding 'symbiotic networks of experts, offices, and salaries'.[42] While bureaucrats may well be blinded by (their own) discursive straightjacketing, it is the dimension of the unconscious that explains more adequately why institutional power is able to sustain itself and multiply: the latter is not only produced discursively in an almost impersonal and anonymous way (i.e. an anti-politics machine), but is able to take hold and expand through libidinal attachments. Or to put it differently, institutional growth is not simply about the circulation and congealment of power, but about how that power is savoured and passionately charged by bureaucratic subjects. There is not-to-be-missed enjoyment, then, in the dissemination of power.[43]

Moreover, what Ferguson sees as 'failure' of projects (which nonetheless result in bureaucratic expansion) can be seen as 'success' from the perspective of unconscious desire. Such outward 'failure' is less the 'unintended' outcome or 'side-effect' of conscious decision-making than the unavoidable other side of rationality – its dirty, secretive, excessive, sometimes even sadomasochistic underside which ensures institutional growth no matter if projects succeed or fail. The 'failure' of projects and the resulting aggrandisement of bureaucratic power are thus the symptoms of the institutional excess and enjoyment; they are proof of the success of unconscious desire.

Finally, from the psychoanalytic perspective, the development bureaucracy appears to be less a 'machine' than a dysfunctional cyborg: intelligent perhaps, but complexly divided; making 'rational' decisions, but being overwhelmed and undermined by the excesses of desire and enjoyment; and deploying knowledge and power in the service of development, but doing so passionately, woundedly or possibly sadomasochistically, but not coldly, automatically or impersonally.

Insecure responses: surrendering to global capitalism

As already emphasised, Foucault's reliance on an immanent notion of power leaves little room for social change and agency. This poses a significant conundrum for Post-Development, doubly so given its stinging critique of development and desire for a radical alternative. Following Foucault, Escobar and Esteva turn to localised forms of resistance, while Ferguson counts on a re-working of governmentality. Yet both responses, I will argue, are unpersuasive if not insecure, ultimately representing an (unconscious) acceptance of the status quo.

Championing social movements and local autonomy: anxious defence?

As is now well known, rather than 'agency', which he sees as relying too much on the Enlightenment myth of the rational subject, Foucault offers up 'resistance'. '[T]here are no relations of power without resistances', he famously pens, envisaging not 'total revolution' but specific and localised struggles to resist the multiple capillaries of power.[44]

True to form, Escobar and Esteva adhere to this Foucauldian logic, calling for the need to 'resist development interventions'[45] and defending grassroots movements and local autonomy. Thus, Escobar writes, 'To the multiplicity of forms of power, we must respond with a multiplicity of localised resistances and counteroffensives'.[46] Esteva, for his part, appears to give up on the (development) state, characterising it as 'naturally ... unjust and arbitrary'.[47] The goal instead is to build decentralised, autonomous spaces as counter-powers to the state.[48] He sees the Zapatista movement as embodying this 'radical democratic' struggle, focusing not on 'seizing State power' but creating local, autonomous spaces that can create 'new political relations'.[49]

However, Escobar and Esteva's arguments are over-confident, with little evidence to support them. There is, first, the issue of whether smaller, localised power struggles can (and do) significantly affect broader structural transformations. Esteva appears to answer in the affirmative: 'a world struggle against GATT or the World Bank, at their headquarters ... seems to be useless ... [Instead] an accumulation of local struggles may well produce the formulation of a new set of arrangements'.[50] But he supplies no corroborating data. There are indeed many cases across the global South of local (and transnational) social movements successfully blocking specific development projects (mining, oil, dams, etc.) backed by, say, the Bank or multinational corporations (MNCs), but to date little to show that such action has significantly undermined the latter's broader, global operations: for example, reversing Western powers' control of the Bank or the Bank's commitments to neoliberal economic policy; or seriously threatening global MNC profits or the goal of capitalist accumulation.[51] Escobar admits as much, appearing to contradict his earlier defence of the local: 'social movements are unlikely to radically transform large structures of domination or dramatically expand elite democracies'.[52]

Post-development's championing of popular movements is further undermined by the fact that many of these movements' issues have been co-opted by the mainstream. As the last three decades have shown, liberal democratic capitalism can so often blunt these movements' effectiveness by culturalising and commodifying their demands. Thus, multiculturalism, while providing civil rights protection and cultural recognition, has often tamed or ignored key socioeconomic demands (e.g. indigenous land claims, economic equality, labour rights). And corporate capitalism has successfully exploited social movement causes by niche-marketing products for the likes of LGBTI groups, young women, 'ethnic' communities, organic food lovers and so forth.[53]

But the glaring glitch in this Post-Development universe is the absence of the state. Escobar barely gives it any place in his work, while Esteva, as pointed out above, is so critical of it that he appears to ignore it altogether in his proposals for a radical democratic alternative. Yet in the absence of a state, what is the authority for coordinating, controlling or protecting against political claims and power? How would locally autonomous spaces withstand the forces of globalisation, particularly capital? What is most glaring, in fact, is that the Post-Development alternative *needs and assumes the state*. A complex network of material, legal and institutional conditions must exist and be maintained in order for 'autonomous' spaces (and social movements, for that matter) *to* function.[54] Decentralisation, equitable land tenure, cultural autonomy and democracy itself would be meaningless without a state that provides safety, security, justice, education, health care and the like. Post-Development might well be highly critical of governmentality and the development state, but it provides no substitute for such a state, all the while surreptitiously (i.e. unconsciously) requiring one.

Given the above gaps – a weak theoretical basis for social transformation (i.e. resistance rather than agency), a lack of adequate evidence and argumentation for a radical alternative to development – Post-Development ends up resorting to inflated claims. Psychoanalytically speaking, I want to suggest in fact that such inflation is an anxious defence against these shaky foundations. To be sure, for Lacan, anxiety is closely connected to a lack/gap; it is a way of sustaining desire – in this case the desire for a credible alternative – despite an absence.[55]

Post-development's first anxious defence is the tendency to romanticise the local. This is a well-known critique that I need not rehearse here. Suffice it to say that critics point to Post-Development's inclination to conflate the 'global' and the 'state' with everything bad, and 'social movements' and the 'local' with everything good (an inclination we noted earlier in relation to 'development', which it similarly rejects outright).[56] Accordingly, Ray Kiely sees Post-Development as the 'last refuge of the noble savage', emphasising how it celebrates the local while downplaying such problems as internal disagreements, gender violence, exploitation or inequality.[57] Esteva is to be especially singled out in this regard: his published work on the Zapatistas and other indigenous movements is mostly a paean to them; he barely has anything negative to say about them and hardly mentions their weaknesses or internal conflicts.[58] Such romanticisation, such black-and-white construction, it seems to me, is camouflage; it is a remedy – an anxious compensation – against weak arguments. It is also, as I have contended elsewhere,[59] a way of consolidating the Self: the desire for the Other as hero is at the same time an anxious desire for the intellectual to appear benevolent or progressive, to ingratiate himself to his audience (or critics).

A second anxious defence is Post-Development's moralistic and inflated rhetoric. This is likely more a question of style and tone than content, although it points once again to an ardent desire for a 'worthy' alternative. In Escobar it is evident in repeated calls for the need to resist, of which here is a sampling: 'localised resistances … *must* be of a radical and uncompromising character … the strategy *must* be aimed at developing a network of struggles, points of resistance, and popular bases'.[60] This 'ought', this appeal to act 'radically', it seems to me, has no discursive grounding; rather, contrary to Foucauldian logic, it is an *extra-discursive* moral exhortation that Escobar is obliged to resort to precisely because of the weak basis for resistance. Indeed, Foucault has himself been taken to task for too simply linking resistance to power without providing an ethico-political basis for which people *would* resist.[61] No wonder, then, that in Escobar this translates into an anxious recourse to a categorical imperative.

The problem is even more pronounced in Esteva's work. His style and tone tend to be rhetorical, if not polemical, with many of his publications written like political manifestos (his co-authored 2013 book is subtitled, *A Radical Manifesto*).[62] Like Escobar, his writing is littered with moral imperatives (e.g. 'It is time to stop the dominant insanity' or 'It is essential that Mexicans adopt new political forms'); but more than Escobar, he engages in exaggeration, if not hyperbole (e.g. 'The Zapatistas activated millions of discontents … with one single word: Enough [Basta]!' or 'An epic is unfolding at the grassroots').[64] Here, it is not just the bravura but its relative intensity and pervasiveness that is psychoanalytically telling: Esteva's insistent repetition is about anxiously searching for the lost object (a radical, alternate politics of development) yet never being able to find it (given, among other things, shaky theoretical grounds and evidence). The result is more – and more insistent – bravura.

Finally, Esteva's moralistic stance is reflected perhaps nowhere better than in the very movement that he most champions – the Zapatistas (EZLN).[65] This is a movement that, at least at its origins in 1994, appeared subversive, instigating a 'revolution' and declaring 'war' against the Mexican state. But since then, it has gradually traded in its uncompromising stance for a more transactional position, mixing negotiation with the state with unilateral declarations of autonomy for Chiapas. It has become notably media-savvy and celebrity conscious, relying on its ubiquitous spokesman, the masked Subcomandante Marcos, to issue a series of calls for social justice and 'declarations' in favour of alternative democratic elections, women's rights and indigenous cultural and political autonomy.[66] It has thus begun to play moral authority, challenging the state and global capitalism mainly symbolically, and being embraced more and more by the mainstream (i.e. political elites, corporate media, advertising, etc.). In this sense, it has become, as Žižek claims, not a counter-point to the state but its 'shadowy double':[67] the EZLN's moralistic protest now places it in an increasingly unthreatening, symbiotic relationship with the state (and capital). In hindsight, as a result of this ultimately placid and conscientious politics, the EZLN could even be seen, not as posing a threat to NAFTA[68] – the movement's main objective at NAFTA's inauguration in 1994 – but helping facilitate NAFTA's integration. This is certainly Žižek's view:

> with Zapatista help, Mexico got the first post-revolutionary government, a government that cut the last links with the historical heritage of Zapata and fully endorsed Mexico's integration into the neo-liberal New World Order.[69]

This is not to disparage the notable struggles of the Zapatista movement or to take away from its successes in gaining a degree of local autonomy. But these local successes have done little to transform wider sociopolitical power. The movement certainly appears to have failed in reaching its initial goals of defeating the Mexican state and dismantling NAFTA. If anything, the EZLN's increasingly unthreatening moralistic stance has let the Mexican state off the hook, allowing the latter to concede a degree of local autonomy to Chiapas but at the same time substantially increase Mexico's integration into NAFTA (of which the recent constitutional privatisation of much of the country's energy sector is a sobering reminder).

The Zapatistas thus illustrate Post-Development's inherent political problem – having to rely on an ineffectual moralistic position to compensate for an equally ineffectual local politics of resistance (at least in terms of effecting broader structural change). Escobar and Esteva's search for a radical alternative to development may be laudable, but their hype, admonitions and rhapsodic tone appear as little more than an anxious cover for a lack of adequate political resources to muster this alternative.

Universal basic income: more welfarism?

If the state is absent in Escobar and Esteva's politics, it is very much present in Ferguson's broader conception of governmentality. His earlier work on bureaucratic politics was highly critical; but his most recent work (especially his 2015 book, *Give a Man a Fish*) is a more hopeful re-working of governmentality, which he characterises as a new Left 'mechanism' or 'art' of government intended to rethink contemporary capitalism and 'conceive of real political alternatives in these neoliberal times'.[70] He sees neoliberalism as a field of governmental techniques that can be 'repurposed' and 'put to work in the service of political projects very different from those usually associated with that word'.[71]

The 'real political alternatives' he has in mind are universal basic income programmes, which are increasingly being discussed and instituted around the world (e.g. Brazil, Alaska, parts of Europe, and most recently in Switzerland, where it was put to a referendum that was defeated). Ferguson's focus is southern Africa, but he writes that the programmes are 'happening in several African countries … [and] in a great many [other] postcolonial states … where leftist and rightist regimes alike have seen fit to introduce policies that transfer cash directly into the hands of the poor'.[72] Thus, a basic income grant (BIG) in South Africa and Namibia is provided to all citizens (with payments to high-income earners recouped through progressive taxes). Grants are unconditional – recipients can choose whether or not to engage in productive labour – and sufficient to cover minimal expenses for such items as food, housing, health care and education.[73]

For Ferguson, these programmes are not charity or social assistance but a 'rightful share'. Citizens become rightful owners of the national wealth, 'of which they have been unjustly deprived'. Thus, the 'most basic citizenship right is … understood not as a right to vote but as a right "to partake in the wealth of the nation"'.[74]

Admittedly, there is much to extol in these programmes. They are distributive in allowing the poorest sections of society in particular to spend more on social goods (nutrition, housing, etc.) and turn down unacceptable or poorly paid jobs. They also help jettison the welfarist and productivist assumptions of mainstream government assistance schemes which, as Ferguson underlines, are so often accompanied by moral opprobrium (e.g. treating recipients as 'welfare bums' or 'parasites') and strict conditions (e.g. obliging people to undergo skills training and seek market employment). Ferguson's Foucauldian loyalties come through in his critique of the surveillance and paternalistic dimensions of traditional 'nanny state' programmes, which he contrasts with the BIG programme's enablement of the poor to actively choose whether and how to participate in society and the market.[75]

Yet, as Žižek points out, while basic income programmes may better help reconcile freedom and equality, we remain very much 'within capitalism – social production remains predominantly capitalist, and redistribution is imposed from the outside by the state apparatus'.[76] This means that it is business as usual for the (transnational) corporate sector which, in the southern African context especially, results in the continued production of socioeconomic inequalities, unevenness and environmental destruction (particularly given the heavy presence of, and reliance on, extractive industries there).[77] Basic income schemes help tinker with liberal democratic capitalism, adding an extra element of social redistribution, but nonetheless posing little threat to the overall framework. Ultimately, such schemes appear to let capitalism off the hook, allowing for its continued smooth functioning.

The problem here is that Ferguson fails to show how neoliberal governmentality is being 're-purposed' or in which way so-called 'radically *distributive* politics'[78] can help transform capitalism in southern Africa. Towards the end of his book he even admits as much, confessing to the limits of existing programmes: 'it is not clear how the southern African BIG campaign is capable of achieving the sort of political traction that would be necessary to achieve its goals'.[79] He stops short, then, of providing the necessary evidence or arguments to show how basic income can challenge (or help the marginalised mobilise against) liberal political economy. Instead, what he offers is a 'capitalism with a human face': a system made more socially responsible but left fundamentally intact; a programme that attends to the worst manifestations of neoliberalism (e.g. the dispossession of the poor) yet thereby ensures its prolongation.

In the end, Ferguson simply gives us more welfarism (or social democracy). The social stigma of such welfarism has perhaps been attenuated,[80] but the overall bureaucratic, bourgeois state-led schema remains. Ironically, his redistributive politics depends on a relatively strong bureaucratic state, the very one whose politics of survival/expansion he was previously critical about. Nowhere does he explain how and why such a top-down set up would acquiesce to anything that deviates from the mainstream or threatens the power (and desires and enjoyments) of bureaucrats. Most importantly, his basic income idea continues to count on the liberal/social democratic compromise with capital that *is* welfarism – give the poor a small piece of the pie, but first ensure capital accumulation; leave the market mostly intact … and attend to its socioenvironmental problems only *after* the fact.

None of this should come as a surprise since, as mentioned earlier, Ferguson touts at the outset how both 'leftist and rightist regimes alike' have embraced basic income. Rather than a hopeful sign, to my mind this underscores precisely the liberal democratic compromise that his basic income proposal cannot escape (rightist regimes are unlikely to compromise on anything that overly threatens market capitalism).

Fetishistic disavowal: capitalism is bad … but it's here to stay

Post-development may well aspire to a radical Left politics, yet what emerges from the above is its avoidance of the traumatic Real, that is, its notable evasion of any direct confrontation with the state or capital. Instead, in the vein of John Holloway's plea to 'change the world without taking power',[81] what Escobar and Esteva resort to is an anxious defence of local resistance and autonomy that outwardly withdraws from the state yet, as emphasised earlier, unconsciously needs and materially depends on it. The two analysts back social movements, yet the latter's localised and moralistic politics tends to be increasingly tolerated if not embraced by the state and capital, thus constructing a relationship of 'mutual parasitism'.[82]

Ferguson similarly refrains from adequately transforming (let alone threatening) the state by offering up a quasi-welfarist politics that operates within the rules already laid down by liberal democratic capitalism. His re-worked governmentality essentially amounts to capitalism with a human face, relying on the bureaucratic bourgeois state to address the worst manifestations of inequality, all the while maintaining the very market economy that creates such inequality. The proof of the pudding is his conception of basic income as a 'rightful share' of national wealth: why is he proffering such a mysteriously abstract conception, which obfuscates the nature and quantity of both 'share' and 'national wealth' (how would one legitimately determine 'real' national wealth or the worth of a just share?), as opposed to something more concrete and precise such as corporate or workplace shares, which would give the poor much more substantive control over their jobs and the economy? The answer surely is that such abstractness allows him to avoid the traumatic Real of (liberal democratic) capitalism. He gentrifies his distributive politics so as not to have to address the key social antagonisms that pit the poor against the wealthy or the proletariat against the bourgeoisie. He anesthetises redistribution against the messy politics of dispossession and inequality by simply extending bureaucratic bourgeois welfarism.[84]

Why such avoidance on the part of Post-Development? Why the unwillingness to confront the Real? I want to suggest that, psychoanalytically speaking, it is a case of fetishistic disavowal (defined earlier). Escobar, Ferguson and Esteva call for a radical politics of development, but end up relying on liberal political economy; they want to resist neoliberal capitalism, but ultimately tolerate if not require the bourgeois state and market. In other words, despite their critique, they have unconsciously surrendered to global capitalism. They may tinker at the edges of it, but they have silently accepted that neoliberal economy, along with its political arrangement – liberal democracy – are here to stay. Hence their avoidance of the traumatic Real of capitalism.

Psychoanalysis points to the unconscious libidinal investments we make so that, in spite of knowing better, we act against our best interests. Unconscious desire trumps knowledge; enjoyment overwhelms reason or intention. Thus, the Post-Development analysts appear to have unconsciously bought into (i.e. fetishised) neoliberal capitalism, despite their outward intellectual protestations and condemnations. This is because, as I have been suggesting, they neither attend to the libidinal underpinnings of power nor have the theoretical inclination or resources to do so, given their Foucauldian orientations. The result is a 'return of the repressed': Post-Development's disavowal of unconscious desires paves the way for its ultimate acquiescence to global capitalism.

If this is true, then we should not be surprised when the likes of Escobar and Esteva resort to hyperbole and romanticisation, as stressed earlier. The latter are an anxious acting out of, an over-compensation for, the weak grounds for resistance to capitalism and the absence of a psychoanalysis to adequately confront the Real (excess, antagonism) of their desires.

However, I do not want to suggest that these Post-Development analysts are uniquely fetishistic. I side with Žižek in claiming that fetishistic disavowal is the key ideological phenomenon of our age.[85] Global capitalism seduces us all by producing fantasies/objects that libidinally capture us, despite our best intentions; this is why not just the subjects of development, but also the very critical (Post-Development) analysts who study them can (and do) easily succumb to its charms. Žižek takes several key Left figures to task (including Antonio Negri, Simon Critchley, Yannis Stavrakakis and Ernesto Laclau) for their seemingly radical yet ultimately reformist politics. According to him, all tend to yield to a polite, unthreatening and half-hearted politics, and the proof is that the status quo tolerates, acknowledges and even accedes to many of their so-called radical demands ('third way' social democracy, gay rights, local cooperatives, autonomous collectives, etc.). All deplore and criticise capitalism and its attendant penchant for inequality and unevenness, but ultimately, for Žižek, all manifest a secret desire that nothing too much must change.[86]

The great challenge, then, is acknowledging and squarely facing the Real of our age. Knowledge and critical intellectual distance are not nearly enough, it seems. If we are to conceive of an 'alternative to development', to be able to meaningfully look beyond the immensely dominant horizon of global capitalism, psychoanalysis suggests that, as first step at least, we need to recognise and confront our unconscious desires.

Conclusion

I have claimed that Post-Development ignores to its own peril the role of desire in its critique of capitalist development. By not considering unconscious passions, it cannot explain how people enjoy rather than reject development, so that capitalism continues to flourish, not perish, globally. Moreover, by not attending to the Real of its own desires, Post-Development ends up buying into global capitalism. Despite its critique of both state and capital, it not only fears confronting them but also winds up relying on them.

I have suggested that part of the problem is Post-Development's dependence on Foucauldian discourse analysis, which provides meagre resources for resistance to capitalism, while also refusing any form of transcendence (e.g. the psychoanalytic Real) that would enable stronger forms of agency. Post-development suffers precisely from this lack of grounding for a radical politics. Yet my proposal that Post-Development engages in fetishistic disavowal points to a more endemic problem: that discourse analysis is itself a surrender to global capitalism, and that it offers only resistance, not radicalism or agency, precisely to honour this surrender. This aligns with Fredric Jameson's argument that postmodernism is but the cultural logic of late capitalism and hence critical but unthreatening.[87] It also adheres to Gillian Hart's claim concerning Post-Development: it is part of the development of capitalism. Recalling Polanyi's notion of capitalism's 'double movement', whereby market forces unleash social havoc that in turn generates demands for social justice, she characterises Post-Development critiques as 'expressions of the opposing forces contained within capitalism'.[88] For her, Post-Development's so-called radicalism is thus integral to the development of development. I agree, except that I would want to supplement her political economy analysis with a psychoanalysis.

Disclosure statement

No potential conflict of interest was reported by the author.

Acknowledgements

Many thanks to the anonymous reviewers, and to Maria Eriksson Baaz and the editor of this special issue, Aram Ziai, for their valuable comments. I also wish to thank Arturo Escobar for his warmth and intellectual generosity. I am forever grateful to Kent Murnaghan for his support and perspicacious insights.

Notes

1. Ferguson, *The Anti-Politics Machine*, 20, italics added.
2. Towards the end of *The Anti-Politics Machine*, 275–276, Ferguson makes fleeting reference to Deleuze and 'desire', even mentioning the 'unacknowledged' and 'non-discursive' structures embedded in development discourse. But he refrains from elaborating these ideas or their psychoanalytic implications. In other words, by evading the psychoanalytic route, he appears to implicitly accept the Foucauldian notion of desire as discursively produced, as opposed to seeing desire as an unconscious, non-discursive remainder à la Lacan.
3. de Vries, "Don't Compromise."
4. Escobar, *Territories of Difference*, 175.

5. I will use the terms 'global capitalism' and 'liberal democratic capitalism' interchangeably as, in my view, both global capitalism and liberal democracy go together: liberal democracy is the political arrangement for (global) capitalism.
6. It should be noted that, while both Escobar and Ferguson have mostly stuck to their Foucauldianism, their more recent work does diverge, with Escobar embracing a more utopic decoloniality perspective (e.g. Mignolo and Escobar, *Globalisation and the Decolonial Option*) and Ferguson a more realist welfarism.
7. Ziai, "The Ambivalence of Post-Development"; Brigg, "Post-Development, Foucault." For example, while Foucault advocates a historically contingent and sensitive notion of discourse, Esteva tends to view development discourse as monolithic, seeing power exercised, not biopolitically as Foucault would have it, but by a single 'Western' force. Esteva, "Development," 6, 17; Brigg, "Post-Development, Foucault," 424–425.
8. Esteva's "Regenerating People's Space" (1987) is perhaps his most Foucauldian, using the term 'development discourse' and citing Foucault (137, 146). His later works make more fleeting references to Foucault, although still identifying with 'post-modern' ideas more generally (as witnessed, for example, by the title of his 1998 co-authored book, *Grassroots Post-Modernism*).
9. Foucault, *Archaeology of Knowledge*, 49.
10. Escobar, "Discourse and Power in Development," 384; Escobar, *Encountering Development*, 9, 11. Escobar's statement closely follows Said's famous definition of Orientalism as 'the enormously systematic discipline by which European culture was able to manage – and even produce – the Orient politically, sociologically, militarily, ideologically, scientifically, and imaginatively during the post-Enlightenment period'. Said, *Orientalism*, 3.
11. Esteva, "Regenerating People's Space," 146; Ferguson, *The Anti-Politics Machine*, 8.
12. Escobar, *Encountering Development*, 215; Esteva, "Development," 6, 8; Ziai, "Post-Development," 846.
13. Esteva, "Regenerating People's Space," 146; Esteva, Babones, and Babcicky, *The Future of Development*, 105; Foucault, *Power/Knowledge*, 81.
14. Foucault, "Governmentality."
15. Escobar, "Discourse and Power in Development," 387–388; Escobar, *Encountering Development*, 17, 21ff., 216; Escobar, "Beyond the Search"; Escobar, *Territories*, 69ff. See also Esteva, Babones, and Babcicky, *The Future of Development*, 115.
16. Ferguson, *The Anti-Politics Machine*, 70.
17. Esteva, "Development," 6, 16.
18. Ferguson, *The Anti-Politics Machine*, xvi, xv, 275.
19. Escobar, *Encountering Development*, 6.
20. Foucault, *Power/Knowledge*, 156, italics added.
21. Lacan, *Ecrits*, 287. See also Homer, *Jacques Lacan*, 71–72; Kapoor, "Psychoanalysis and Development: Contributions," 1122.
22. Copjec, *Read My Desire*, 19. Note that Lacanian psychoanalysis focuses not on some essentialised and separate 'individual' mind or psyche (and is in fact very critical of behavioural psychology on this score) but on a transindividualised 'subject' (of language), which it sees as split, that is, a subject of lack, always troubled and divided by a gap, an excess (i.e. the unconscious). Kapoor, "Psychoanalysis and Development: Contributions," 1123.
23. Foucault, *History of Sexuality*, 15ff., 129–130. In his later work, Foucault is quite critical of psychoanalysis, seeing it (along with medicine generally) as a normalising technology in the service of our disciplinary societies.
24. Copjec, *Read My Desire*, 14. See also Žižek, *Enjoy Your Symptom*, 81; Vighi and Feldner, *Žižek*, 18–23.
25. Harstock, "Foucault on Power," 168–170; Sawicki, "Feminism and the Power of Discourse"; Fraser, *Unruly Practices*, 31.
26. Lacan calls the Real 'extimate' (*extimité*), that is, intimately external or internally transcendent. Lacan, *The Seminar, Book VII*, 71. Žižek illustrates the idea this way: 'What all epochs share is not some trans-epochal constant feature; it is, rather, that they are all answers to the same

deadlock [the Real]. I think this is the only consistent position' (Žižek and Daly, *Conversations With Žižek*, 76).

27. Kiely, "The Last Refuge," 30.
28. Escobar, *Encountering Development*, 215, 226.
29. Esteva, "Development," 6; Ziai, "The Ambivalence of Post-Development," 1048.
30. Kiely, "The Last Refuge"; Storey, "Post-Development Theory," 42; Ziai, "Post-Development," 839.
31. Rigg, *Southeast Asia*, 36.
32. Kiely, "The Last Refuge", 44.
33. Esteva and Prakash, *Grassroots Post-Modernism*, 25.
34. CSPI, "Soda Companies."
35. Žižek, *How to Read Lacan*, 79.
36. Žižek, *The Sublime Object of Ideology*, 18, 32–33.
37. Lacan, *The Seminar, Book XI*, 273.
38. Kapoor, "Psychoanalysis and Development: An Introduction," 1118–1119.
39. Ferguson, *The Anti-Politics Machine*, 19–21, 254–255.
40. Ibid., 19, 21.
41. Kapoor, *Celebrity Humanitarianism*, 34; Kapoor, "Psychoanalysis and Development: Contributions," 1130–1132; Wilson, "The Joy of Inequality." Note that associating *jouissance* with sadomasochism is wholly within the Lacanian tradition; the term denotes excessive, irrational pleasure, after all. Lacan, *The Seminar, Book XI*, 185.
42. Ferguson, *The Anti-Politics Machine*, 269. Note, as the rest of this paragraph/section underlines, that I am not trying to replace Ferguson's argument, but enrich and complicate it with a psychoanalytic argument. As I shall claim later (see Universal basic income), the fact that there is a not-to-be-missed passionate enjoyment in bureaucratic politics further undermines Ferguson's recent attempt at 'repurposing' neoliberal governmentality: it is improbable that bureaucrats passionately invested in the system (and their own bureaucratic power/privilege) would be easily amenable to change, and Ferguson fails to specify otherwise.
43. Institutional expansion can be explained more precisely by what Lacanians call 'drive', which is to be distinguished from desire: while both desire and drive arise as a result an impossible striving for fullness, desire is a futile attempt to fill the void with particular objects that never satisfy, while drive is a constant circulation around objects, deriving satisfaction (*jouissance*) from the futility of searching. Drive thus feeds off always frustrated desire. Hence my suggestion that institutional growth happens through the enjoyment of power (i.e. drive). Kapoor, "What 'Drives' Capitalist Development?"
44. Foucault, *Power/Knowledge*, 142, 99.
45. Escobar, *Encountering Development*, 11, 215, 218.
46. Escobar, "Discourse and Power in Development," 377; see also Escobar and Alvarez, *The Making of Social Movements*; Alavarez, Dagnino, and Escobar, *Cultures of Politics*.
47. Esteva, "The Zapatistas and People's Power," 165; see also Esteva and Prakash, *Grassroots Post-Modernism*, 161.
48. Esteva, "The Zapatistas and People's Power," 163, 155ff.; Esteva, "The Meaning," 126. See also Esteva, Babones, and Babcicky, *The Future of Development*, 124ff.; Esteva and Prakash, *Grassroots Post-Modernism*, 152ff., 172ff.
49. Esteva, "The Zapatistas and People's Power," 173.
50. Esteva and Prakash, *Grassroots Post-Modernism*, 31, 34.
51. Kirsch, *Mining Capitalism*; della Porta, *Social Movements*; McMichael, *Development and Social Change*, 213ff.; Aronowitz, *Left Turn*, especially 1ff., 109 ff.
52. Escobar and Alvarez, *The Making of Social Movements*, 325–326; see also Escobar, *Encountering Development*, 226.
53. Žižek, *The Ticklish Subject*, 355; della Porta, *Social Movements*.
54. Žižek, *Organs without Bodies*, 179.
55. Lacan, *Anxiety*, 16ff., 157ff.
56. Kiely, "The Last Refuge"; Nederveen Pieterse, "After Post-Development"; Storey, "Post-Development Theory"; Hart, "Development Critiques in the 1990s," 655; Ziai, "Post-Development."

57. Kiely, "The Last Refuge," 46.
58. Esteva, "The Zapatistas and People's Power"; Esteva, "The Meaning"; Esteva and Prakash, *Grassroots Post-Modernism*.
59. Kapoor, *The Postcolonial Politics of Development*, 51–53.
60. Escobar, "Discourse and Power in Development," 381, italics added. See also a series of similar statements on page 393, including: 'a strategy of resistance *must* develop' and 'the discourse of development *must* be dismantled' (italics added); in Escobar, *Encountering Development*, 98, 110, 209, 222. This is an illustrative, not exhaustive list, as is the case with the examples from Esteva's work listed in notes 63 and 64 below.
61. Harstock, "Foucault on Power," 170.
62. Esteva, Babones, and Babcicky, *The Future of Development*.
63. Esteva, Babones, and Babcicky, *The Future of Development*, 70; Esteva, "The Meaning and Scope," 142. Other examples of moral exhortation can be found in Esteva, Babones, and Babcicky, *The Future of Development*, x, 117; Esteva, "The Zapatistas and People's Power," 169; Esteva and Prakash, *Grassroots Post-Modernism*, 42ff.
64. Esteva, "The Zapatistas," 162; Esteva and Prakash, *Grassroots Post-Modernism*, xiv. Other examples of such generalisations and bravura can be found in Esteva, "The Zapatistas and People's Power," 162, 174; Esteva and Prakash, *Grassroots Post-Modernism*, 8, 204; Esteva, "The Meaning and Scope," 139. Esteva rationalises his 'broad brush strokes' by stating that he aims at 'breaking the prison of academic disciplinary boundaries' in order to speak to 'non-specialists' (Esteva and Prakash, *Grassroots Post-Modernism*, 8). But I am suggesting they are more likely an unconscious cover/compensation for ineffectual arguments and theoretical grounding.
65. Esteva has worked as an advisor to the Zapatista Army for National Liberation (EZLN) in Chiapas, especially in connection with its negotiations with the Mexican government. So perhaps it is no coincidence that the EZLN's moralistic politics has rubbed off on him, or indeed that his own moralistic stance has been, at least to a small degree, reproduced in the EZLN.
66. Esteva, "The Zapatistas and People's Power."
67. Žižek, *Organs without Bodies*, 177.
68. North American Free Trade Agreement.
69. Žižek, *Organs without Bodies*, 178.
70. Ferguson, "The Uses of Neoliberalism," 173; Ferguson, *Give a Man a Fish*, 32, xiii.
71. Ferguson, "The Uses of Neoliberalism," 183.
72. Ibid., 173.
73. Ferguson, *Give a Man a Fish*, 15, 17.
74. Ibid., 24, 26, 56.
75. Ibid., 19, 36, 38ff., 177; Ferguson, "The Uses of Neoliberalism," 174.
76. Žižek, *Living in the End Times*, 236, italics added. It should be noted that, ironically, Ferguson marshals Žižek's statement that universal basic income is 'arguably the Left's only original economic idea of the last few decades' (Žižek, *Living in the End Times*, 233) to back up his case (Ferguson, *Give a Man a Fish*, 193), but he does so disingenuously since Žižek is in fact highly critical of the idea, despite it seeming attractive.
77. Mensah, *Neoliberalism and Globalisation in Africa*; Bond, *Looting Africa*.
78. Ferguson, *Give a Man a Fish*, 198, italics in original.
79. Ferguson, *Give a Man a Fish*, 200. Ferguson's book is scattered with sentences that favour what he calls a certain 'empiricism' and 'inductivism' so that, according to him, his project can start from what people do 'instead of from some theorist's idea of what they ought to do' (Ferguson, *Give a Man a Fish*, 140; on p. 32 he even approvingly quotes Foucault on the need for 'a certain empiricism'). Yet by the same token, given his admission of the currently unfavourable record of basic income in southern Africa, his arguments must succumb to these same empiricist predilections.
80. The paternalism Ferguson is worried about may be reduced through basic income programmes, but it would by no means be eliminated. Society would still be divided into 'basic income' and (let's say) 'productive' citizens, so that hierarchical distinctions and social stigma and resentment would still remain. Žižek, *Living in the End Times*, 240–241.

81. Holloway, *Change the World*.
82. Žižek, *In Defence of Lost Causes*, 349.
83. Per-capita income could be one measure, but as is well-known, this is not an unproblematic indicator, given its tendency to hide sometimes wide inequalities (in income, gender and racialised positioning, etc.) and the environmental costs of development.
84. Japhy Wilson accuses Ferguson's variant of Post-Development of being 'complicit in the reproduction of relations of domination' by excluding the dimension of desire and the Real; Wilson, "Fantasy Machine," 1156.
85. Žižek, *The Sublime Object*, 18, 32–33.
86. Žižek, *In Defence of Lost Causes*, 337ff.
87. Jameson, *Postmodernism*.
88. Hart, "Development Critiques in the 1990s," 650. Ray Kiely also makes a similar argument in "The Last Refuge," 48.

Bibliography

Alavarez, Sonia, Evelina Dagnino, and Arturo Escobar, eds. *Cultures of Politics/Politics of Cultures: Re-Visioning Latin American Social Movements*. Boulder: Westview Press, 1998.

Aronowitz, Stanley. *Left Turn: Forging a New Political Future*. New York: Routledge, 2006 (republished 2016).

Bond, Patrick. *Looting Africa: the Economics of Exploitation*. London: Zed, 2006.

Brigg, Morgan. "Post-Development, Foucault Metaphor." *Third World Quarterly* 23, no. 3 (2002): 421–436.

Copjec, Joan. *Read My Desire: Lacan against the Historicists*. Cambridge, MA: MIT Press, 1994.

CSPI (Center for Science in the Public Interest). "Soda Companies Turning to Low- and Middle-Income Countries to Replace Sagging US Soda Sales." https://cspinet.org/new/201602091.html.

della Porta, Donatella. *Social Movements in Times of Austerity*. Cambridge: Polity Press, 2015.

de Vries, Pieter. "Don't compromise your desire for development! A Lacanian/Deleuzian Rethinking of the Anti-Politics Machine." *Third World Quarterly* 28, no. 1 (2007): 25–43.

Escobar, Arturo. "Discourse and Power in Development: Michel Foucault and the Relevance of his Work to the Third World." *Alternatives* 10 ([1984] 1985): 377–400.

Escobar, Arturo. *Encountering Development: the Making and Unmaking of the Third World*. Princeton, NJ: Princeton University Press, 1995.

Escobar, Arturo. "Beyond the Search for a Paradigm? Post-Development and beyond." *Development* 43, no. 4 (2000): 11–14.

Escobar, Arturo. *Territories of Difference: Place, Movements, Life, Redes*. Durham: Duke University Press, 2008.

Escobar, Arturo, and Sonia Alvarez, eds. *The Making of Social Movements in Latin America: Identity, Strategy, and Democracy*. Boulder: Westview Press, 1992.

Esteva, Gustavo. "Regenerating People's Space." *Alternatives* 12, no. 1 (1987): 125–152.

Esteva, Gustavo. "Development." In *The Development Dictionary*, edited by W. Sachs, 6–25. London: Zed, 1992.

Esteva, Gustavo. "The Zapatistas and People's Power." *Capital and Class* 23, no. 2 (1999): 153–182.

Esteva, Gustavo. "The Meaning and Scope of the Struggle for Autonomy." *Latin American Perspectives* 28, no. 2 (2001): 120–148.

Esteva, Gustavo, and Madhu Suri Prakash. *Grassroots Post-Modernism: Remaking the Soil of Cultures*. London: Zed, 1998 (2014 edition).

Esteva, Gustavo, Salvatore Babones, and Philipp Babcicky. *The Future of Development: A Radical Manifesto*. Bristol: Policy Press, 2013.

Ferguson, James. *The Anti-Politics Machine: 'Development', Depoliticization, and Bureaucratic Power in Lesotho*. Minneapolis, MN: University of Minnesota Press, 1990.

Ferguson, James. "The Uses of Neoliberalism." *Antipode* 41, no. S1 (2009): 166–184.

Ferguson, James. *Give a Man a Fish: Reflections on the New Politics of Distribution*. Durham, NC: Duke University Press, 2015.

Foucault, Michel. *The Archeology of Knowledge*. Translated by A. M. Sheridan Smith. New York: Pantheon, 1972.

Foucault, Michel. *Power/Knowledge: Selected Interviews and Other Writings 1972-1977*. Edited by C. Gordon. New York: Pantheon, 1980.

Foucault, Michel. *History of Sexuality*. Vol. 1. Translated by Robert Hurley. New York: Vintage, 1990.

Foucault, Michel. "Governmentality." In *The Foucault Effect: Studies in Governmentality*, edited by G. Burchell, C. Gordon, and P. Miller, 87–104. Chicago, IL: University of Chicago Press, 1991.

Fraser, Nancy. *Unruly Practices: Power, Discourse and Gender in Contemporary Social Theory*. Minneapolis: University of Minnesota Press, 1989.

Hart, Gillian. "Development Critiques in the 1990s: Culs de Sac and Promising Paths." *Progress in Human Geography* 25, no. 4 (2001): 649–658.

Harstock, Nancy. "Foucault on Power: A Theory for Women?" In *Feminism/Postmodernism*, edited by L. Nicholson, 157–175. New York: Routledge, 1990.

Holloway, John. *Change the World without Taking Power*. London: Pluto Press, 2010.

Homer, Sean. *Jacques Lacan*. London: Routledge, 2005.

Jameson, Fredric. *Postmodernism, or, The Cultural Logic of Late Capitalism*. London: Verso, 1991.

Kapoor, Ilan. *The Postcolonial Politics of Development*. London: Routledge, 2008.

Kapoor, Ilan. *Celebrity Humanitarianism: The Ideology of Global Charity*. London: Routledge, 2013.

Kapoor, Ilan. "Psychoanalysis and Development: Contributions, Examples, Limits." *Third World Quarterly* 35, no. 7 (2014): 1120–1143.

Kapoor, Ilan. "Psychoanalysis and Development: An Introduction." *Third World Quarterly* 35, no. 7 (2014): 1117–1119.

Kapoor, Ilan. "What 'Drives' Capitalist Development?" *Human Geography* 23, no. 5 (2015): 66–78.

Kiely, Ray. "The Last Refuge of the Noble Savage? A Critical Assessment of Post-Development Theory." *The European Journal of Development Research* 11, no. 1 (1999): 30–55.

Kirsch, Stuart. *Mining Capitalism: The Relationship Between Corporations and Their Critics*. Oakland, CA: University of California Press, 2014.

Lacan, Jacques. *Écrits: A Selection*, Translated by Alan Sheridan. New York: W.W. Norton, 1977.

Lacan, Jacques. *The Seminar, Book VII: The Ethics of Psychoanalysis, 1959-60*. Translated by D. Porter. London: Routledge, 1992.

Lacan, Jacques. *The Seminar, Book XI: The Four Fundamental Concepts of Psychoanalysis, 1964*. Translated by A. Sheridan. New York: Norton, 1998.

Lacan, Jacques. *Anxiety: The Seminar of Jacques Lacan, Book X*, edited by J.-A. Miller. Cambridge: Polity Press, 2014.

Mignolo, Walter, and Arturo Escobar. *Globalization and the Decolonial Option*. London: Routledge, 2010.

McMichael, Philip. *Development and Social Change: A Global Perspective*. 6th ed. Thousand Oaks, CA: Sage, 2017.

Mensah, Joseph, ed. *Neoliberalism and Globalization in Africa: Contestations on the Embattled Continent*. New York: Palgrave Macmillan, 2008.

Nederveen Pieterse, Jan. "'After Post-Development'." *Third World Quarterly* 21, no. 2 (2000): 175–191.

Rigg, Jonathan. *Southeast Asia: The Human Landscape of Modernization and Development*. London: Routledge, 1997.

Said, Edward. *Orientalism*. London: Penguin, 1978.

Sawicki, Jana. "Feminism and the Power of Discourse." In *After Foucault: Humanistic Knowledge, Postmodern Challenges*, edited by J. Arac, 161–178. New Brunswick: Rutgers University Press, 1988.

Storey, Andy. "Post-Development Theory: Romanticism and Pontius Pilate Politics." *Development* 43, no. 4 (2000): 40–46.

Vighi, Fabio, and Heiko Feldner. *Žižek: Beyond Foucault*. Basingstoke: Palgrave Macmillan, 2007.

Wilson, Japhy. "Fantasy Machine: Philanthrocapitalism as an Ideological Formation." *Third World Quarterly* 35, no. 7 (2014): 1144–1161.

Wilson, Japhy. "The Joy of Inequality: The Libidinal Economy of Compassionate Consumerism." *International Journal of Zizek Studies* 9, no. 2 (2016): 1–26.

Ziai, Aram. "The Ambivalence of Post-Development: Between Reactionary Populism and Radical Democracy." *Third World Quarterly* 25, no. 6 (2004): 1045–1060.

Ziai, Aram. "Post-Development: Premature Burials and Haunting Ghosts." *Development and Change* 46, no. 4 (2015): 833–854.

Žižek, Slavoj. *The Sublime Object of Ideology*. London: Verso, 1989.

Žižek, Slavoj. *The Ticklish Subject: The Absent Centre of Political Ontology*. London: Verso, 1999.

Žižek, Slavoj. *Enjoy Your Symptom! Jacques Lacan In Hollywood and Out*. London: Routledge, 2001.

Žižek, Slavoj. *How to Read Lacan*. London: Granta, 2006.

Žižek, Slavoj. *In Defense of Lost Causes*. London: Verso, 2008.

Žižek, Slavoj. *Living in the End Times*. London: Verso, 2008.

Žižek, Slavoj. *Organs without Bodies: On Deleuze and Consequences*. London: Routledge, 2012.

Žižek, Slavoj, and Glyn Daly. *Conversations with Žižek*. Cambridge: Polity, 2004.

Worlds beyond the political? Post-development approaches in practices of transnational solidarity activism

Kalpana Wilson

ABSTRACT

This article considers some ways in which one strand of post-development thinking has influenced non-governmental organisation (NGO)-led activist discourses and practices of transnational solidarity. It argues that there has been a tendency for these discourses and practices to rearticulate racialised constructions of unspoiled and authentic 'natives' requiring protection which are historically embedded in colonial practices of governance. In turn, this has meant the failure to acknowledge indigenous histories of political organisation and resistance. Further, the characterisation of development in binary terms as both homogeneous and always undesirable has meant the delegitimisation of demands for equality as well as the neglect of the implications of the decisive shift from developmentalism to neoliberal globalisation as the dominant paradigm. Drawing upon a discussion of aspects of the local, national and transnational campaign to prevent proposed bauxite mining in the Niyamgiri hills in Odisha (India), I argue that given that international NGOs are themselves embedded in the architecture of neoliberal development and aid, their campaigning activities can be understood as facilitating the displacement and marginalisation of local activists and silencing their complex engagements with ideas of development. This potentially defuses and depoliticises opposition to neoliberal forms of development, while transposing collective agency onto undifferentiated publics in the Global North, processes which, however, continue to be actively resisted.

Introduction

Like other theoretical trends within international development, post-development has emerged from particular processes of struggle and contestation over development policies and practices. Unlike others, however, its central project is the deconstruction of development itself, which is characterised as 'a pervasive cultural discourse with profound consequences for the production of social reality in the so-called Third World'.[1] For post-development writers, this deconstruction leads to 'the possibility of imagining a post-development era, one in which the centrality of development as an organizing principle of social life would no longer hold'.[2] Post-development has thus sought to transcend debates about the ways in which development could be best achieved and to question the very desirability of development as a goal, however it was conceived. Much post-development thinking drew inspiration from the 'new social movements' of the 1990s[3] which while resisting the manifestations of neoliberal globalisation such as displacement, dispossession and environmental destruction tended to invoke community rather than class identities, unlike other radical movements with similar concerns which were led by left political parties (although in reality this distinction was not always clear cut) and to eschew prescriptions for social transformation. For Escobar, this was epitomised by 'the Zapatistas' slogan of "one no and many yeses", with the no being to neo-liberal globalisation and to the European modernity model underlying it, and the many yeses being region-specific, movement-specific'.[4] I argue that despite this affinity with one strand of radical social movements, in the intervening period, specific elements of post-development thinking have been selectively appropriated within the discourses and practices of international non-governmental organizations (NGOs) which are embedded in the architecture of mainstream development. This article explores the implications of this for the discursive and material practices of transnational solidarity in which these NGOs engage, and suggests that there are specific aspects within post-development thought which have made it particularly amenable to this incorporation within contemporary dominant development discourses.

I focus here on three critiques of post-development and examine their implications for transnational solidarity activism. These are, firstly, the tendency in one strand of post-development to romanticise and essentialise the local and traditional in ways which reproduce and reinforce racialised colonial discourses[5]; secondly, post-development's failure to engage with demands for development, conceived in multiple ways, articulated by poor and marginalised groups[6]; and, thirdly, the neglect within post-development scholarship of the transition from developmentalism to neoliberalism as the dominant development approach, and its material and discursive implications.[7]

In his seminal post-development text *Encountering Development*,[8] Escobar warns against the romanticisation of knowledges and practices constructed as 'local' and 'traditional' and the elision of the inequalities, histories and power relations which shape them, arguing that

> one must be careful not to naturalise 'traditional' worlds, that is, valorize as innocent and 'natural' an order produced by history … These orders can also be interpreted in terms of specific effects of power and meaning. The 'local' moreover, is neither unconnected nor unconstructed, as is thought at times'[9]

However, arguably one strand within post-development thinking continued to reproduce precisely these elisions and naturalisations. Ziai[10] makes a distinction between 'sceptical' post-development, which he suggests 'does not generally reject all elements of modernity but promotes cultural hybridization, is critical towards cultural traditions, abstains from articulating desirable models of society and employs a dynamic, constructivist conception of culture',[11] and a 'conservative', 'neo-populist' post-development which 'promotes the return to (often idealized) subsistence communities, employing an essentialised conception of culture'.[12] This latter approach is epitomised perhaps by Rahnema and Bawtree's frequently cited description of development which decries how

> under the banner of development and progress … a merciless war was fought against the age-old traditions of communal solidarity. The virtues of simplicity and conviviality, of noble forms of poverty, of the wisdom of relying on each other, and of the arts of suffering were derided as signs of 'underdevelopment'.[13]

This approach is evidently structured by many of the binary oppositions which charac-terise colonial discourses: tradition vs modernity, simplicity vs sophistication, communality vs individuality, spirituality vs rationality. As Maria Eriksson Baaz points out, 'while Post-Development and the Eurocentric modernization approach are on one level based on oppos-ing strategies, the two discourses share a central discursive strategy – representations of *difference*'.[14] On one level, then, 'conservative Post-Development' can be understood simply as reversing the hierarchy and revaluing the attributes which are ascribed to the 'derided' Other. But, arguably, it can also be seen as rearticulating and updating elements which are in fact already pervasive within colonial discourse.

Racialised colonial representations of the 'noble savage' of the Americas tragically but inexorably doomed to extinction, the 'dignity' of the 'Pathan warrior' or the 'innocence and simplicity' of the Indian 'hill tribes' are just some of many which produced subjects who were simultaneously romanticised and infantilised. Postcolonial theorists like Bhabha[15] have high-lighted this ambivalence which pervades colonial stereotypes, highlighting how the colo-nised 'Other' can also be the (forbidden) object of desire. Striking continuities between Western dissatisfaction with European modernity which produced the trope of the 'noble savage' and a comparable projection by post-development thinkers onto the 'local' and 'traditional' has been noted.[16] As we will see, contemporary narratives about poor people in the Global South emerging from a broadly post-development framework operate within racialised regimes of representation[17] in which the desire for the racialised other[18] can be understood as repressed or, in more Foucauldian terms, as *produced* by colonial discourse.[19] Yet while marked by ambivalence, such representations also directly and indirectly informed strategies of governmentality and facilitated the extraction of resources. The 'savage' char-acteristics of nobility, dignity and simplicity were continually contrasted not only with those of the European rational man with complex individual needs and desires, but also with those of other colonised subjects who were constructed as lacking these premodern virtues. For example, many of the *adivasi*/indigenous peoples of India were designated by British colonial administrators as 'primitive tribes' at risk of exploitation by 'cunning' and 'avaricious' 'Hindus' from the plains and therefore requiring the protection of the colonial state. This obscured the role of colonialism in exploiting and dispossessing adivasi groups, both directly, and indirectly through local usurers, traders and landlords. It denied the underlying reasons for the series of adivasi uprisings against forced dispossession of land, oppressive taxation, forced and indentured labour and reservation of forests,[20] while it also legitimised strategies of surveillance and control over adivasi populations through special regulations which 'at best amounted to paternal despotism'.[21] It also constructed the colonial state as protecting adivasi communities from exposure to the materially and morally destructive effects of modernity and progress, effects which are constructed in a way which can be understood as prefiguring elements of the post-development critique.

This discourse, however, co-existed with and complemented the dominant strand within colonial discourse in which 'primitive', 'backward' groups were viewed as the objects of mis-sions to civilise and develop, justifying brutal repression when they resisted. This is evident, for example, in colonial ethnologist W.W. Hunter's explanation of the uprising by the adivasi Santhal community in 1855: 'The inoffensive but only half tamed highlander had tasted blood, and in a moment his savage nature returned'.[22] I argue that this co-existence also characterises contemporary development interventions, and has partially enabled the incorporation of one strand of post-development critiques within dominant discourses of development.

While Escobar explicitly critiques the coloniality of this discourse[23] and has come to be more closely associated with ideas of decoloniality which have developed in Latin America[24] through the work of Walter Mignolo, Maria Lugones and Anibal Quijano among others, I suggest that it is the strand of post-development thinking which remains rooted in notions of timeless traditions and undifferentiated communities which has been most influential within NGO-led transnational solidarity activism.

This version of post-development again raises the spectre of 'authenticity' and, like its colonial predecessors, abrogates to itself the power to identify it. Postcolonial feminist writers have explored the ways in which the construction of the 'authentic native', 'the unspoiled African, Asian or Native American who remains more preoccupied with his/her image of the real native – the truly different – than with the issues of hegemony, racism, feminism and social change'[25] sustains and reproduces contemporary racialised relations of power. The notion of 'inauthenticity' also becomes a weapon of dominant groups with an interest in maintaining the status quo. In the Indian context, conservative forces have long mobilised it in attempts to discredit transformative politics such as those of Marxism and feminism as 'alien';[26] recently we have seen right-wing Hindu nationalist ideologues explicitly mobilising the ideas of post-development theorists like Ashis Nandy[27] in their promotion of an upper caste Hindu supremacist project which, ironically, is not only colonial in origin, but today is inseparable from the corporate-driven predatory neoliberal version of 'development' pursued by the Narendra Modi government.

If the tendency to romanticise and essentialise the 'local' and 'traditional' in post-development thinking is arguably more visible within the 'conservative' strand of its proponents, a more pervasive (though related) problem is post-development's understanding of critiques of poverty and global economic inequality as themselves an effect of development discourse. As Arturo Escobar summarised the post-development position:

> Poverty on a global scale was a discovery of the post-World War II period. If within market societies the poor were defined as lacking what the rich had in terms of money and material possessions, poor countries came to be similarly defined in relation to the standards of wealth of the more economically advantaged nations.[28]

This approach has been seen as leading to a failure to engage with the struggles of poor and marginalised communities which are actually articulated in terms of needs and desires for development,[29] albeit quite differently conceived from the notion of 'development' being promoted by global capital. I argue in this article that this failure has particularly marked implications for practices of transnational solidarity activism. In particular, the incorporation of some elements of post-development thinking within the discourses and practices of international NGOs has actually contributed to displacing and marginalising local activists and defusing the potential for a transnational politics of solidarity and resistance to neoliberal forms of development.

Further, in highlighting the continuities in the 'meta-narratives' of development and the continuing centrality of discourses of progress, improvement and meeting goals, post-development approaches obscure the very substantial changes in global patterns of capital accumulation, and relatedly in the dominant development approaches, which have marked the period since 1945. Post-development as well as postcolonial critiques have highlighted the Eurocentrism of a monolithic developmentalism based on planning and characterised by 'the construction of roads, hydroelectric projects, schools, hospitals and factories'.[30] But this does not recognise the decisive shift since the 1980s from the 'developmental state' to neoliberal 'accumulation by dispossession'[31] which, by contrast, has witnessed the destruction of such public services and infrastructure, and under which 'development' is more likely to entail unplanned and untrammelled incursions by footloose corporate capital seeking to extract and export resources.

This neglect of historical changes in development is particularly problematic because of the capacity of neoliberal discourses to flexibly incorporate critical ideas. Increasingly, the notions of 'difference' and multiple subjectivities which poststructuralists have used to counter hegemonic constructions of knowledge have, like the notion of agency, been appropriated, transformed and redeployed within neoliberal discourses of development. They reappear in the context of an emphasis on 'choice', individual 'empowerment' through the market and users' control over (for which read responsibility for) social provision, legitimising policies of liberalisation, privatisation and outright corporate plunder, and marginalising questions of inequality, oppression and exploitation.[32] More fundamentally, development is no longer primarily discursively constructed in the universalising terms of 'catching up with the West' which have been the main focus of critique by post-development theorists, but also offered possibilities for appropriation by progressive and left forces in the Global South.[33] As Duffield has noted, the rise of sustainable development as the dominant development paradigm marked a break with the 'aspirational goal' of modernisation theory which claimed that living standards in the 'underdeveloped' world would eventually come to resemble those in the 'developed' countries.[34] In the era of the Sustainable Development Goals, North/South inequality is instead assumed to be necessary to sustainability, and the emphasis is now on 'adaptation' and 'resilience', in the interests of containment of the Global South and maintaining the security of the Global North.[35] While capital has always functioned through differentiation as well as homogenisation,[36] 'difference', is now explicitly affirmed in dominant development discourses in the form of this permanent global inequality, which is seen as a requirement for sustainability.

In what follows, I will explore the themes outlined above through a discussion of aspects of the local, national and transnational campaign to prevent proposed bauxite mining in the Niyamgiri hills in Odisha (India). I first examine and discuss the way the sustained resistance of the Dongria Kond people in the region to the mining corporation Vedanta has been represented internationally, how this mobilises tropes which are also present in some post-development discourses, and the possible relationship between these representations and the structural position of international NGOs within the contemporary architecture of development. The article then goes on to explore these questions further though a reflection on some contesting practices of solidarity which emerged in the British-based campaign against mining in Niyamgiri. Lastly, I consider an alternative set of representations of the movement against mining in Niyamgiri, discussing the analysis put forward by participants in the Niyamgiri movement in the independently produced film *Wira Pdika*, and, in particular, their complex engagements with questions of development.

Niyamgiri: solidarity or protection of the 'authentic'?

Vedanta is a London Financial Times Stock Exchange (FTSE) 250 listed Mining Corporation. It is 67.99% owned by Anil Agarwal and his family (as of January 2014) through a series of tax havens and holding companies. The UK's Department for International Development (DfID) and Department of Trade and Industry helped launch it on the London Stock Exchange in 2003. Vedanta has mines, refineries and factories in various states in India – as well as in Zambia, Liberia, South Africa, Namibia, Australia and Ireland. It has recently expanded its activities from aluminium to iron ore, copper, zinc and oil.[37] Vedanta's aluminium refinery at Lanjigarh in Odisha has been held responsible for polluting fertile agricultural land over a vast area in a region which has seen starvation deaths every year since 2007; contaminating drinking water sources by dumping fly ash and toxic red mud into river streams; and displacing thousands of people from their homes. For more than a decade, people who live in this region, mainly belonging to Dongria Kond adivasi communities, have been waging a sustained struggle against the company's incursions in the region, resisting Vedanta's plans for a 73-million-tonne bauxite mine in the Niyamgiri hills and a sixfold increase in the Lanjigarh refinery's capacity, with massive blockades and protests. The Dongria Konds depend on the hills and their complex ecology for their livelihoods, and consider the mountain targeted for mining to be sacred. Their movement has won some important victories, most notably in 2013 when Vedanta was stopped from mining the Niyamgiri hills for bauxite, costing the company up to $10 billion USD. But the struggle against the corporation, which is still pressing to be allowed to mine for bauxite and to expand its refinery, continues. Since then, the state has stepped up repression of the movement, and appears to be seeking to replicate strategies of militarisation and police and army terror adopted to pave the way for corporate exploitation in other mineral-rich Indian states by falsely labelling local activists as Maoists and Naxalites.[38] Recent protests against this wave of arrests, torture and false cases in Niyamgiri have also been highly critical of the role of NGOs in the movement, with banners reading 'Niyamgiri Suraksha Samiti demands that all foreign and local NGOs in the area duping us should Go Back!' and 'we rejected NGOs'.[39]

As this suggests, a range of transnational actors have engaged in campaigning and advocacy in opposition to Vedanta's activities in Odisha, including a number of international NGOs, as well as unfunded activist campaigns and organisations,[40] and this has led to the production and circulation of a variety of representations of the movement against Vedanta.[41] Among these is an article published in June 2010 by the British *Observer* newspaper, written by the celebrity environmental campaigner Bianca Jagger and entitled 'The Battle for Niyamgiri'. Jagger had visited the Indian state of Odisha on a trip organised by the international NGO Action Aid, to meet local Dongria Kond adivasi people who are overwhelmingly opposed to the proposal by Vedanta to mine for bauxite in the Niyamgiri hills.

The article provides an interesting example of the way racialised constructions of the 'authentic other' have been mobilised in the context of NGO-led solidarity initiatives. In the article, Jagger explains the situation with Vedanta, and the destructive impact of the aluminium refinery set up by Vedanta in neighbouring Lanjigarh, and then goes on to describe her 'sudden' meeting with 'a large gathering of more than 100 members of the Dongria Kondh':

> A group of smiling women surround me and put their arms around my waist, leading me to my assigned seat. They give me a bouquet of scented flowers and welcome everyone by putting the traditional 'tika' on our foreheads, made with the paste of turmeric and rice. The women and girls are wearing their traditional colourful clothes, beaded jewellery, hairpins, ear- and nose rings, and head necklaces. In contrast, the men wear plain dhotis. Many have long hair tied into a knot in the nape of their necks. Some are carrying axes on their shoulders and in their hands. One can already see the influence of 'development' in some of the young men wearing shirts and T-shirts.[42]

Many of the binary oppositions discussed above are in play here – the undifferentiated 'smiling women', the repeated use of the word 'traditional' which recurs throughout the article, and the detailed description of the 'colourful' clothes and 'beaded' jewellery worn by the women, combine to produce an image of the Other both exotic and childlike. The reader is invited to share the experience and the anthropological gaze of the intrepid Western visitor, honoured and respected by these 'natives' who, we have been told earlier, are 'considered an endangered Primitive Tribal Group and are recognised as "a people requiring particular protection."'[43] Thus, while the article is framed as an appeal for support for the resistance of the Dongria Konds to the depredations of a British corporation, it does this in part by inter-textual reference to a whole canon of narratives of white European exploration, 'discovery', conquest and benevolent trusteeship of 'primitive' peoples.

Consistent with these earlier accounts, there is a preoccupation with racialised embodied difference: the clothing and ornaments of the 'beautiful young girls' are emphasised, but, notably, it is in Jagger's description of the Dongria Kond men that this is most evident. The references to the men's 'plain dhotis', 'long hair tied into a knot in the nape of their necks' 'axes on their shoulders and in their hands' and (in an earlier passage) 'hand-made drums' conjure up the full panoply of associations with the 'noble savage' of colonial imagination and his racialised masculinity, and the desire which this evokes. Echoing the post-developmentalists, Jaggar appears to mourn the baneful influence of 'development' – not in the destruction of rivers and mountains and livelihoods which the Dongria Konds have organised to resist, but in the affective loss of embodied authenticity which she experiences when she sees 'some of the young men wearing shirts and T-shirts'.

But it is by combining discursive critique of texts like these with analysis of the material relations within which Action Aid (which organised Jagger's visit) and other development NGOs are positioned, and what this has meant for the struggle against Vedanta, that, I suggest, we can gain important insights into the implications of this incorporation of elements of post-development discourse into NGO-led interventions.

The role of the NGO sector in neoliberal development models has been the subject of in-depth analysis and critique.[44] The 1980s saw NGOs beginning to take over the role of service provision in the wake of the dismantling of existing forms of social protection by the state, and mobilising people's – and particularly women's – unpaid labour to fill the gap. The period from the 1990s onwards, coinciding with the rise of the 'good governance' agenda, has seen them simultaneously play a much wider role as the chosen representatives of 'civil society' as conceptualised in dominant neoliberal approaches. In some contexts, this takes the form of actively mobilising and expressing support for neoliberal economic policies or imperial intervention.[45] But they have also, it has been argued, played a key role *within* broad movements of people's resistance to the depredations of global capital, a role which has centred around delinking this resistance from political ideology and coherent visions of social transformation. This depoliticisation operates both at the level of the way this resistance is represented by NGOs, who by virtue of the scale of their funding have considerable control over the production and circulation of information, and at the level of direct intervention into and attempts to control people's movements.[46] These multiple roles, and the big international NGOs' central positioning within the architecture of development (which also incorporates the donor governments which fund them as well as transnational corporations and 'philanthrocapitalist' organisations like the Gates Foundation) makes their apparently contradictory actions easier to understand.

These contradictions have appeared to be particularly marked in the case of Action Aid. It has been publicly critical of neoliberal policies, and publicises its involvement in campaigns like that of Niyamgiri. At the same time, activists have argued that particularly through its close links with (and funding from) the British government's international aid department DfID, it is implicated in facilitating corporate exploitation, with notable inconsistences in its approach:

> Action Aid appeared to be campaigning vigorously against Vedanta only to apparently change course from time to time: on August 14th 2010, as part of its Corporate Social Responsibility project 'Partners in Change' it was part of a jury which awarded Vedanta the 'Best Community Development' for its 'good work' around the Lanjigarh refinery at Niyamgiri hills, as advertised proudly on Vedanta's website (accessed 25/7/11). Four days later Vedanta's Lanjigarh project was damned by the Indian government's Saxena Report for violations of tribal rights and illegal land grabbing.[47]

The ambiguous role of NGOs in the context of aluminium mining in Odisha has been examined in detail by Padel and Das.[48] They point out that while Action Aid 'has been one of the most pro-active' in the campaign against Vedanta in Niyamgiri, it also receives funds from DfID, which has actively promoted the company. In 2000, as Whittel[49] notes, the government of Orissa (now Odisha)

> was guaranteed World Bank and DfID money to address its fiscal deficit, as long as it undertook 'a program to reform the business and direction of government'. … In conjunction with a series of reforms commercialising the water and power sectors, the Industrial Policy Resolution and the Orissa Rehabilitation and Resettlement Policy, jointly written and funded by the DfID in 2001 and 2006 respectively, encouraged companies such as Vedanta, POSCO and Tata to come and mine the bauxite, coal and iron ore under the state's lands, paying rates of tax that do little to fill the state's already depleted coffers and displacing thousands of people.

Padel and Das trace the long-term relationship between Action Aid's Indian organisation and corporate capital which has developed in tandem with India's adoption of neoliberal economic policies since the early 1990s:

> as the New Economic Policy was coming into effect, Action Aid India [AAI] formed a Corporate Partnership unit in 1993, which became 'Partners in Change' in 1995, with funding from the Ford Foundation, DFID and Novib, laying the ground for MoUs [Memorandums of Understanding] with Sterlite (part of the Vedanta Group) ICICI (one of its major investor banks) and other corporate houses: business partnerships that raise questions about AAI's involvement in the movement to save Niyamgiri.[50]

These apparent contradictions and other similar ones which followed seem be consistent with the understanding put forward by unfunded local campaigning organisations like the Niyamgiri Suraksha Samiti that the interventions of international NGOs sought to manage and limit rather than support resistance to corporate capital. The sense that these NGOs were attempting to bypass existing peoples' organisations and 'handpick' individuals to represent the community in international campaigns, in order to depoliticise and defuse them, further contributed to the anger towards NGOs expressed during recent protests.

NGOs and 'aliens' in the London anti-Vedanta protests

The role of NGOs in movements such as that around Niyamgiri also raises questions about practices of transnational solidarity, requiring further engagement with the ways in which processes of racialisation are embedded within them. In this section I discuss aspects of the campaign in solidarity with the struggle in Niyamgiri in Britain in order to reflect on this further.

The protest which took place outside Vedanta plc's 2010 Annual General Meeting near Westminster in Central London brought together a range of groups and individuals with diverse political approaches. As a participant in this protest (and similar ones in 2009 and in following years) I was struck by several aspects of it, which I explain below.

This protest and others like it can be understood as examples of the way power operates spatially on a micro level. Firstly and more obviously, this takes place through the reproduction of the boundary between the shareholders' meeting where decisions are taken inside a building guarded by the police (and which was on this occasion infiltrated by a number of activists who had bought shares in order to raise questions inside the meeting), and the street outside where protestors raised the demands of the people whose lives were most directly affected by the decisions. But it is also interesting to consider the unacknowledged and racialised boundaries within the space of the protest itself, and its reproduction of the wider positioning of NGOs in relation to people's movements.

In many ways the protest felt like a space within which two very different types of political action, each with its own political imaginaries, and material and discursive practices, overlapped, without quite touching.[51] The non-NGO protestors, mainly members of non-funded campaigning organisations and individuals, and many of South Asian origin, held huge hand-painted placards with photographs of Anil Agarwal, under the slogan 'Wanted – for Vedanta's Murders and Environmental Crimes'; they angrily yelled slogans like 'Anil Agarwal – blood on your hands' and 'Who Killed Arsi Majhi? [one of the leaders of the movement in Niyamgiri] Vedanta did!' Other placards targeted then British Prime Minister David Cameron for his collusion with Vedanta's crimes. On either side of this group of protestors stood two smaller groups, whose manner was quite different. On one side, members of Survival International stood quietly and slightly apart, all wearing yellow t-shirts printed with the Survival logo and holding matching printed placards with the slogan 'Vedanta's Profits – Dongria's Destruction' and the name of the organisation prominently displayed.[52] On the other side, again slightly apart, stood another group of about half a dozen protestors, all in red t-shirts printed with the Action Aid logo. From time to time, this group launched into a group chant of their own which ran: 'One: we are the people, Two: a little bit louder, Three: we've got to get Vedanta out of here!'

However, a great deal of the publicity generated by the protests focused on the presence of two actors, who had been hired by Survival International to attend the protest in blue body paint to represent members of the Na'vi tribe – the inhabitants of the planet Pandora from the then recently released science fiction film *Avatar* (2009). The two actors were photographed holding placards reading 'Save the Real Avatar Tribe'. This parallel had first been drawn by Survival International in February of that year, when they placed an advertisement in entertainment magazine *Variety* invoking the idea that 'Avatar is fantasy … and real' and appealing to James Cameron, *Avatar*'s director, to 'please help the Dongria'.[53] This notion of the 'real *Avatar* tribe' was taken up extensively in the media (including in India newspapers) and became a very popular theme of campaigning around Niyamgiri.

Campaigners on Niyamgiri were not the only ones to make use of the *Avatar* theme. As Deuze explains, in Bil'in, a Palestinian village located in the central West Bank, where weekly protests have been taking place against the Israeli state's *construction* of a wall around its territory, five protestors wore Na'vi costumes in February 2010.[54] A statement on Bil'in's website explained: '[l]ike Palestinians, the Avatars fight imperialism, although the colonizers have different origins. The Avatars' presence in Bil'in today symbolizes the united resistance to imperialism of all kinds'.[55] But these two contexts in which the Avatar parallel was invoked have very different implications for questions of agency and representation. Significantly, in contrast to the Palestinian case, members of the Dongria Kond community have never dressed up as Na'vi themselves: whereas, as their statement clearly explains, the Palestinian protestors mobilised Avatar as a political metaphor, the Dongria Konds are represented by others as literally resembling the Na'vi.

We must ask, then, how people in India who are organising to resist the plunder of their environment by corporate capital come to be represented in this way by their supporters in Britain and elsewhere? What does this imply for notions of solidarity? What are the particular discursive and material relationships which make this kind of representation possible, and which in turn are reproduced by its circulation?

Part of the effectiveness of the comparison with the film clearly stems from the parallels between the situation in Niyamgiri and the plot of *Avatar*, which revolves around a corporate/military mission from Earth to drive the 'native humanoid' Na'vi from their homes in order to mine for the valuable 'unobtainium ore'. But the parallel is taken much further: the focus in this campaign is not actually on the aggressors but on the irreducible 'otherness' of the Dongria Konds themselves – who have been represented as the embodiment of the 'real-life' Na'vi to the extent where several online photographic images used in campaigning fused the face of a young Dongria Kond girl with that of one of the blue-skinned Na'vi characters in a 'mirror' image. Further, the Avatar campaigning strategy 'worked', I would argue, precisely because the portrayal of the Na'vi in *Avatar* (unlike other science fiction portrayals of 'aliens', sympathetic or otherwise) is clearly based on markers more often associated with racialised groups. The Na'vi have evidently human features which include large, widely spaced eyes, flat noses and high cheekbones – and wear their hair in braids and beads. Their blue skin evokes the body painting practiced by certain indigenous groups in the Global South, while their lifestyle 'in harmony' with nature is also clearly intended to indicate their equivalence to these groups. Significantly, notwithstanding the use of makeup and computer-generated imagery (CGI) in creating the Na'vi on screen, none of the actors selected to play the main Na'vi characters are white. I would argue that the emphasis on racialised 'otherness' in the mobilisation of the *Avatar* parallel foregrounds a colonial ethos of morality, where people in the 'developed world' are made aware of an obligation to act to protect both the environment and those whose lives are lived in harmony with it and are apparently as yet untouched by 'development' – people who are assumed to live (as the Na'vi literally do) 'on another planet' from those campaigning on their behalf, a world beyond the political. Even more significantly, it forecloses certain kinds of political approaches – those which recognise the collective political resistance organised by the people affected and take this as the starting point for actions based on an ethos of solidarity, linking it with struggles taking place in the Global North.

While the Dongria Konds are recognised to be overwhelmingly opposed to Vedanta's plans in NGO-produced materials, there is little acknowledgement of the existence of organisations among them or their initiation of and sustained participation in political action and advocacy. Whereas some observers characterise such tendencies as 'oversimplification', a side effect resulting from international NGOs' compulsion to attract public support in their home countries and compete with each other to raise funds, I would suggest we need to look at them more carefully.

The construction of the members of the Dongria Kond community within NGO discourses as pre-modern, innocent and uncorrupted 'noble savages' appears to preclude consideration of their engagement in sustained political organising which has made possible the series of protests, marches and blockades which prevented mining from 2002 onwards; their historic and present relation to political structures such as the various levels and arms of the Indian state and its colonial predecessor; or their articulation of any visions of the future which depart from a narrative of restoration of 'traditional' lifestyles and livelihoods. By contrast, the possibility of collective action to bring about change by an undifferentiated British public is emphasised and valorised by the major NGOs involved in the Vedanta campaign. This public is expected to act on behalf of, rather than alongside, poor people in the Global South, a transposition of agency epitomised by the British Action Aid volunteers' adoption of the 'we are the people' chant which originated in South Africa. The celebration of popular agency which the chant articulates here comes to be framed in terms of moral obligation towards 'other' worlds rather than a political project of transformation of one's own, an obligation also implied in Survival International's slogan 'Their Future is in Your Hands'. Mutual solidarity, alliances between different but related struggles, or even the process of identifying shared interests in change – all of which require a much more extensive and committed engagement with actually existing struggles in the South, representing what for Spivak is 'not just a problem of knowledge but a call to a relationship'[56] – are precluded in this framework in which the British public is called upon to prevent the primordial desecration of the 'unspoiled'.

Increasingly, while development discourses bestow 'agency' upon people – and specifically women – in the Global South in the form of individual entrepreneurialism and the moral imperative to help oneself,[57] collective agency is located in and largely restricted to undifferentiated publics/civil society in the Global North, and here the imperative is again a moral one, to help – or rescue – less-fortunate others. In this model, connections between campaigners in the North and those for whom they advocate can only be configured along two axes: that of the 'heroic rescue narrative',[58] and that of obligation based on the benefits to the Global North of unequal trade, resource extraction and environmental destruction in the South. The possibility of complicating and blurring this North/South dichotomy by acknowledging that the 'public' in the Global North is itself structured by a highly unequal distribution of these benefits along lines of class, race and gender in particular, and that there may be struggles taking place there which are confronting the same forces which are ravaging the Global South, is ruled out in this model. This is particularly dangerous since it not only limits the scope and effectiveness of campaigning, but with its reiteration of immutable difference, it actively reinforces the currently dominant 'development/security' model of relations between people in the Global North and South in which people in (or entering from) the South are identified primarily as a racialised threat to those in the North, which can only be contained through neoliberal forms of development. While campaigning international NGOs articulate this differently, they arguably mobilise the same logic, which also contributes to the exclusive re-imagining of the 'British public' as a homogeneous entity with shared national interests, in a manoeuvre characteristic of imperialism.[59]

As portrayed in British-based NGO-led campaigns, then, the struggle over Niyamgiri appears to epitomise the binary opposition which characterises conservative post-development theorising – with Vedanta as the harbinger of development on the one hand and the Dongria Kond community representing tradition, simplicity and harmony with the natural world on the other. This narrative is repeated in a range of NGO-produced material on Niyamgiri online and in print and broadcast media.[60]

However, there are also other representations which have emerged from the people's struggle in Niyamgiri and the surrounding area, which suggest that what people in Niyamgiri are actually saying is considerably more complex and does not fit neatly into these categories. In the following section I consider one of these, the film *Wira Pdika* (2005).[61]

'We want permanent development': counter-narratives from Niyamgiri

Independently produced and directed by Amarendra Das and Samarendra Das and released in 2005, *Wira Pdika*'s title is in the Kui language spoken by the Konds. In Odia, the film is called *Matir Poko, Company Loko*. Both translate as *Earthworm, Company Man*, the film's English title.

In this film, which does not contain any narration or voiceovers, people from the Dongria Kond and Majhi Kond communities across a wider region which includes Niyamgiri speak about their lives and their struggles against 'the company'. As the film shows, a series of aluminium companies have been attempting to mine bauxite in the region since the early 1990s, and faced sustained resistance from the people living there. It should be clear that this discussion of *Wira Pdika* does not seek to present some representations as 'more authentic' than others in the sense we have already referred to. The film does not make claims to present an 'unbiased' view of events; on the contrary, it is an example of politically committed filmmaking seeking to produce work which can be widely used as a tool in the struggle. Rather, I seek in this section to demonstrate the existence of ideas and perspectives which have been silenced in mainstream representations that incorporate elements of post-development thinking, and to provoke reflection on how this silencing relates to particular political projects and structures of power.

The film conveys a number of ideas which counter the dominant NGO narrative in relation to the region. The Kond people's opposition to corporate mining has been sustained and organised and is informed by a history of struggles going back to the colonial period, with a long and often bitter experience of interactions with politicians of major parties, the state in the form of the District and Block administrations and the police, and NGOs. For example, Kond activist Bhagaban Majhi, a spokesperson of the movement against mining in the area, describes the prelude to the launch of the movement against corporate projects to mine bauxite in the area 13 years earlier[62]:

> Anantaram Majhi, the Congress Party MLA [Member of Legislative Assembly], came to our meetings, he spoke against the company … he said he will help us if we vote for him. We elected him but nothing changed, he didn't speak for us but took the company's side. That is how the movement started. (*Wira Pdika*)

As this suggests, while marginalised and excluded on multiple levels, the Konds are in fact not isolated from the outside world as Survival's notion of a 'remote tribe' implies, but have been compelled to negotiate relations with other groups and with the state over several centuries. They are incorporated into the lowest levels of a social formation structured by caste and class. The people interviewed in *Wira Pdika* convey this powerfully in their frequent references to the discrimination and contemptuous attitudes towards adivasis which they face, and the way these attitudes are used to suppress dissent:

We, the people of 12–13 villages wrote an application to the district administration saying 'We are not going to give up our water and forests, we won't part with our Niyamgiri'. Then (they said) – 'Who has written this? A pig or a goat? Does he have a name or an address?' (Daisingh Majhi, Niyamgiri Surakshya Samiti, [Save Niyamgiri Campaign] Belamba, in *Wira Pdika*)

They ridicule us and say 'what are the Konds up to? What do they know?' (Bhima Majhi, Niyamgiri Surakshya Samiti, Turiguda, in *Wira Pdika*)

In addition, while people express a sense of the sacredness of Niyamgiri, this is articulated in combination with an emphasis on their material dependence on the mountain, and also with an analysis of the possible ecological impacts of its destruction, in the context of already precarious livelihoods. In the same interview cited above, Bhima Majhi explains,

> We are resisting for our motherland, for our mountain. The summer is very hot already. It will get hotter if [Vedanta] Sterlite comes. You won't get rain then. The summer is so hard for us already, so we want them to stop. So we oppose Sterlite, we oppose the government. (*Wira Pdika*)

Similarly, Bhagaban Majhi explains that

> we are tribal cultivators (*chasi adivasi*) … earthworms (*matir poko*) … we want permanent development (*sthahi unnati*). Provide us with irrigation for our land. Give us hospitals and medicines, give us schools and teachers. Give us our land and forests. We don't need the company. Get rid of the company. We have been saying this for 13 years but the government is not listening. (*Wira Pdika*)

Further, as this makes clear, the Konds' struggle against Vedanta is not primarily conceived as a struggle against development and in favour of maintaining the status quo, or what Rahnema and Bawtree call 'noble forms of poverty'.[63] In fact, the notion of 'development' (*unnati*, which can also be translated as 'progress') is one which they frequently mobilised to make concrete demands for change: for education, healthcare, irrigation – resources which the state has consistently failed to provide to their communities. The discourse which pervades *Wira Pdika*, then, is one in which people make claims not against development, but about the kinds of development which they do and do not want. In this context, the post-development-influenced approach deployed by NGOs which constructs contact with the outside world as polluting the purity of the Konds' lifestyle acts to silence these demands and construct them as inauthentic and illegitimate.[64] As Eriksson Baaz writes,

> the problem of the Post-Development approach … is not only located in the risk of relegating questions of poverty and economic inequality to the margins by an infatuated interest in the authentic and the unspoiled. It is also about the ways in which demands for economic development and equality are delegitimized.[65]

Lastly, many of the people interviewed in the film make it clear that they conceptualise the activities of companies like Vedanta as representing not development, but plunder. The opposition to 'the company' is articulated over and over again in terms of resisting the expropriation and seizure of resources – water, land, forests and mountains, destruction and environmental degradation.

While, as we have suggested, it has been neglected in post-development thinking, for those resisting 'the company' in Odisha, the distinction between a developmental state and one which merely exists to facilitate 'accumulation by dispossession' is extremely significant. As Bhagaban Majhi asks:

> Where will the people go once the construction is over? Is this development? You say you are here for development – how many high schools, colleges, engineering colleges, health centres

will you set up? When we ask these questions, they stay silent ... Destroying age-old resources is not development ... Over the 23 years (which the bauxite will last) the government will get Rs 12–13 billion – but the company will grab Rs 2880 billion in 23 years. They will build red mud tanks and ash ponds – they will pollute our environment and export our resources abroad. How does our government benefit, the public benefit? Whereas the company benefits so much. He had no answer. (*Wira Pdika*).

But fighting on this difficult terrain in which the notion of 'development' itself becomes a site of contestation also requires an awareness of how the people's demands for 'stable' (*sthai*) development – for education, healthcare, irrigation and other forms of state provision – too can be appropriated and manipulated. In *Wira Pdika* we hear how the companies used the familiar practices of Indian state developmentalism, with its preoccupation with enumeration and classification inherited from the colonial state, in order to gather information for its own purposes:

Earlier when company people came, they would disguise themselves as veterinary doctors. They would get the information they required from us on the pretext of doing surveys about our cattle, sheep and chickens. They also came to us as auxiliary nurses and midwives (ANM) to ask about statistics of village population ... how many women, how many children ... After many such surveys, we became suspicious and would not let them carry out further surveys. (Bhagaban Majhi, in *Wira Pdika*).

After this strategy failed, the mining corporates set up their own NGOs, forming an organisation called Utkal Rural Development Society (URDS).[66]

They started free health check-up camps, free seed donation camps, free adult education. We saw they ... were really company people. They aimed to win people's confidence and to divide people. So we protested against this organisation. Then they brought in Business Partners for Development – we also opposed them. After this there was repression, jail, false cases, police beating up protesters ... (Bhagaban Majhi, in *Wira Pdika*).

Conclusion

This article has identified three main elements associated with a section of post-development thinking which are visible in the discourse and material practices of international NGOs engaged in transnational campaigns against mining in Niyamgiri. Firstly, through both campaigning discourses (such as those in Bianca Jagger's article discussed above) and practices (such as the use of the *Avatar* parallel) they reproduce racialised representations of the 'noble savage' in need of protection in order that they may remain isolated from and untainted by modernity. Secondly, and following on from this, they do not acknowledge the history and present of sustained political organising and resistance among the adivasi people of the region, and the specific demands for social and economic change as well as potentially counter-hegemonic articulations of 'development' which emerge from this. Thirdly, they reproduce a narrative based on binary oppositions which, by constructing development as a pernicious and homogeneous metanarrative, obscures changes in the dominant model of development which have facilitated the current unrestrained exploitation and appropriation of the region's resources by footloose transnational capital.

The experiences and analyses articulated by adivasi activists in the film *Wira Pdika*, I suggest, provide a counter-narrative which directly challenges these understandings and elisions. We also need to consider the work which these understandings, selectively appropriated from post-development, do in paradoxically displacing and marginalising local activists and silencing their complex engagements with ideas of development, potentially defusing and depoliticising resistance to neoliberal forms of development, while transposing collective agency onto undifferentiated publics in the Global North. As I have suggested, this requires not only an engagement with the discourses produced by international NGOs, but also a recognition of how they are materially embedded within the contemporary architecture of neoliberal development, illustrated for example, in the case of Niyamgiri, by the complex interrelationship between Action Aid, DfID and Vedanta. It is this recognition which has led, as we have noted, to a direct rejection of NGO intervention by local activists in Niyamgiri.

In the mid-1990s, post-development thinkers drew inspiration from a wave of 'New Social Movements' which they saw as autonomous, polyvalent and, unlike those which had preceded them, not geared towards systematic structural transformations. Two decades on, not only have movements against neoliberal global capital multiplied and intensified, but their articulation of collective visions of transformation, albeit often multiple ones, has become impossible to ignore. The practice of transnational political solidarity with these movements, I would suggest, requires a sustained engagement with these visions, and a decisive break with the colonial discursive and material relations which continue to structure NGO campaigning.

Disclosure statement

No potential conflict of interest was reported by the author.

Acknowledgements

I would like to thank Aram Ziai, Maria Eriksson Baaz and two anonymous reviewers for their helpful comments on an earlier draft of this article. I would also like to thank Samarendra Das for his comments on my earlier writing on this subject.

Notes

1. Escobar, "Beyond the Search."
2. Ibid., 11.
3. See for example Esteva and Prakash, *Grassroots Post-Modernism*.
4. Escobar and Ciobanu, "Latin America in a Post-development Era."
5. Eriksson Baaz, *Paternalism of Partnership*; Wilson, *Race, Racism and Development*.
6. Andreasson, this volume; Eriksson Baaz, *Paternalism of Partnership*.
7. Wilson, *Race, Racism and Development*.
8. Escobar, *Encountering Development*.
9. Ibid.,170.

10. Ziai, "Ambivalence of Post-Development"; Ziai, "Post-Development: Premature Burials."
11. Ziai, "Post-Development: Premature Burials," 837.
12. Ibid., 837.
13. Rahnema and Bawtree, *Post-Development Reader*, x.
14. Eriksson Baaz, *Paternalism of Partnership*,160, italics in original.
15. Bhabha, "The Other Question."
16. Eriksson Baaz, *Paternalism of Partnership*.
17. Hall, 'Spectacle of the "Other."'
18. Fanon, *Black Skins White Masks*.
19. Stoler, *Race and the Education of Desire*.
20. Das, *Republic of Bihar*, 69; Sundar, *Subalterns and Sovereigns*.
21. Das, *Republic of Bihar*, 60.
22. Hunter, *Statistical Account of Bengal*.
23. Escobar, "Beyond the Search."
24. Ziai, "Post-Development: Premature Burials."
25. Trinh, *Woman, Native, Other*, 88; see also Chow, *Writing Diaspora*.
26. Narayan, *Dislocating Cultures*.
27. See for example Juluri, "Hinduism and its Culture Wars"; Shah, "Against Caste in British Law."
28. Escobar, *Encountering Development*, 22–4.
29. Eriksson Baaz, *Paternalism of Partnership*; Kapoor, this volume; Andreasson, this volume.
30. White, "'Gender Lens': A Racial Blinder?", 56.
31. Harvey, "'New' Imperialism: Accumulation by Dispossession."
32. See Wilson, "Towards a Radical Re-appropriation" for a discussion of this in the context of gender, development and neo-liberal feminism.
33. Ahmad, "Politics of Literary Postcoloniality"; Cooper "Modernizing Bureaucrats," cited in Ziai, "Post-Development: Premature Burials."
34. Duffield, "Getting Savages to Fight Barbarians," 152.
35. Wilson, "Re-centring 'Race' in Development.
36. Hall, "Gramsci's Relevance," 24.
37. Foil Vedanta, https://www.foilvedanta.org/about/
38. Tripathi, "Activists Object to Home Ministry."
39. Foil Vedanta, 'Niyamgiri Decries State Human Rights Abuses."
40. The latter notably includes Foil Vedanta, which has been opposing Vedanta's activities in India, Zambia, South Africa and elsewhere.
41. See for example web pages such as that of Survival International on Niyamgiri, https://www.survivalinternational.org/tribes/dongria
42. Jagger, "Battle for Niyamgiri."
43. Ibid.
44. See for example Manji and O'Coill, "Missionary Position"; Hearn, "African NGOs: The New Compradors"; Choudry and Kapoor, *NGOization*; Wallace, "NGO Dilemmas."
45. Robinson, *Promoting Polyarchy*; Chandler, *From Kosovo to Kabul and Beyond*.
46. In the case of Niyamgiri, it was these attempts to intervene in and redirect the movement which led to the protests against NGOs reported in 2016.
47. South Asia Solidarity Group, 'Strange Bedfellows for Action Aid.
48. Padel and Das, *Out of this Earth*.
49. Whittel, "Dodgy Development: DfID in India."
50. Padel and Das, *Out of this Earth*, 523–4.
51. For a discussion of a spatial approach to protest, see Kaika and Karaliotas' "Spatialization of Democratic Politics" in which the authors discuss the co-existence of two distinct political imaginaries in the 'Indignants' protests in Athens' Syntagma Square.
52. This is not intended to reproduce ideas about authentic or inauthentic protestors (or placards!).
53. Cameron did not respond to Survival's appeal. He did go to the Amazon rainforest with another group, US-based Amazon Watch, to meet the Kayapo people threatened by a dam planned by the Brazilian government.

54. Deuze, "Survival of the Mediated."
55. Bil'in Popular Committee, 2010, cited in Deuze, "Survival of the Mediated," 6.
56. Landry and MacLean, *Spivak Reader,* 5.
57. Wilson, "Towards a Radical Re-appropriation."
58. See for example Nash, "Global Citizenship as Show Business," on the Make Poverty History campaign.
59. This is accompanied by the exclusion from 'Britishness' of those who are constructed as not sharing these 'national' interests.
60. For example, in Survival's online film *Mine: Story of a Sacred Mountain* (narrated in the hushed tones usually reserved for wildlife films by the quintessentially upper-class-English voice of actress Joanna Lumley), the emphasis is on the isolated existence of the 'remote tribe' and the idyllic environment in which they had been living until the advent of the mining company.
61. Dir. Amarendra Das and Samarendra Das, 2005, India.
62. The first of these was Utkal Alumina International Ltd. (UAIL) which sought to mine bauxite deposits covering 10 or more square kilometres on top of the mountain Bapla Mali. UAIL was formed by Indal and Tata in a joint venture with Norway's Norsk Hydro; Padel and Das, *Out of this Earth,* 109.
63. Rahnema and Bawtree, *Post-Development Reader,* x.
64. Similar processes can be observed in a variety of contexts: for example, McNeish's discussion of indigenous protests in Bolivia against the Morales government's road building project in the TIPNIS [*Territorio Indígena y Parque Nacional Isiboro Secure* (Isiboro Sécure National Park and Indigenous Territory)] region highlights that 'In contrast to the information provided by supporting environmental organizations and analysts, the indigenous leaders stated that their protest was not intended to indefinitely stop all development projects in their territory, but rather to oppose the irresponsible building of a highway that, given its routing, would clearly not benefit local communities in the TIPNIS ... Johnny, an Osomomo leader who had taken part in the protest, reported to Al Jazeera that "if they build it correctly, so that it skirts the reserve, a road could be a good thing. For example, we have very few health supplies and doctors here and it could help keep our children healthy"'(McNeish, 'Extraction, Protest and Indigeneity', 228–9)
65. Eriksson Baaz, *Paternalism of Partnership,* 163.
66. The URDS was set up by Utkal Alumina International Limited. According to Padel and Das, the World Bank 'listed it as a model project in its Business Partners for Development scheme (BPD) a worldwide scheme promoting "tri-sectoral partnerships" between government, companies and civil society. The UK was the only government that became officially involved, through. DfID'; Padel and Das, *Out of this Earth,* 115.

Bibliography

Ahmad, Aijaz. "The Politics of Literary Postcoloniality." *Race and Class* 36, no. 3 (1995): 1–20.
Bhabha, Homi K. "The Other Question: Stereotype, Discrimination and the Discourse of Colonialism." In *The Location of Culture,* 68–84. London: Routledge, 1994.
Chandler, David. *From Kosovo to Kabul and beyond: Human Rights and International Intervention.* London: Pluto Press, 2006.
Choudry, Aziz, and Dip Kapoor, eds. *NGOization: Complicity, Contradictions and Prospects.* London: Zed Books, 2013.
Chow, Rey. *Writing Diaspora: Tactics of Intervention in Contemporary Cultural Studies.* Bloomington: Indiana University Press, 1993.
Das, Arvind N. *The Republic of Bihar.* Delhi: Penguin, 1992.
Deuze, Mark. "Survival of the Mediated." *Journal of Cultural Science* 3, no. 2 (2010): 1–11.
Duffield, Mark. "Getting Savages to Fight Barbarians: Development, Security and the Colonial Present." *Conflict, Security & Development* 5, no. 2 (2005): 141–159.
Eriksson Baaz, Maria. *The Paternalism of Partnership: A Postcolonial Reading of Identity in Development Aid.* London: Zed Books, 2005.

Escobar, Arturo. *The Making and Unmaking of the Third World*. Princeton, NJ: Princeton University Press, 1995.

Escobar, Arturo. "Beyond the Search for a Paradigm? Post-Development and beyond." *Development* 43, no. 4 (2000): 11–14.

Escobar, Arturo, and Claudia Ciobanu. "Latin America in a Post-Development Era: An Interview with Arturo Escobar." *Open Democracy*, November 6, 2012.

Esteva, Gustavo, and Madhu Suri Prakash. *Grassroots Post-Modernism: Remaking the Soil of Cultures*. London: Zed Books, 1998.

Fanon, F. *Black Skin, White Masks*. New York: Grove Press, 1967 (1952).

Foil Vedanta. "Niyamgiri Decries State Human Rights Abuses and Rejects NGOs." 2016. https://www. foilvedanta.org/news/niyamgiri-decries-state-human-rights-abuses-and-rejects-ngos/

Hall, Stuart. "Gramsci's Relevance for the Study of Race and Ethnicity." *Journal of Communication Inquiry* 10, no. 2 (1986): 5–27.

Hall, Stuart. "The Spectacle of the 'Other.'" In *Representation: Cultural Representation: Cultural Representatives and Signifying Practices*, edited by S. Hall, 225–279. London: Sage, 1997.

Harvey, David. "The 'New' Imperialism: Accumulation by Dispossession." *Socialist Register* 40 (2004): 63–87.

Hearn, Julie. "African NGOs: The New Compradors." *Development and Change* 38, no. 6 (2007): 1095–1110.

Hunter, W. W. *A Statistical Account of Bengal*. London: Trubner and Co., 1875.

Jagger, Bianca. 2010. "The Battle for Niyamgiri." *The Observer*, June 13.

Juluri, Vamsee. 2013. "Hinduism and Its Culture Wars." *The India Site*, May 19. https://www.theindiasite. com/hinduism-and-its-culture-wars/.

Kaika, Maria, and Lazaros Karaliotas. "The Spatialization of Democratic Politics: Insights from Indignant Squares." *European Urban and Regional Studies* 23, no. 4 (2016): 556–570.

Landry, Donna, and Gerald Maclean. *The Spivak Reader*. New York: Routledge, 1996.

Manji, Firoze, and Carl O'Coill. "The Missionary Position: NGOs and Development in Africa." *International Affairs* 78, no. 3 (2002): 567–584.

McNeish, John-Andrew. "Extraction, Protest and Indigeneity in Bolivia: The TIPNIS Effect." *Latin American and Caribbean Ethnic Studies* 8, no. 2 (2013): 221–242.

Narayan, Uma. *Dislocating Cultures: Identities, Traditions, and Third World Feminism*. New York: Routledge, 1996.

Nash, Kate. "Global Citizenship as Show Business: The Cultural Politics of Make Poverty History." *Media Culture Society* 30, no. 2 (2008): 167–181.

Padel, Felix, and Samarendra Das. *Out of This Earth: East India Adivasis and the Aluminium Cartel*. Delhi: Orient Blackswan, 2010.

Rahnema, Majid, and Victoria Bawtree, eds. *The Post-Development Reader*. London: Zed Books, 1997.

Robinson, William I. *Promoting Polyarchy: Globalization, US Intervention, and Hegemony*. Cambridge: Cambridge University Press, 1996.

Shah, Prakash. *Against Caste in British Law: A Critical Perspective on the Caste Discrimination Provision in the Equality Act 2010*. Basingstoke: Palgrave Macmillan, 2015.

South Asia Solidarity Group. "Strange Bedfellows for Action Aid." August 13, 2011. https://www. southasiasolidarity.org/2011/08/13/strange-bedfellows-for-action-aid/.

Stoler, Ann. *Race and the Education of Desire: Foucault's History of Sexuality and the Colonial Order of Things*. Durham, NC: Duke University Press, 1995.

Sundar, Nandini. *Subalterns and Sovereigns: An Anthropological History of Bastar, 1854–1996*. New York: Oxford University Press, 1997.

Trinh, Minh-Ha. *Woman, Native, Other. Writing Postcoloniality and Feminism*. Bloomington: Indiana University Press, 1989.

Tripathi, Bhasker. 2017. "Activists Object to Home Ministry Linking Niyamgiri Hills Struggle to Maoists." *The Wire*, April 21. https://thewire.in/126626/mha-niyamgiri-hills-maoist-vedanta-mining/

Wallace, Tina. "NGO Dilemmas: Trojan Horses for Global Neoliberalism?" *Socialist Register* 40 (2004): 202–219.

White, Sarah. "The 'Gender Lens': A Racial Blinder?" *Progress in Development Studies* 6, no. 1 (2006): 55–67.

Whittel, Richard. 2010. "Dodgy Development: DfID in India." *Corporate Watch*, January 28. https://corporatewatch.org/news/2010/jan/27/dodgy-development-dfid-india

Wilson, Kalpana. *Race, Racism and Development: Interrogating History, Discourse and Practice*. London: Zed Books, 2012.

Wilson, Kalpana. "Towards a Radical Re-Appropriation: Gender, Development and Neoliberal Feminism." *Development and Change* 46, no. 4 (2015): 803–832.

Wilson, Kalpana. "Re-Centring 'Race' in Development: Population Policies and Global Capital Accumulation in the Era of the SDGs." *Globalizations* 14, no. 3 (2017): 432–449.

Ziai, Aram. "The Ambivalence of Post-Development: Between Reactionary Populism and Radical Democracy." *Third World Quarterly* 25, no. 6 (2004): 1045–1060.

Ziai, Aram. "Post-Development: Premature Burials and Haunting Ghosts." *Development and Change* 46, no. 4 (2015): 833–854.

The making and unmaking of development: using Post-Development as a tool in teaching development studies

Wendy Harcourt

ABSTRACT

This article explores the ways in which western modernity, as Boaventura De Sousa Santos suggests, can play tricks on intellectuals when we try to teach revolutionary ideas in reactionary institutions. I reflect on my efforts to use Post-Development (PD) as a tool to engage students in critical reflections on development in a post graduate course in 2015/2016. One of their assignments was to create an International Institute of Social Studies (ISS) Development Dictionary emulating the Sachs's collection. The results were mixed. On the one hand, they produced wonderful digital collations of concepts, ideas and critiques, but on the other hand, many felt that learning about PD had turned their world upside down. Given the strong reactions of the students, and also my colleagues, I reflect on the possibilities and also the problems of using PD as a tool to teach development studies to international students (most of whom are from the Global South). My experiment in asking students to engage in their own 'unmaking of development' recorded in their evaluations, a series of interviews, and my own and other colleagues' reflections sets out the difficulty of unsettling apparent truths of development processes even in progressive institutes at the interface of activism and academe.

Introduction

One of the tricks that western modernity plays on intellectuals is to allow them to produce revolutionary ideas in reactionary institutions.[1]

You have to understand that we have different points of view, you are hermetic and even eurocentric while I, I'm free and without center, however, we are discovering 'us' and we are recovering our mutual confidence. I have no fear that our friends Empower Ment and Parti Cipation watch my feelings for you, Gender Gender (Posting from Arturito Escobar to Gender Gender[2]).

I fully agree with your comment concerning analysis of social relations within communities participating in development projects/initiatives. … It is very important to establish what is 'just and fair' within each community and country, as their understandings may differ from Western perspectives due to unwritten norms, values and cultural differences…. we need to understand how agency and structure cooperate or clash within different societies and how these processes affect power relations between genders (Posting from Ethno Graphy to Gender Gender).

My essay reflects on the continuing relevance of the *Development Dictionary*[3] by describing how I was inspired to use it as a core text in the 2015/2016 academic year in the International Institute of Social Studies (ISS) 'General Course'. The course used Post-Development (PD) as a tool to engage 152 international post-graduate students in development studies in their own critical reflections on development practice. As the postings from the Facebook page above suggest, the attempt moved the discussion beyond the reading and studying of texts and into the realm of critical deconstruction and imagination using different forms of social media that the students took up, intuitively, in relation to the questions and discussions being posed. The experience raised for me important questions about the role of critical pedagogy[4] in a neoliberal climate and what kind of space PD can have in an increasingly cautious academic environment.

In this article, I reflect on the course, in response to the quote from De Sousa Santos above, exploring how critical pedagogy, as a political practice, can be part of the 'unmaking' of development in a process of teaching to transgress.[5] The *Development Dictionary* was used by students in a peer-to-peer learning exercise in order to make their own Development Dictionary presented in a short video to the whole class, and later, individually, in an essay.

The article is also a personal story about creating transgressive spaces in teaching institutions. In this sense, the article uses ethnography[6] in order to contribute to discussions on the 'doing' of teaching in academe today, and specifically the politics of teaching critically about mainstream development processes[7] with all the funding implications for managing institutions, scholarships and job security. It is a story of learning (and unlearning) for teachers, as well as students, and of how difficult it is to unsettle truths of mainstream development in places like the ISS of Erasmus University, where this experiment was carried out, which has a long history at the interface of activism and academe as well as being a beneficiary of development funding to European institutions in order to teach students from former colonies.

The research for this essay is qualitative[8]; most of the material for the essay comes from the participants' experiences recorded in the formal course evaluations. I quote the students' contributions to the evaluation their essays and the videos they produced.[9] In addition I refer to internal group discussions with some of the students and staff, held in person, on the official Intranet and Facebook (FB), and via Whats App, as well as internal teaching reviews.[10] Writing this paper is in itself part of a learning, self-reflective process and demands an openness about my positionality as a teacher at ISS. I see reflections on the how of doing teaching, and experiments in critical pedagogy, as important to knowledge production. In this, I am inspired by feminist writers such as Donna Haraway,[11] who sees all knowledge as 'situated'. I see this essay as part of the politics of ontology, 'the doing of PD',[12] as I explore how the self and the field are co-constitutive and reflect on the highly political process of the production of knowledge (what counts as knowledge, who has the authority to teach, in which language, from which history).[13] The politics of ontology is about how the operations of power – institutional and discursive – have produced marks of difference, ie how race, gender, ability, age, etc. have been produced as essential categories in development teaching and practice. I find this 'reflexive turn'[14] on pedagogy welcome, if also problematic,[15] as it demands courage to scrutinise what goes on in the classroom.

Outline of the paper

I realized that every aspect in our day-to-day life and activities is a form of development or means to development. Before learning about bodies, places and Glocality, little did I know that funerals can be related to development. (Q2.4 S 2)[16]

Section one describes how the course operated, and the pedagogical methods used. I give a brief outline of the course activities, with a specific focus on how the course was designed from a PD perspective using PD as a tool to understand development encounters, in particular peer learning as students put together their different ISS *Development Dictionaries*.

Section two analyses the responses of the students to the course. I reflect on the teaching as a process of 'unlearning' transformation and transgression individually and collectively, with a focus on what I judge to be the most provocative and troubling themes discussed in the lectures and workshops.

Section three analyses the strategy to use PD as tool for teaching as I set out what I learnt from trying to teach a transgressive and transformative methodology. I examine the continuing challenge for development studies to be progressive, and how hard it is to question development given the backdrop of dwindling resources as well as broader pessimism about increasing global inequalities, economic and ecological failures. I also reflect on the tension around privilege, race, gender bias, and the politics of knowledge production.

The conclusion responds to the intriguing questions informing this *TWQ* Special Issue:

Does PD produce more progressive theory and practice by fundamentally questioning 'development', or does it distract from pragmatic and down-to-earth reforms of development cooperation?

Has PD been far-sighted and prophetic in its critique of economic and ecological models, or did it get wrong some basic facts, for example that most people in the South are very much interested in Western-style models and little concerned with 'alternatives to development'?

Section one: introducing the general course

The writings of Arturito Escobar and Wolfgang Sachs. They have opened a world for me. I am extremely intrigued. I hope to one day be able to take part in such an inspiring movement'. (Q7.1 S82)

The course was taught at the ISS in The Hague, the Netherlands, a well-known European post-graduate institute offering degrees in development studies. Founded in 1952, the ISS has been for most of its history an independent institute funded by the Dutch government to do capacity-building and post-graduate (adult) education, as well as research, pioneering a number of critical development courses over the years.[17] In 2009, the ISS joined Erasmus University, Rotterdam. The focus of ISS is now more firmly anchored within mainstream academe, competing on various levels with other universities in Europe for students, undertaking societally relevant research with less emphasis on capacity training as part of the focus on teaching the Global South, and competing with other Dutch agencies for funding. There is now a growing emphasis on winning large research grants rather than on capacity-building projects. In joining Erasmus, the ISS has had to adjust to the demands of a competitive academic environment.

The ISS master's in development studies takes 15 months, and there is a period where 'batches' of students overlap as one group begins the course and another completes their master's thesis. The General Course, taught in this period, is the only obligatory course that all the students take. The large majority of students are from the Global South, and that year the intake was 152 students from 57 different countries. The majority of students have scholarships, and many take a year off jobs in government, non governmental organisations (NGOs) and universities to do the master's degree.

It was my first time teaching the course, and my fourth year at the ISS. The Deputy Rector of education gave me a free hand to design the course and encouraged my idea to experiment by adopting a PD approach. It was not the first time PD was taught at the ISS, but it was the first time it was the main pedagogical tool for the only compulsory course at ISS. My preparations the summer before the course began included a meeting in Helsinki on PD research in European institutes, and visits during my holidays with different development studies departments in the UK, the USA and Australia. Their interest, and I have to say warnings, made me aware that what I was planning to do was ambitious and challenging.

The course took place over 12 weeks, with lectures and workshops, and using Moodle as an online platform as well as social media. The course is co-taught. The teaching team included two other academic staff, 12 'old batch' MA students who were hired to run the workshops, and a post-doctoral student who had just completed her PhD. There were weekly lectures (co-taught by the teaching team and with five guest lecturers) and workshops (facilitated by the 'old batch' MA students), and continuous online discussion groups. The course used participatory methodology, and where possible aimed to flip the classroom in order to encourage dialogue and to create space for students to speak about their own knowledge and experience of development.

The course outline and introduction explained that it was using PD thinking, methods and critiques of development to approach development studies. The course was designed so that space was created for the debate and discussion informed by the students' own experiences and interest. The readings were offered as jumping-off points for discussion, and the lectures were designed as short reflections on main concepts. During the lectures there were 'buzz' groups and interactive debate. More in-depth discussions were expected to happen in peer-learning processes, both on- and offline in the 12 working groups facilitated by the old-batch MA students. In addition, there was a general online discussion group for all teachers and students that we used for information-sharing rather than dialogue and debate. The teaching team communicated via Facebook and WhatsApp. As a result of the focus on dialogue and interaction there is a huge digital trail of discussion and debate during the course, as well as a midterm review and two-hour end-of-year review by the students. In addition, there were three internal reviews by the teaching team with teachers and the 12 workshop facilitators.

Two texts played a particularly important role in the teaching – *Encountering Development*[18] and *The Development Dictionary*.[19] The Escobar text guided the first essay, and the one compulsory exam question, and Sachs was used in the group assignment and final essay.

The first assignment asked students to: 'reflect critically on a personal experience of living and doing development …. Your task is to write a narrative essay of a particular place in your life where you have encountered the making of development. In the essay, we invite you to respond to Arturito Escobar's call for "the unmaking of development through the intervention of new narratives, new ways of thinking and doing"'.

The second assignment asked students to work in groups of 10 in order to: 'prepare, write and present 5 Entries for an ISS General Course Development Dictionary designed for a specific audience'. Each group had to prepare a 5–7-minute pitch to the audience in plenary – in the form of a video. The videos had to show an understanding of development as a cultural, political, economic and historical process, and had to be produced collaboratively in a multidisciplinary and multicultural context with emphasis on creativity as well as clarity.

Section two: turning the world upside down?

I don't know, I feel like I have not learned anything in this class, besides questioning everything and everyone, which is useful … but now what? (Q7.3 S 74)

A reflection on two moments in the course

Just as I was about to leave the classroom after the second lecture, a female student in her mid-30s (who I later found out was a business consultant from Colombia) came up to me and said, 'You have turned my world upside down'. I felt troubled but also just a bit pleased to hear it. In fact, it was a refrain I was to hear often during the course, in different tones, ranging from thanks to accusation. All these responses, in and outside the classroom, made for a dynamic course.

Such were the pressures of setting up a new course that the teaching team met every week, continually adjusting the course, the readings, and the approach. We began by flipping the classroom, which meant asking students to read the texts and watch (music) videos related to the themes before the lecture, and began each session with a video of a song and buzz groups where students divided into groups of two and three to discuss issues raised. We co-taught, taking time to tell students who we were, where the authors they were reading came from, what institutions and backgrounds produced these texts (academe, World Bank, NGOs, social movements), and where the places and people were situated in the development debates. We began the course by presenting development as a highly contested term. We spoke about the different and conflicting explanations of development – why travelling along roads, migrants, funerals and mobile technologies were an important part of the development process. We asked them to see the course as discussing partial truths of development in order to challenge the homogenising nature of the dominant development project.[20] We taught that there were many understandings of development.[21] We pointed to the conflicts, contradictions and potential cracks in these understandings, including their own. We wanted them to learn from each other's views of development by sharing their own experiences. We saw ourselves together with the students as co-producers of knowledge in the classroom. It was exciting for some, but the response was decidedly mixed. Some met the whole process of the course (its approach and content) with disbelief and confusion followed by demands for the facts and figures and the 'real development' story. These students did not want to be part of an experiment. They wanted the teachers to tell them what development was about; they had not come to the ISS to problem-solve with other students. Some of the negative responses about the course revealed this:

Go back to the old way of teaching, it may help us learn much more (Q7.4 S 22), or *I still do not get most of the materials in the course. Workshops must help us to understand, instead of doing nonsense things* (Q7.4 S 25).

Some of the response, I realise now, was due to the fact that students coming from 57 countries have experienced very different pedagogical processes. The ones that were bemused by our approach came from backgrounds where teachers taught and students listened, and knowledge was from books, not songs or videos or stories. For them, flipping the classroom in the lectures and interactive pedagogy were not working. In an informal midterm review where we distributed 'Post-it® Notes' and asked students to comment, we decided it was best to drop the flipping, and move to a more standard teaching format in the lectures while keeping a participatory and transgressive peer-led pedagogy in the workshops. As one student commented:

I think students should be better prepared for what to expect from this course – the structure of the course came as a surprise to them and was frustrating and bewildering for many as this is not a style of learning with which they are familiar. (Q7.3 S 36)

As course leader it was considerable work for me to keep the teaching team believing in the process and in the possibilities of what peer learning could produce.

The second moment on which I want to share my reflections comes from the last session of the course. Again I felt that sense of trouble, mingled with achievement. Students were fully in charge of the last session; they instructed the teachers to join only at the end. So, as the class was held, I sat in a meeting of the ISS Institute Council receiving 'WhatsApp' photos and videos from the MA facilitators who were running the 'treasure hunt' where students were going from clue to clue at different 'stations' in the building. From the noise and the photos, it seemed the institute was itself being turned upside down as the students were carrying out games and doing rap dances to concepts such as glocality, power, participation, culture and coloniality of gender. It was riotous and fun, and a lot was being discussed in the process. But, while I was very happy to see all this going on, I was also very conscious of the Rector and the rest of the ISS management team who were in the meeting. They were clearly not so sure. When we joined the students in the attic to award a prize to the group that won the treasure hunt, the teaching staff were also, to our surprise, given gifts, and were filmed doing our own rap. Something had worked.

Using PD as a tool for understanding development

Name two things you learnt from the course:

The source, origin and birth of the word and concept of 'development' and the way it has been contextualized. Development differs from place to place due to or based on the background of a particular place as well as social, economic and political factors. (Q2.4 S 55)

The course provided other perspectives on seeing development narratives. That there is no single story about development. People live in different spaces, cultures and times, so that we have to be more critical when doing development agendas. (Q2.4 S 78)

As these two examples suggest, the course did provide students with the tools to examine critically development processes. We used PD as a tool to do so, while trying not to give an authoritative and definitive view of what development was as such. We defined PD through references to different texts or 'stories' as being critical of the development discourse. We followed Escobar in understanding development as an 'extremely efficient apparatus for producing knowledge about, and the exercise of power over, the Third World'.[22] We examined different practices of development and modernity using PD as a tool to look at how power operates in development processes. We opened up the debate around development as Eurocentric, authoritarian and hegemonic, but also in this process we asked the students to understand that there is the possibility to create spaces for transformation and change. We asked them to look at 'alternatives to development' by building in the course a shared critical stance towards global development discourse that was inspired by alternatives to development at the local level. The concept of glocality was introduced as a major concept, taken from the work of Arif Dirlik.[23] Glocality, we explained, defines development as glocal phenomena, involving transactions and flows at very large scales but also necessarily defined by context and the particularities of place. We spoke about how place constitutes people's experience of development, and encouraged students to look at glocality when understanding modes of domination at both global and local levels in a module called 'People and places'. We suggested that diversities inform and build resistance, and are dynamic and fluid rather than place bound. In our approach to PD we were inspired by Katherine McKinnon's definition of PD not as a 'cohesive movement' but rather as a 'set of debates ... grounded in a particular way of thinking about the nature of truth and knowledge'.[24] We deliberately did not present first the dominant stories of development and then dismantle it but tried to teach through the lens of PD as a critical conceptual stance in order for students to re-think the way they have experienced and observed development being been done in their lives, and in sharing those experiences to think together about new narratives.

It was an uphill battle. The questions that came, the debates, and the silences, in the first lectures and workshops, showed that the dominant development narrative for some of the students was difficult to question, and to see as a narrative. For them development was about 'underdeveloped' countries learning how to follow the development path to progress, modernity, success and wealth. The tools they asked for were not critical theory but practical information about how to do development better back home in their governments, NGOs and business so they and their country could benefit. They were inscribed within development discourse in ways that made it difficult to look at it critically. They did not see the value of discussing experiences, ideas and diverse narratives; they wanted to know how development worked, not to change it, but so that they could, once home, make it work better, in particular for the poor.

As several suggested in the evaluation, there was a need for:
More concrete examples of the work (good and bad) done by the big development organisations eg United Nations, International Monetary Fund, World Bank, United States Agency for International Development (Q7.4 S 59).

Or:

Perhaps we could also invite people from mainstream, such as World Bank, to lecture students (Q7.4 S 82).

The first assignment on encountering development, inspired by Escobar, coming early in the course (week 5) was a key moment. When setting the essay, we imagined that it would be easy for students to speak to their own experience of development, assuming that students coming to study at the ISS would welcome the chance to share their own history and colonial experience, and then, as a course, we would learn from their 'encounters'. We asked them to read the Escobar's text, and watch some carefully chosen YouTube videos such as Chimamanda Ngozi Adichie's 2009 speech 'The Danger of a Single Story',[25] as well as look at the introduction to the *Development Dictionary*. We proposed that these writers and thinkers represented just some of many narratives and encounters of development. We wanted the essay to be a space for students to write their narrative, speaking about their lives and entanglement with development.

Some students wrote brilliant essays, voyages of discovery and curiosity about how to use PD as a tool to unpack assumptions. One deeply felt essay spoke to the metaphor 'don't cross the river before you get to the bridge' and how 'culture' is essential in the making of development. S/he argued that we need to 'remake the meaning of development and then through our practices and in the context we live, get deep inside the water' (Student Essay B, November 2015). Another student wrote an evocative essay about his/her travels across histories and landscapes on his/her way to the ISS, reflecting on the contradictions of development encounters in his/her life, concluding:

I arrive at The Hague looking to imbue those experiences with theoretical rigour. Travelling across the development spectrum has given me a more nuanced view of poverty. Here, I've been encountering academics who translate this multi-layered reality into a general, if diverse, theory. (Student Essay C, November 2015)

But several students found it impossible to write in the first person. They were unsettled by the idea of writing narratives, firm in their belief that development was economics and progress, prescribed by academics and practiced by development experts. Their interest was in the conceptual tools about how to measure and analyse development; they did not see the relevance of socio-cultural understandings of self and community. For them, writing about how they experienced development, rather than being told what it was from lecturers and textbooks, was not a valuable learning experience. Some did not understand what a development encounter could be, and thinking about how they have experienced development rather than being taught it made some anxious, and others simply angry.

In response to the question about how they saw the first assignment, there were some interesting answers ranging from somewhat tongue in cheek to deeply anxious:

For example, I learnt *development issues, evaluation of my own life and experiences, putting thoughts together, concepts of "mental furniture", "unmaking", etc., referencing, discipline, hard work, reading etc., etc., etc* (Q2.4 S 102); *I learnt to work under tremendous pressure and anxiety* (Q2.4 S 110); *For me, it was confusing. I am not sure if I actually learnt something out of it* (Q2.4 S 87); or just *how to get confused?* (Q2.4 S 92)

Though there were others who enjoyed it:

It was very enriching to write the first narrative essay, since it made me reflect on my work and study experiences and understand the connection with historical processes that I can know recognize and explain with consciousness and critical view. It also helped me to identify the authors that I align my thoughts with and to go deeper in the course readings. (Q2.4 S 67)

It was a very interesting exercise for me to connect the un-making of development and what the Japanese farmer I met the in rural area showed me as their way of living in their community. I felt that respect to the local people can be one of the missing element[s] in many of development projects. (Q2.4 S 48)

Peer-to-peer pedagogy

Half-way through the course, after the first essay and midterm review, one could feel a sense of settling in; the lecturers, while continuing to use videos, dropped the buzz groups and delivered more standard lecturing. The 'flipping' of the classroom was done in the workshops which began to function well as they moved into creative work ranging from writing poetry, to sharing songs, role plays and online discussion with photographs and blogs, and there was more ease now with open-ended questions and challenging assumptions about the doing of development. PD as a tool to question and critique development had begun to work, at least for some.

At this stage they began to look at the *Development Dictionary* and discuss the different concepts there, comparing them with lectures and readings. An example comes from an online posting which described the student rethinking their engagement in relation to 'participation' in a project on HIV/AIDS.

We asked the community (in a village meeting) how we could reduce the HIV infection. The community replied to us "to construct a bridge". ... we had no idea how to understand their answer. The reason they gave us is that they had to go very far to reach the market in the town, so that many people had [a] night stop on the half-way where many sex-workers were. Thus, if a bridge can be constructed linking their village with the town located on the other side of the river, they were expecting to reduce the rate of HIV infection (Student Group A).

Human rights were discussed as both a necessary and a contested issue, based on students' experiences. For example, one Nigerian student led a debate on 'What is human rights?' when the state cannot be trusted to secure the rights of students. S/he described how in a town in Oyo State, university students were arrested by police when coming back to their hostels ferried on motor bikes the night before their exams. The police placed them (and the motor bike carriers) in gaol and tried to extort money from the students' relatives, knowing there was pressure for them to be released in order to do the exams the next day (and for the motor bike carriers to earn their livelihood). After intervention by the Students' Union to the local government they were released. The student used this example to argue that human rights require law and order which is not always possible if the police were corrupt, something that resonated throughout the group discussion (Student Group D).

Writing and performing the ISS Development Dictionary

The group assignment was wonderful and awesome, based on the multicultural fora and backgrounds here at ISS. (Q2.6 S 42)

This was [a] fascinating assignment, I learnt how to work with excellent people from different backgrounds and cultures, it taught us how diversity matters in making development. (Q2.6 S 82)

It was during the presentations that I understood what development study was all about. (Q2.6 S 33)

PD as a tool of analysis came into its own when students moved into making their group 'ISS Development Dictionary'. The students were divided into 12 groups and took around a month to produce their dictionaries. Modelled on the original, it was up to them to select the concepts and produce the dictionary as a 'pitch' to a particular audience.

From the reviews, the group assignments were the most appreciated aspect of the course. Students were excited that they could 'create our own concept, taking into account what is the direction that we wanted to go'. (Q2.6 S 45)

Another student from the Arturito Escobar group stated:

It was wonderful. We learned from each other, our perspectives on the course topics and concepts, we shared experiences and were able to clarify aspects that we did not understand through our Facebook discussions. (Q2.6 S 52)

With reference to the opening quote, this group explored different processes of othering by playing with identities, genders and meanings within and outside the development processes, teasing in written and visual forms the teachers and the authors they were reading.

The students worked hard; as one stated:

It challenged me to integrate other points of view, different to mine, with respect and inclusiveness. I learnt to work with a very diverse group in terms not only of culture but also professional perspectives and expectations regarding our studies at ISS. (Q2.6 S 32)

However, at least one person passionately did not like it: 'NO GROUP ASSIGNMENT WITH 11 PEOPLE … that was the worst experience of my life'. (Q7.3 S 80)

What they produced was written texts and short, seven-minute videos – these were shown in a five-hour session which was attended by all, and the atmosphere was electric. Combined with the videos were some extremely funny skits as well as emotionally moving film and statements. The creativity and imagination were impressive, as was the use of music and quality of the filming. One film involved parents and friends back home, via Skype. Another showed development in The Hague through a day in the life of a student. Several recreated Truman's Speech, from showing black and white pictures to reenacting it. One had a skit reversing sexism, and another showed how modernity was perceived from different viewpoints, using music. There were two animations with drawings done by hand. The students could choose their audience, and three groups chose future ISS students; the best was shown to the next General Course students, and the rest were online.[26]

Section three: reflections – teaching revolutionary ideas in reactionary institutions?

'Unmaking' development can only serve any purpose if we subsequently remake it somehow. (Student Essay November 2015)

What did you learn? What did I learn? (And unlearn?)

It was difficult to design a class that could enable people coming from such diverse geographies, histories, religions, cultures and educational processes to debate different experiences of development. Their understanding of development was constituted by very different people and places. There were hierarchies and simmering dislikes, and there was shyness due to language barriers. There was always a hovering question about the facts and requests to tell the 'real' dominant and 'needs to be known' development story.

Even if the group assignments undoubtedly worked well, there was a polarisation of students who liked or disliked the course. The internal reviews and end-of-year evaluation showed a division between those that said things like 'the lectures were totally not helpful' (Q2.4 S 28), and 'From the beginning it was hard but I learnt to write and relate it to my own experience on how development is being made' (Q2.5 S 11), and those who stated: *I liked everything in the course. I learnt that development cannot be a one-way process, that is from the more privileged to the less.* (Q2.5 S 20)

One particularly thoughtful feedback from a student was the following:

I really enjoyed the methodology implemented and the experimental approach within a very diverse group of students. I believe that even those who did not enjoy or understood completely the course, will in the long term, conscious or unconsciously, enrich their understanding and approach to development in an innovative and wider view. (Q7.1 S 82)

This kind of comment pointed to how using PD as a tool to deconstruct mainstream development ended up silencing some of the very people we were trying to give the space to explore and experience partial truths and alternative stories. Asking people to let go of the dominant story or development blueprint, whether it be questioning the Millennium Development Goals (MDGs) or arguing that not all development led to improvement, human rights, or to an end of poverty and inequality, was difficult and created contestations and led to some unruly and volatile discussions.

Throughout the course, there was a friction around the differences of authority among the students and the teachers based on gender, class and race. Judging from the many detailed comments in the course reviews, in the end the majority of students liked the class. [27] But there was a solid core of students who refuted the 'unsettling' and 'unmaking' of development.[28] This discomfort with the course was directed at the lecturers, and in particular me, as a course leader. My identity – age, Global North, white and female-gendered status – was seen by a few as not desirable in a teacher; I was not what was expected. Maybe I embodied the confusion about what authority was[29]; particularly my willingness to expose my own doubts and concerns about the development process was questioned. Several students raised this issue and discussed it with me sympathetically at different times during the course. They were highly conscious of the divide among the class as to my approach and methods, and also how some students perceived me as biased, as a feminist researcher, PD scholar and former activist. A critique of subjectivities in development processes – Who were the recognised development actors, institutions and power players? – extended to a critique of me as course leader and of the course itself. As one student commented later: *Why did you want us to see development in the same way that you were looking at it? … There is a big power relation inside teaching: Who gets to teach and why? What are the interests behind teaching certain knowledges?*[30]

Was it appropriate to turn students' 'world upside down' or unmake development without giving them a clear set of tools to remake it? This was not fully solved in the course, for students who were not sympathetic to our views. We reminded them that other courses in ISS would enable students to re-orient themselves and get the tools that could help them engage differently with mainstream development practices. I admit I felt saddened but wiser about comments such as:

The knowledge I got is like a gloomy cloud. I cannot get the clear answer about "development" solutions but at least I think we got the tools to find the answer later. (Q7.3 S 44)

However, I also saw that students who had enjoyed the course understood our starting point:

That there is no single story about something. People live in different spaces, cultures and times, so that we have to be more critical when doing development agendas. (Q2.4 S 45)

Using PD as a critical tool

We have all encountered development at one point or another. The task for us as development workers is to critically assess and unpack development. (Student Essay C, November 2015)

One of the main lessons I learnt was the difficulty of creating spaces of transgression. It was not easy to ask people who had come to The Hague to study development studies to confront immediately critiques of development. The responses of the students forced me to reflect on the role I played as teacher in a Dutch academic institute. In the same way that the course was asking the students to position themselves as development workers, I had to consider where ISS is positioned in the development processes. The course was designed to challenge authoritarian and hegemonic ideas, and to make visible the impact of modernity and coloniality in development processes, but, awkwardly, both teachers and students were bound by the same hegemonic structures of development and education processes. We were part of the privileged mainstream of development discourses we were wanting to challenge. Even if there was a tension around the different forms of privilege in our course interactions, we were, as De Sousa Santos points out in this essay's opening quote, trying to produce revolutionary ideas in a reactionary institution. As well as the obvious hierarchy of teacher and student, we were teaching in English, the institution was Dutch with its specific colonial history, and the scholarships were given by the Dutch government with the expectation that students who would come to our institution were being trained in how to do development.[31] There was the underlying assumption, in using PD as a pedagogical tool, that students could be taught to question development, and we expected them to find an appeal in the texts and narratives that were being taught. Yet by teaching it, we were inviting them to reproduce what we said in exams and in marking their essays. There was something highly contradictory in saying that knowledge is partial and yet examining it. And in the lectures it was a very forced dialogue – How could one speak freely with teachers who were given authority to grade and judge? We were not trying to test knowledge that students should reproduce, which was perhaps what students found so hard. We tried to exploit the limited space we had within the exam regulations. Even though it was limited, we used the space to look for alternatives to development, and asked students to question development practices in order to explore the possibility of change in their own engagement in development outside the classroom. We were conscious of the politics of teaching in this attempt to close the disconnections between the spaces of teaching/learning and the realities of the world beyond.

One deliberate way that we chose to be transgressive in our teaching methods was by asking questions and not telling answers. Though we spoke about alternatives at the community level, social movements and radical networks, we did not address directly what to do with the 'big development' picture, even if we were evidently critical of it because we spoke about partial truths. We were keen to follow Freire in this regard, seeing education as 'the practice of freedom, the means by which men and women deal critically and creatively with reality and discover how to participate in the transformation of their world'.[32]

We asked the students to learn to adopt the lens of critical development thinkers. Our aim was not to force them into solidarity with social movements, feminism or radical alternatives, but to invite them to reflect on their privileges. In this we used, along with PD, decoloniality and feminist pedagogies to consider how best to engage in western-dominated models of development. We tried to create a safe space where epistemic violence could be countered through ethical engagements with other students, a connection that could extend beyond the classroom.

Teaching PD in ISS also provoked a tense reaction among ISS teaching staff. As a member of the teaching team commented: 'the course was criticised by a good number of colleagues.

Who, I suspect, were undermining the authority of the course and its teachers in discussions with students.'[33] This corridor talk – as none of my ISS colleagues spoke to me directly – was one of the most difficult aspects of the whole process. There are many reasons for such a reaction. To begin with we are living in a time where there is uncertainty about development studies in general and specifically funds and staff security. There were on-going talks about the future of the institute, with threats of cuts and continuing moves towards more conservative competitive academic practices. Maybe it was not a conducive time to do something new. Beyond the ISS, but informing the daily lives of the students and staff, were the increasing anti-migrant, anti-refugee public behaviours and a rise in right-wing politics in the Netherlands, accompanied by explicit racism. These issues, perhaps, were seen as needing to be addressed in different ways than by PD calls for alternatives to development. Beyond corridor politics, the resistance to the course also reflected years of colonial education that positions teachers as hierarchal providers of knowledge. Perhaps colleagues' criticism of PD as a central approach to the 'flagship' course in ISS was also unconsciously about the unsettling of their privileges as 'experts' on development who see their job as providing a professional set of prescriptions to students.

Conclusion

To conclude, let me turn to the questions mentioned in the introduction that define this *TWQ* Special Issue: Does Post-Development distract from pragmatic reforms of development cooperation? Does Post-Development ignore the fact that many people in the South desire western-style models of development? Both questions are very pertinent to the responses of the students in this experimental first year of the General Course. A solid group of students (the 30% who rated the course below 3.5) looked for pragmatic and down-to-earth reforms of development and were not interested in alternatives to western-style models of development. They were representative of the privileged middle class from the Global South who were used to western lifestyles. They did not see the point of looking for alternatives; they wanted improvements in development that could reach all people. They saw in the course a major hypocrisy to criticise something of which most people in the room were the beneficiaries. For them PD was a distraction from reforms, and they wanted prescriptions on what to do. But at least we got them to think that there might be the need for reforms that do not just include, but listen to, others.

More positively, there were the other students who embraced PD because it gave them the chance to construct something different from the mainstream and to ask questions of what and how. For those students, applying a PD lens gave them a profound critique of western-dominated development enterprise. They took up the question of how to create alternatives to the injustices inherent in modern western development by looking for the possibilities to shift dominant western power and knowledge structures.[34] However critical PD is in declaring the need for absolute alternatives to development, there is still the underlying belief that we can correct global inequalities and that it is possible to make the world a better place.[35]

When I watched the students' Development Dictionary videos, I saw how it was possible to link the classroom to spaces of activism beyond the academy through pedagogical practices that highlight the politics of the possible. In using PD as a tool to understand development, the course helped students see the importance of recognising profound injustices and, at the same time, to consider doing things differently. This required them to challenge western domination in development and to find their own voice and agency in doing so. Returning once more to the opening challenge of De Sousa Santos, perhaps the trick is to ensure that these revolutionary ideas born in reactionary institutions come to fruition by supporting our students as they move outside the classroom to make the needed and crucial social-economic and political transformations in today's shockingly 'post-truth' era.

Disclosure statement

No potential conflict of interest was reported by the author.

Acknowledgements

I would like to acknowledge and thank the students and staff of this 'experimental' year of the general course and in particular those who read this in draft form. I take full responsibility for the text.

Notes

1. De Sousa Santos, *Epistemologies from the South*, 3.
2. Taken from the Facebook Page 'Arturito Escobar' set up by Group B1 with pseudo-names Arturito Escobar, Gender Gender, Em Powerment and Parti Cipation as part of the group assignment in the 2015–2016 General Course, December 2015 https://wwwfacebookcom/profilephp?id=100010721888584 accessed 5 November 2016.
3. Sachs, *Development Dictionary*.
4. The course aimed to give students a first step into a process of unlearning or 'unmaking' of development, aiming at pedagogy of positionality and transition. My understanding of critical pedagogy comes from Freire, *Pedagogy of the Oppressed*, who argues for pedagogy to treat students as co-creators of knowledge.
5. Hooks, *Teaching to Trangress*.
6. I use ethnography as a qualitative research method to reflect on my personal experience and connect these self-reflections on teaching to wider political and social understandings of education.
7. I see development as having many definitions; one of the concepts underlying the course was Phil McMichael's analysis of the different historical moments of the global 'development project' – McMichael, *Development and Social Change*.

8. There is some quantitative information about the students. In terms of nationality and gender of the students: 19.5% of the students were from Latin America, 29% from Africa, 40% from Asia, 7.6% from Europe, 2.6% from the Middle East and 1.3% from North America; 39% were men and 61% were women (no other gender identity was registered). The majority of the students were in their 30s (53%), with 20% in their 20s and the rest over 40. There was one student with disabilities.

9. The quotes from students come from a detailed Final Course Evaluation held 1 February 2016 before the grades were released, organised by one of the ISS staff using a computer generated EvaSys package. The evaluation is compulsory and grades are withheld if the student does not answer; 126 students answered the survey. I designed the questionnaire with the staff member. There were seven questions with several sub-questions, making a total of 22 questions. There were 16 questions that involved giving a rating of 1–5, and six questions that asked for written responses (of the 34-page survey report, 31 of the pages are written responses; the staff member commented that this amount of written feedback was highly unusual). The section with quotes is from a study of all 31 pages as well as online written reports. As the entry is a personal, anonymous reflection it was not possible to differentiate which students said what. I selected the most articulate comments.

10. Drafts of the article were shared with a selection of 152 students and 16 teaching staff and facilitators involved. A short version of the piece was also presented at the Development Studies Association Conference in Oxford September 2016. I take full responsibility for the views expressed here. Note that most of the material I quote is only available on institutional servers or social media that cannot be accessed by the public.

11. Haraway, "Situated Knowledges."

12. Ziai, *Exploring Post Development Theory*.

13. Icaza and Vazquez, "Coloniality of Gender."

14. Kobayashi, "GPC Ten Years On."

15. Icaza, "Testimony of a Pilgrimage."

16. Throughout the essay I refer to many of the students' comments from the evaluation, as explained above. As all comments were anonymous I refer to them by a question number (Q), and a number (S) that refers to the location of the student answer in the list of answers to that particular question.

17. For more on the ISS visit its website at http://www.iss.nl/about_iss/

18. Escobar, *Encountering Development*.

19. Sachs, *Development Dictionary*.

20. McMichael, *Development and Social Change*.

21. Ziai, "Concluding the Exploration," 226.

22. Escobar, *Encountering Development*, 9.

23. Harcourt and Escobar, *Women and the Politics of Place*.

24. McKinnon, *Development Professionals in Northern Thailand*, 14.

25. https://www.ted.com/talks/chimamanda_adichie_the_danger_of_a_single_story?language=en, accessed 5 November 2016.

26. We had a hard time grading them, our first impulse being to give them all distinctions.

27. In the final evaluation, 71% gave it 3.5/5 or more, with 15% giving it 5, though it should be noted that ISS students tend to score quite high and in ISS it is expected to have 3.5 overall.

28. In the final evaluation, 10% gave 1 to the question 'In general I appreciated this course favourably' and 5% gave 1 to the question 'During the course I could usefully reflect on my own life and work experience'.

29. As one of my female colleagues commented, I was the first woman to be given the leadership of the course, due to my personal trajectory, whiteness, age, experience, etc.; as she noted, prior to me, men had led the course.

30. Personal correspondence with student from 2015–2016 Course, 11 November 2016.

31. Currently, one-third of the fellowships at ISS come from the Dutch government. ISS is now getting more and more students with fellowships (or study loans) from governments located in the South. Every year ISS has seven fellowships from the World Bank.

32. Freire, *Pedagogy of the Oppressed*, 34.
33. E-mail correspondence with colleague, 30 November 2016.
34. De Sousa Santos, *Epistemologies of the South*.
35. McKinnon, *Development Professionals in Northern Thailand*, 3.

Bibliography

De Sousa Santos, B. *Epistemologies of the South: Justice against Epistemicide*. Boulder: Paradigm Publishers, 2014.
Escobar, A. *Encountering Development. The Making and UnMaking of the Third World*. Princeton: Princeton University Press, 2012.
Freire, P. *Pedagogy of the Oppressed*. New York: Continuum, 2000.
Haraway, D. "Situated Knowledges. the Science Question in Feminism and the Privilege of Partial Knowledge." *Feminist Studies* 14, no. 3 (1988): 575–599.
Harcourt, W., and A. Escobar, eds. *Women and the Politics of Place*. Bloomfield CT: Kumarian Press, 2005.
Hooks, B. *Teaching to Trangress: Education as the Practice of Freedom*. NY/London: Routledge, 2014.
Icaza, R. "Testimony of a Pilgrimage. (Un)Learning and Re-Learning with the South." In *Women in Academia Crossing North-South Borders: Gender, Race and Displacement*, edited by M. Barahona and Z. Arashiro, 1–26. Lanham, Maryland: Lexington Books, 2015.
Icaza, R., and R. Vázquez. "The Coloniality of Gender as a Radical Critique of Developmentalism." In *The Palgrave Handbook on Gender and Development: Critical Engagements in Feminist Theory and Practice*, edited by W. Harcourt, 62–76. London: Palgrave, 2016.
Kobayashi, A. "GPC Ten Years on: Is Self-Reflexivity Enough?" *Gender, Place & Culture* 10, no. 4 (2003): 345–349.
McKinnon, K. *Development Professionals in Northern Thailand: Hope, Politics and Power*. Singapore: ASAA Southeast Asia Publications Series, Singapore University Press, 2011.
McMichael, P. *Development and Social Change. A Global Perspective*. Fifth Edition. Thousand Oaks, CA: Sage, 2012.
Sachs, W., ed. *The Development Dictionary: A Guide to Knowledge as Power*. Second Edition. London: Zed Books, 1992/2010.
Ziai, A., ed. *Exploring Post-Development: Theory and Practice, Problems and Perspectives*. London: Routledge, 2007.
Ziai, A. "Concluding the Exploration: Post Development Reconsidered." In *Exploring Post-Development: Theory and Practice, Problems and Perspectives*, edited by A. Ziai, 226–234. London: Routledge, 2007.

'I am not a Post-Developmentalist, but…' The influence of Post-Development on development studies

Aram Ziai

ABSTRACT

During the course of the 1990s, the Post-Development school emerged as an innovative though controversial approach in development studies. The article examines its critical reception in the textbooks and the extent to which its authors and arguments have become influential. It argues that the relationship between development studies and Post-Development is characterised simultaneously by (sometimes explicit, sometimes implicit) rejection and integration. Examining a number of current development studies textbooks, it illustrates the growing influence of Post-Development arguments and how they have been tacitly or consciously taken up while often rejecting Post-Development per se.

Introduction

Since it became prominent during the 1990s, the Post-Development (PD) school in development theory[1] has criticised the concept of development as Eurocentric and imbued with colonial and neo-colonial relations of power. PD has given rise to intensive criticism[2] and debate.[3] Some commentators in this debate have suggested that as long as PD fails to offer a constructive political programme for dealing with Third World poverty, it will be stuck in ineffective agnosticism and thus remain dispensable in development studies.[4] My hypothesis is that this position underestimates the influence of PD on the discipline. In this article the influence of PD writers and arguments on development studies textbooks and overviews shall be systematically examined. I will argue that PD has in fact exerted considerable influence on development studies,[5] although this influence is not always acknowledged as such.

After some methodological considerations, core arguments of PD will be identified, before their presence (or absence) in development studies books will be investigated. After that, I will try to systematise the observations and present typical ways of dealing with PD in development studies – leading to the conclusion that PD has at the same time been rejected and integrated in development studies: while the majority of works criticise the PD approach, its central arguments can – in varying degrees – be found in most of them as well. Slightly exaggerating, one might frame this attitude with the phrase 'I am not a Post-Developmentalist, but the discourse of development is Eurocentric, paternalist and imbued with relations of power'. At the end of the article, I will speculate about the historical role of PD in development theory.

Methodological considerations

If the research question is: 'What is the influence of PD on development studies?', methodological considerations are needed at least in respect to three questions: (1) What is seen as development studies, or, to be more precise: How is the sample representing development studies constituted? (2) What exactly is defined as PD and PD influence? (3) How exactly is the influence of PD being examined?

As for the first question: I have confined myself to textbooks or general overviews on development studies or development theory. The sample is constituted by 36 works which were available in the German university library system (resulting from a keyword search of these concepts in 2016) and therefore certainly not exhaustive. They include monographs as well as edited volumes or readers and a small number of works from development economics and development anthropology, as well as a small number of textbooks from the South. The search yielded a number of works focusing on development cooperation, which have been excluded because they usually do not engage in theoretical debates where PD might be expected to be discussed. Specialised works on aspects of development theory or development studies which did not qualify as textbooks or general overviews were also excluded.

The influence of PD will be examined through content analysis. PD will be defined through specific authors and specific arguments linked to this school. While the specific arguments of PD (eg the 'invention of underdevelopment', 'development as amoeba', critique of Eurocentrism, knowledge as power and the economist worldview) will be discussed at length in the next section, the choice of PD authors was guided by taking the *Development Dictionary* as the first major PD publication as reference.[6] However, only a handful of these authors were repeatedly mentioned in the development studies books when they were discussing PD, as were two others not present in this publication. On the basis of the sample, the following writers are perceived as representative of this school of thought: Arturo Escobar, Gustavo Esteva (occasionally together with Madhu Suri Prakash), Wolfgang Sachs, Vandana Shiva, Majid Rahnema (partly together with Victoria Bawtree), Gilbert Rist and James Ferguson.[7] The latter two were not present in the *Development Dictionary*.

The third question – How exactly is the influence of PD being examined? – is the most difficult to answer. Strictly speaking, we cannot conclude a PD influence from the presence of PD arguments – after all, the authors might have endorsed these arguments on their own, without or before having been influenced by PD writers, as is probably the case if textbooks published at the same time as the *Development Dictionary* or earlier include what we identify as PD arguments. However, if PD arguments are encountered in combination with an explicit reference to the PD school of thought or its writers, this is regarded here as evidence of PD influence. Note that this also opens up the possibility of development studies books being influenced by PD but not acknowledging it – in this case, the influence is hard to prove. There is also the possibility of PD arguments being falsely attributed to PD influence if the authors came up with them by themselves *and* quote PD writers.

Core arguments of Post-Development

The following arguments of PD will be considered central for the approach, as they are shared by several of the writers taken here to be representatives of PD.[8]

The first core argument of PD is that 'underdevelopment' was invented by US president Truman in his inaugural address in 1949, as part of a political campaign to maintain or increase Western influence in Africa, Asia and Latin America (now dubbed 'underdeveloped areas') in the context of the Cold War and processes of decolonisation through a 'program of development' consisting of investments, technical progress and aid, and promising improvements in the standard of living (the invention of underdevelopment).[9] The thrust of this argument is to realise the historicity of the concept and to locate it in the geopolitical context of its time, leading some to talk about an 'ideology of development' which legitimises neocolonialism.[10]

Another central argument is that the content of the concept of 'development' is ambiguous, contested and far from clear. Because in the second half of the twentieth century the concept underwent frequent redefinitions and was used to refer to just about any kind of measure officially intended to improve people's lives, from building roads to economic reforms, environmental protection or empowering women, PD authors argue, its contours are blurred and it has become a shapeless, amoeba-like concept (development as amoeba).[11]

The subtitle of the *Development Dictionary* indicates another central argument: that knowledge about and representations of the social world are not neutral, but have a certain perspective and imply relations of power. Knowledge about 'development' therefore always implies a claim on how other ('underdeveloped') people should live and how their lives can be improved, and thus a justification of intervention (knowledge as power).[12] Some PD writers go further and argue that these interventions in the context of development cooperation suggest that problems of poverty can be solved by technical knowledge, ignoring relations of power and oppression and thus depoliticising poverty.[13] And the – very few – feminist PD authors add that this universal and technical developmentalist knowledge is not neutral but closely related to patriarchy and its dichotomous thinking.[14]

By characterising the majority of the world population as primarily 'underdeveloped', the West (comprised mainly of Europe and its former settler colonies in North America, Australia and New Zealand) defined its own society as standing at the top of a universal scale of progress and other societies as deficient, perceiving difference merely as backwardness and disregarding non-Western cultures, contexts and conceptions of a good society. This is possible only by employing Eurocentric standards as universal standards (Eurocentrism).[15]

Many PD writers claim that the promises of 'development' turned out to be empty, and that the processes, projects and programmes undertaken in its name did not lead to an improvement in standards of living, but to increased inequality, experiences of exclusion and impoverishment at least for significant parts of the population (development as impoverishment). The main reason is that subsistence economies were undermined or destroyed, while the modern cash economy did not provide secure livelihoods for all.[16] Again, PD feminists have pointed out that women suffered most from the enclosure of the commons and the 'war against subsistence'.[17]

According to some PD authors, the worldview of economics and its notions of markets, production and labour should be seen as a contingent expression of cultural values, not as a universal science (economics as culture). They argue that this worldview is focused on growth, productivity and the satisfaction of infinite needs for material goods and based on the model of economic man (*Homo oeconomicus*), but that it is very short-sighted or ignorant in regard to different dimensions of economic activity: the relation to Mother Earth, one's ancestors or the community, for example, which may play an important role in agricultural labour and determine why and how people work; or the idea of sufficiency, to have enough and require no more goods; or ideas of hospitality, solidarity and sharing, which are at odds with the maximisation of personal gain. They criticise the reductionist view on work and on what is perceived as valuable and productive and what not.[18]

The last central argument of PD concerns the claim that an increasing number of people in the South, disappointed by the promise and excluded from the project of 'development', resist Westernisation, reject this economic worldview, engage in alternatives and turn to models of the economy, politics and knowledge based on local culture and difference or at least on hybrid models, not based on catching up with the 'developed' countries (alternatives to Development).[19]

The presence of Post-Development arguments in development studies

As the investigation included 36 books, it is not possible to discuss the presence of PD core arguments in development studies in detail. Therefore, the results of the investigation need to be presented in the condensed format of a table (Table 1).

Contrary to my expectations, there is no conclusive evidence for the strong hypothesis that PD has been recognised as an important approach in development studies and that in recent years no development studies textbook can afford to ignore it. There are some that in fact mostly or entirely do without the PD debate and focus exclusively on more traditional questions of development studies. It may be not surprising that this is the case with authors from economics (Mavrotas/Shorrocks, Khambhampati), but some cases can also be found in sociology (Blumberg/Cohn, Petras) and political science/international relations (Williams, Brett). Nevertheless, this group has become a minority by now. Of the 18 books which were published during the last decade (since 2007), 12 discuss PD arguments on at least five pages, mention at least five PD texts and include at least five elements of PD arguments. For the 18 books in the sample published earlier than 2007, the respective number is a mere three. In this respect, there is indeed a historical trend of increasing recognition of PD in development studies.

In this respect, it is interesting to compare different editions of the same book published in different parts of the time period covered here. In the sample, there are two of these instances (Allen/Thomas and Nederveen Pieterse), plus two cases where it is not strictly speaking a new edition, but a very similar book published a few years later by the same author (Haynes, Corbridge). While there is hardly any difference concerning PD in the new edition of Nederveen Pieterse's book (he intensively discusses PD already in the 2001 edition), we find significant changes in the other cases. Haynes does not discuss PD works in 2002, but mentions (and discusses) five PD texts in 2008.[20] The widely used Open University textbook by Allen/Thomas does not discuss PD in the 1992 edition – before the publication of the *Development Dictionary*, PD was practically a non-issue in development studies: there were only a few texts from this perspective, written by some renegades, which received little attention outside the (growing) PD community. In the 2000 edition, the number of PD works mentioned rises from zero to 10, and the approach is debated on 13 pages. There are also significant differences between *Development Studies. A Reader* of 1995 and *The Development*

Table 1. Presence of Post-Development arguments in development studies textbooks.

Author(s)	Year	PD topics	PD works	CA 1	CA 2	CA 3	CA 4	CA 5	CA 6	CA 7	PD elements	Eval.
Larrain	1989	0	0	o	o	o	o	o	o	o	0	o
Webster	1990	2	0	x	x	x	x	x	o	x	6	o
Allen/Thomas	1992	3	0	o	x	x	x	o	o	o	3	o
Hettne	1995	28	3	x	x	x	xx	xx	x	x	9	+
Corbridge*	1995	18	1	xx	x	xx	xx	x	o	o	9	+/−
Hoogvelt	1997	6	2	xx	o	xx	x	x	o	xx	8	+
Martinussen	1997	1	1	o	x	o	o	x	o	o	2	−
Swanepoel/De Beer	1997	2	1	o	o	x	x	o	o	o	2	o
Allen/Thomas	2000	13	10	xx	x	x	x	xx	xx	o	9	+/−
Nederveen Pieterse	2001	28	38	xx	x	xx	xx	x	x	x	10	+/−
Haynes	2002	3	0	o	x	x	o	o	o	o	2	o
Kothari/Minogue	2002	13	38	x	o	xx	xx	x	o	o	6	+
Petras	2003	2	5	x	o	o	o	o	o	o	1	−
Muia/Otiende	2004	5	2	o	o	x	o	x	o	x	3	o
Khambhampati	2004	4	2	o	x	o	x	o	o	o	2	o
Olivier de Sardan	2005	2	5	x	o	x	x	o	o	o	3	−
Simon*	2006	38	7	x	x	o	o	o	o	o	2	o
Elliott	2006	2	3	o	o	x	xx	xx	o	o	5	+/−
Greig et al.	2007	12	14	xxx	o	xx	o	xx	o	o	7	+/−
Mavrotas/Shorrocks	2007	2	1	o	x	o	x	o	o	o	2	+/−
Desai/Potter	2008	8	10	x	o	x	x	x	x	o	5	+/−
Potter et al.	2008	12	6	xx	xx	xx	xx	x	xx	x	12	(+)/−
Kingsbury et al.	2008	7	7	xx	x	xx	x	x	x	o	8	o
Chari/Corbridge*	2008	85	8	xxx	x	xxx	xx	x	xx	o	12	+/−
Haynes	2008	9	5	xx	xx	xx	xx	o	x	x	10	(+)/−
Brett	2009	2	5	x	o	o	xx	x	o	o	4	o
Peet/Hartwick	2009	28	43	xx	x	xx	xx	xx	xx	xx	13	+/−
Haslam et al.	2009	20	9	xxx	x	xxx	xx	x	o	xx	12	+/(−)
Johnson	2009	27	25	xxx	x	x	x	x	o	o	7	(+)/−
Nederveen Pieterse	2010	28	38	xx	x	xx	xx	x	x	x	10	+/−
Willis	2011	16	12	xxx	x	xx	xx	xx	o	o	10	+/−
Hopper	2012	11	12	xxx	o	xx	xx	o	x	o	9	+/−
Williams	2012	2	0	x	o	o	o	o	o	o	1	o
Berger/Weber	2014	7	5	xx	o	x	x	o	o	o	4	o
Redclift/ Springett	2015	12	4	o	o	x	o	x	x	x	4	+
Blumberg/ Cohn	2016	3	0	o	o	o	o	x	o	o	1	o

Notes: PD topics: number of pages in which PD arguments (including postmodern or postcolonial critique of 'development') are debated;

PD works: number of PD works (including postmodern or postcolonial critiques of 'development') cited (in readers/collections of texts: included);

x: one element of core argument present;

o: no element of core argument present;

CA 1: Truman address/invention of underdevelopment/development as ideology;

CA 2: development as ambiguous/development as amoeba;

CA 3: knowledge and representation as power/paternalism or trusteeship/anti-politics machine;

CA 4: disregard of local culture/Eurocentrism;

CA 5: negative consequences of development/development as impoverishment;

CA 6: problematisation of economic categories/economics as culture;

CA 7: resistance to development/alternatives to development;

PD elements: number of elements of core PD arguments present;

Eval.: + (moderately) positive, − (moderately) negative or no (o) evaluation of PD;

*: in readers (collections of original texts) only the arguments present in the editor's contribution and only the authors present with an own contribution were listed.

Reader of 2008, edited respectively by Chari and Corbridge. While the earlier edition was already aware of the debate around PD and postcolonialism and included a text by Escobar, the new edition also included texts by Gandhi, Fanon, Ferguson, Mamdani, Mosse, Coronil, Appadurai and Mahmood, testifying to the influence not only of PD, but particularly of the related postcolonial perspective in development studies. Yet already in 1995, there are a large number of PD elements to be found in the editorial texts by Corbridge – it took many other authors another decade to take note of the discussion.

Still, one needs to differentiate between presentation and endorsement of the PD arguments. For example, while few textbooks devote as many pages to PD as Peet/Hartwick (28), these authors also deliver a decisive critique not only of the arguments, but also of their theoretical points of reference.[21] A special case is the book by Hettne, whose coverage of PD arguments (28 pages) far exceeds the coverage of PD texts (three). A closer look reveals that the majority of arguments made about Eurocentrism, development as ideology and development as impoverishment do not stem from a reading of Escobar, Sachs and Esteva, but are developed independently of their work, drawing instead on what Hettne calls the counterpoint paradigm. This counterpoint is characterised by arguing for 'the inherent superiority of small-scale, decentralized, ecologically sound, human and stable models of societal development' and can be traced back to 'romanticism, … anarchism, utopian socialism, populism and other ideologies articulating protests against modernity', Schumacher's 'small is beautiful' being cited as a contemporary formulation. The counterpoint ideal would then be a society that is 'physiocratic' (centred around the earth's natural resources), 'ultrademocratic' and structurally undifferentiated in terms of a division of labour.[22] The case of Hettne resonates with the claim made by Corbridge and Nederveen Pieterse that most PD arguments sound familiar to scholars of development theory aware of the critiques designated as counterpoint.[23] There is no room to discuss the claim in detail here, but even if PD were 'merely' a contemporary formulation of the counterpoint tradition, adding some poignant phrases ('invention of underdevelopment', 'development as amoeba', etc.), this would not lessen the force of its arguments. And, honestly, how many development studies textbooks took note of Illich and Gandhi before the *Development Dictionary*?

One final result of the investigation has to be mentioned which does not find a place in Table 1 above. What is conspicuous when looking at the textbooks is that many of them now include a chapter reflecting on the meaning of 'development', the origin of the concept and the discipline of development studies itself. In earlier publications, such treatises were often either very brief[24] or non-existent.[25] In the 2000s, such chapters appear more and more frequently. To give only a few examples: The new edition of Allen/Thomas has a new section on 'Conceptions of Poverty and Development', comprising chapters on 'Poverty and the "End of Development"' and 'Meanings and Views of Development'[26]; the first chapter of Kingsbury et al. is entitled 'What Is Development?'[27]; in Willis its title is 'What Do We Mean by Development?'[28]; and the opening chapter of Haslam et al. is headed 'Meaning, Measurement and Morality in International Development'.[29] All of these chapters include references to PD. Whereas earlier the meaning of the term 'development' and its pursuit was taken for granted, the critique of PD has sparked a new reflexivity and the desire to clarify what development studies is all about. Some of these reflections on the concept of development explicitly include sections on colonialism and its influence in today's world, highlighting colonial legacies and continuities.[30]

Rejection and integration: dealing with Post-Development in development studies

Regarding the evaluation of PD, it can be observed that there is a slightly increasing tendency in the more recent publications to include a discussion and evaluation of PD in the first place:

in the first half of the sample (up until 2006), eight out of 18 works did not consider PD to be important enough for such an evaluation. In the second half, the number dropped to five. What is more noteworthy is that within the 23 evaluations, the number of positive (four) and negative (three) evaluations presents a minority in contrast to the 16 evaluations which include positive and negative elements. This mixed reaction to PD seems to be the most typical.

Within these mixed reactions, at least two patterns can be discerned. The first pattern, common in texts which do not engage very thoroughly with PD, is that of a dilution of PD arguments. A few of these arguments are mentioned, but often in a weakened version which allows the author(s) to rank PD among different approaches in development theory without discussing the fundamental criticism that PD raises against most of the discipline. In this pattern, PD is reduced to a critique of Eurocentrism and a top-down approach in development studies.[31] Therefore, the central demand of PD can be portrayed as being one for 'sufficient attention [paid] … to the cultural dynamics of incorporating local thinking and practice into the global orthodoxy of economic thought'.[32] This is certainly not wrong, but leaves aside the more fundamental critique of power relations and knowledge formations manifest in the core arguments listed above (invention of underdevelopment, development as ideology, trusteeship, economics as culture, etc.).

The second pattern is based on a far more detailed engagement of PD and therefore deserves more attention. It can be characterised as a sharp criticism of PD coupled with a tacit integration of at least some central arguments of PD, and is present not only in the works of the most well-known critics of PD,[33] but also in a number of other textbooks.

Nederveen Pieterse, who shall be used as the first example of this pattern, claims that 'there is no compelling logic' to PD arguments, and describes it as 'flawed' and 'misconceived',[34] and accuses it of 'dichotomous thinking' and 'exaggerated claims',[35] a 'nostalgia politics of romanticism, glorification of the local, grassroots, community with conservative overtones',[36] 'misleading' claims and 'biased representation',[37] 'deeply conventional' and profoundly conservative' thinking,[38] and of turning discourse analysis into an 'ideological platform'[39] According to him, PD 'invites political impasse and quietism'[40] and merely 'replicates the rhetoric of developmentalism'.[41]

After this amount of criticism, one would not expect endorsement of PD arguments in the rest of the book. Yet Nederveen Pieterse also finds it useful to focus on an 'ideological function' and 'the ideological role of development theory' (but not to 'simply reduce it to ideology'),[42] resonating with a central element of PD's core arguments. He criticises the idea that 'the developed or advanced societies are supposed to be the mirror and guide of less developed societies' as implausible 'unilinear thinking' and 'cognitive colonialism', and advocates the 'decolonization of knowledge' in development theory.[43] He argues that 'the relationship between knowledge and power' is a 'central issue' and claims: 'Reading development theory … is also reading a history of hegemony and political and intellectual Eurocentrism'.[44] Criticising 'developmentalism' (the idea that 'social change occurs according to a pre-established pattern, the logic and direction of which is known'), he observes: 'Those who declare themselves furthest advanced along its course claim privileged knowledge of the direction of change. Developmentalism is the truth from the point of view of the centre of power; it is the theorization (or rather, ideologization) of its own path of development'.[45] The parallels to PD's critique of Eurocentrism and relations of power in knowledge about 'development' are obvious. He goes on to argue that even critical development theories were sharing modernization theories' 'economism, centrism, and teleology', identifies the merging of Christian and Enlightenment with scientific discourses in developmentalism, and comments: 'Resistance to development in the South is also an affirmation of autonomy and an expression of cultural resistance to Western ethnocentrism'.[46] Nederveen Pieterse also agrees with PD in describing 'development' as a 'necolonial discourse' and in the statement 'The assumption that the Western concepts of the nation, state, civil society and representative government are universal increasingly proved invalid'.[47] Here, numerous PD arguments are not merely presented, but employed in the analysis.

A similar case can be made for Corbridge and Peet. In a prominent critique of PD, Corbridge accuses PD of 'non-sequiturs', 'unhelpful binaries', 'false deductions', 'wobbly romanticism', 'self-righteousness', and 'implausible politics'.[48] According to him, PD 'too often trades in dogma and assertion' and its arguments sometimes are 'disgraceful' and 'ludicrous'.[49] Considering the usually more diplomatic customs of academic battles, this amounts to quite heavy artillery.

Yet looking at the editorial contributions in the collection of texts in the *Development Reader* of 2008, some of Corbridge's arguments appear to be subtler versions of PD criticisms. The statement 'For many people in the global North, development is something that happens in the South or the Third World. It is something that happens to other people'[50] already points to the fact that social, economic and political change are called 'development' only if they are happening in the South because we in the North are already 'developed', ie it points to the process of Othering implicit in the paradigm of 'development'. The editors go on to say they want to open up space for 'dissenting voices, like Gandhi, who call into question assumptions about the rightness of development as material progress', stressing 'the importance of standing back from taken-for-granted terms and practices, or ... dominant discourses', which can be seen as acknowledging even the fundamental criticism of PD vis-à-vis modern industrial capitalism. Further, they are inquiring: 'What assumptions does the development business make about those peoples around the world who are to be "developed" ... ? What absences are supposed to define their lives? ... What words and images are we using to structure today's development debates?'[51] These are questions which have prominently been asked by the *Development Dictionary*. Would it really be exaggerating to say that they have entered the debate in development studies primarily through the contribution of PD authors so harshly criticised by Corbridge beforehand? Chari and Corbridge also highlight the importance of knowledge and power in their emphasis on the notion of trusteeship as a significant element of development theory as well as in their critique of development planners' conceit and arrogance.[52] Further, they affirmatively paraphrase Escobar in the statement: 'The Third World was offered development as a cure for its supposed maladies'.[53] This neatly sums up the authoritative claim to diagnose other societies' ills ('cure'), the contingency of the diagnosis ('supposed') and the geopolitical or economic rationale ('offered') behind the concept. Overall, Chari and Corbridge seem to share PD's views in important, although certainly not in all, respects.

Peet and Hartwick are somewhat less polemical, but not softer in their critique of PD. They criticise PD's notion of a 'single developmental discourse' and argue that 'lumping together these critical notions [dependency theory, democratic Marxism and participatory approaches] ... with neoclassical economics, modernization theory, and World Bank policy into a broad, coherent "developmentalism" denies fundamental differences and denigrates the efforts of many brave theorist-activists'.[54] According to them, 'associating any trait with the West is sufficient [for PD] to condemn it without further question'[55] and PD would tend to 'divert attention away from ... class rationalities and material contexts', reminding of 'discursive idealism'.[56] Finally, the PD's social construction of poverty and its ethics of advocating convivial poverty would be 'a cruel hoax – it amounts to telling those about to expire that they are ... rich, that they should die with 'dignity' rather than struggle for life'.[57]

Yet here also we find instances where PD arguments have been adopted. This can be seen in the statement 'Development is a founding belief of modernity' (which in the first edition of the book was followed by the sentence 'Progress has long since replaced God as the icon of our age'), coupled with the observation 'the idea of development can be used to legitimate what in fact amounts to more money and power for a few'.[58] Here, the authors apparently reformulate the 'development-as-ideology' claim of PD on the first page of their book, as they do in writing '"Development" is the kindly face we place on this kind of profit-oriented endeavour wherein economic growth is recast in such terms as "millennium development goals we really should try to reach" ...'.[59] When Peet and Hartwick write 'the deficiency of development lies in its limited aims (an abundance of things), the timidity of its means (copying the West), and the scope of its conception (experts plan it)', they echo a number of PD arguments. The 'abundance of things' as aim criticises the identification of a good life with the ever-increasing production and consumption of material goods. The means of 'copying the West' criticises the Eurocentric conception of non-Western societies lagging behind on a universal scale and the reduction of social change to re-enacting Western modernity. The conception of expert planning points to the fact that the democratic decision-making by the people concerning what kind of society they would like to live in is denied in favour of technocratic decision-making by those who claim privileged knowledge about 'development' – implying specific relations of power.

Now there is nothing wrong with sharply criticising an approach, and an evaluation yields that at least for some PD texts (but not for others), most of the criticisms are in fact justified.[60] But the harshness of the critique is surprising in the light of the number of arguments apparently taken over from PD. PD's radical anti-establishment position is explicitly disavowed, but implicitly some of its tenets are endorsed without giving credit where credit is due.

Post-Development in development theory

So what can be said about PD and its role in the context of development theory? The diagnosis that development theory has reached an impasse is far from new,[61] but is still present in the recent academic debate.[62] It is my contention that the reason for this academic unease extends beyond the usual factors cited – the failure of development theory to achieve significant improvements in living standards for the majority of people in the Global South, the postmodernist critique of the social sciences, and the rise of globalisation preventing solutions on the level of the nation-state.[63] I argue that it lies in the fact that development theory has not sufficiently dealt with the implications of pluralism. Nederveen Pieterse correctly remarks: 'The idea of development as a single forward path ... or generalizing across developing societies lies well behind us'.[64] And he is also right in stating that since the crisis, '[m]ainstream approaches have coopted elements of alternative development like participation'.[65] But the implication of this rejection of 'development as a single path' has not been fully recognised – despite the universal acclaim that Sen's definition of 'Development as Freedom' enjoys.[66] Kothari and Minogue agree with Nederveen Pieterse that 'forms of alternative development have become institutionalized as part of mainstream development',[67] but argue that this type of alternative development 'does not redefine development, but instead questions its modalities, agency and procedures … It is still ultimately about the achievement of Western modernity by developing and transitional countries'.[68] This means that alternative development merely looks for different roads to arrive at the same goal. However, if this goal is defined by modern, industrial capitalist societies, then even alternative development remains firmly grounded in the Western or, more precisely, hegemonic models of politics (nation state and liberal democracy), the economy (neoliberal, globalised capitalism) and knowledge (Western science). Thus we are still assuming a single path forward to a good society, and the potential of non-Western alternatives to these models to improve human well-being remains untapped. If we take the imperative of 'development pluralism'[69] seriously, we need to consider these non-Western alternatives as well in order to redefine development, taking into account not only different paths to modernity but different ideas of a good life altogether. This is why the Post-Development approach which questions these hegemonic models and promotes non-Western alternatives plays a central role in the reinvention of development theory beyond the impasse.

If we differentiate within PD between a neo-populist discourse advocating radical localism and subsistence communities and a sceptical variant more cautious about cultural traditions and less willing to outline 'alternatives to development' (after all, it was for the people themselves to decide whether to pursue a western lifestyle or that of their ancestors or some hybrid model),[70] its role in development theory can be described as follows. Neo-populist PD can be seen as a new formulation of the counterpoint paradigm as outlined by Hettne, rejecting the goal of Western modernity.[71] Sceptical PD, however, opens up the horizon of what Nederveen Pieterse has described as 'development pluralism': While modernisation theory assumed there was one goal of 'development' and one road towards it (economic growth, industrialisation and technology, modernisation), dependency theory and alternative approaches have introduced alternative ways to reach the same goal. Sceptical PD now claims there are multiple goals and multiple roads. However, as the rules of development discourse require anyone who wants to contribute to the debate to say what 'development' is and how we get there, its answer 'the goal of a good society and the means to get there should be the matter of democratic decision-making by the people concerned and not of expert knowledge' is outside of this discourse.[72]

Conclusion

Contrary to the assumption that PD will remain without consequences unless it provides a 'constructive alternative programme', the article has shown PD has indeed become influential in development studies. Not all, but two-thirds of the examined textbooks from 2007 to 2016 discuss PD intensively (as opposed to one-sixth of those from 1989 to 2006). But what does this influence look like? On the basis of the present study, the influence of PD on development studies can be seen to consist in the following points. It has led to more frequent and more intensive reflections on development studies, the meaning of 'development' and the origin of the concept, including the historical context of the Cold War and colonialism. And it has led to increasing recognition that development studies are interwoven with relations of power and Eurocentrism. In discussing PD, these issues have gained a prominence in development studies they have not had before, visible in the significantly increased presence of PD arguments in development studies textbooks of the last decade. While PD has explicitly been rejected by many authors, a number of its central arguments have often been accepted and implicitly endorsed, leading to a curious mixture of rejection and integration. PD's critique of development discourse's Eurocentric and paternalist elements has widely been accepted by the more progressive authors in development studies, while the promotion of 'alternatives to development' finds little support and a constructive engagement with modernity is deemed indispensable. It is possible to describe this as a new 'middle ground' position in development scholarship. PD has shifted the terms of the debate. The challenge is to translate this into practice.

Disclosure statement

No potential conflict of interest was reported by the author.

Funding

This work was supported by the DFG -Deutsche Forschungsgemeinschaft [grant number ZI 759/8].

Acknowledgements

I am grateful to the anonymous reviewers for their constructive and useful comments.

Notes

1. See above all Sachs, *Development Dictionary*; Escobar, *Encountering Development*; and Rahnema with Bawtree, *Post-Development Reader*.
2. See eg Knippenberg and Schuurman, "Blinded by Rainbows"; Corbridge, "Beneath the Pavement"; Kiely, "Last Refuge"; Nanda, "Who needs Post-Development?"; Storey, "Post-Development Theory"; Nederveen Pieterse, "After Post-Development."
3. See eg Nustad, "Development: The Devil We Know?"; Brigg, "Post-Development"; Lind, "Feminist Post-Development Thought"; Matthews, "Post-Development Theory"; Ziai, "Ambivalence of Post-Development"; Simon, "Separated by Common Ground?"; Andrews and Bawa, "Post-Development Hoax?"; Ziai, "Premature Burials."
4. Nederveen Pieterse, "My Paradigm or Yours?," 366; Nederveen Pieterse, *Development Theory* 2nd ed., 122f; Andrews and Bawa, "Post-Development Hoax," 930.
5. Thus, I am supporting the position of Nustad, "Development: The Devil We Know?," who argues that PD's lack of instrumentality for a political programme of development should not lead to sidelining the approach.
6. Sachs, *Development Dictionary*.

7. Of course, this does not do justice to writers like Serge Latouche, Ashis Nandy, Claude Alvares, Frédérique Apffel-Marglin and others.
8. This excludes arguments which are central for one of these writers, but marginal or not present in the work of others, such as Shiva's characterisation of 'development' as a 'project of western patriarchy'; Shiva, *Staying Alive*, 1.
9. Esteva, "Development," 6f; Sachs, "Introduction," 2; Escobar, *Encountering Development*, 3; Rist, *History*, 69–72.
10. Rahnema, "Introduction," ix.
11. Sachs, "Introduction," 4; Esteva, "Metaphor," 79.
12. 'Though development has no content, it does possess one function: it allows any intervention to be sanctified in the name of a higher goal'; Sachs, "Introduction," 4. Li talks about the 'will to improve' in this context (Li, Will to Improve), Cowen and Shenton about 'trusteeship' (Cowen and Shenton, Doctrines).
13. Ferguson, *Anti-Politics Machine*, 256; Escobar, *Encountering Development*, 143; Sachs, "Archaeology," 9.
14. Shiva, *Resources*; see also Saunders, *Feminist Post-Development*; Shiva, *Staying Alive;* Mies and Shiva, *Ecofeminism*.
15. '... development cannot be separated from the idea that all peoples of the planet are moving along one single track towards maturity, exemplified by the nations "running in front". In this view, Tuaregs, Zapotecos or Rajashtanis are not seen as living diverse and non-comparable ways of human existence, but as somehow lacking in terms of what has been achieved by the advanced countries'; Sachs, "Introduction." 3. 'The metaphor of development gave global hegemony to a purely Western genealogy of history, robbing peoples of different cultures of the opportunity to define the forms of their social life'; Esteva, "Development," 9.
16. Sachs, "Introduction," 3; Esteva, "Development," 13; Escobar, *Encountering Development*, 4; Rahnema, "Introduction," x.
17. Bennholdt-Thomsen and Mies, *Subsistence Perspective*; Sittirak, *Daughters of Development*.
18. Esteva, "Development," 17–20; Escobar, *Encountering Development*, ch. 3; Sachs, "Archaeology," 18–22.
19. Esteva, "Development," 20–22; Escobar, *Encountering Development*, ch. 6.
20. Haynes, *Development Studies*, especially 168–71.
21. Peet and Hartwick, *Theories of Development*, 230–9.
22. Hettne, *Development Theory*, 30f.
23. 'For all its protestations of radical difference, there is little in Post-Development that moves beyond Gandhi or Schumacher, Illich or Fanon'; Corbridge, "Beneath the Pavement," 145. Nederveen Pieterse makes a similar point in *Development Theory*, 107.
24. Larrain, *Theories of Development*, 1–3.
25. Hoogvelt, *Globalisation*.
26. Allen/Thomas, *Poverty and Development*, 1–48.
27. Kingsbury et al., *International Development*, 21–50.
28. Willis, *Theories and Practices*, 1–35.
29. Haslam et al., *Introduction*, 1–27.
30. Eg Willis, *Theories and Practices*, 20–6; Haslam et al., *Introduction*, 28–44; Allen/Thomas, *Poverty and Development*, 241–70; Greig et al., *Challenging Global Inequality*, 59–66; Kothari/Minogue, *Development Theory*, 36–40; Berger/Weber, *Rethinking the Third World*, 25–32.
31. Khambhampati, *Development*, 82.
32. Mavrotas and Shorrocks, *Advancing Development*, 45.
33. According to a Google Scholar search for PD and critique, these are Nederveen Pieterse, Kiely and Corbridge; https://scholar.google.de/scholar?q=post-development+critique&btnG=&hl=de&as_sdt=0%2C5 (accessed 10 October 2016).
34. Nederveen Pieterse, *Development Theory* 1st ed., 110f.
35. Ibid., 106f.
36. Ibid., 109.
37. Ibid., 106, 108.

38. Ibid., 106.
39. Ibid., 103, 110.
40. Ibid., 110.
41. Ibid., 111.
42. Ibid., 3.
43. Ibid., 4.
44. Ibid., 8.
45. Ibid., 18.
46. Ibid., 25–7.
47. Ibid., 28.
48. Corbridge, 'Beneath the Pavement', 139.
49. Ibid., 143, 145.
50. Chari and Corbridge, *Development Reader*, 3.
51. Ibid., 7.
52. Ibid., 47, 263.
53. Ibid., 125.
54. Peet and Hartwick, *Theories of Development*, 231f.
55. Ibid., 236.
56. Ibid., 233.
57. Ibid., 285f.
58. Ibid., 1.
59. Ibid., 277.
60. Ziai, "Ambivalence of Post-Development."
61. Booth, "Marxism"; Booth, *Rethinking*; Schuurman, *Beyond the Impasse*; Kiely, *Sociology and Development*.
62. Schuurman, "Impasse."
63. Ibid.
64. Nederveen Pieterse, *Development Theory* 2nd ed., 214.
65. Ibid., 184.
66. 'Development can be seen … as a process of expanding the real freedoms that people enjoy'. Sen, *Development as Freedom*, 3. This definition basically claims that people have to decide for themselves what development understood as the path to a good society looks like – a view shared by sceptical PD. Taking seriously Sen's definition and Nederveen Pieterse's 'development pluralism' thus leads to a position close to PD – suggesting that there is no dichotomy between PD on one side and development studies on the other side.
67. Kothari and Minogue, *Development Theory*, 9.
68. Ibid., 10.
69. Nederveen Pieterse, *Development Theory* 2nd ed., 214.
70. Ziai, "Ambivalence of Post-Development."
71. I expect that the increasing awareness of industrial capitalism's ecological and social consequences will strengthen the position of its radical rejection in the future.
72. Ziai, "Premature Burials," 43.

Bibliography

Allen, T., and A. Thomas, eds. *Poverty and Development in the 1990s*. Oxford: Oxford University Press/ Open University, 1992.

Allen, T., and A. Thomas, eds. *Poverty and Development into the 21st Century*. Oxford: Oxford University Press/Open University, 2000.

Andrews, N., and S. Bawa. "A Post-Development Hoax? (Re-)Examining the past, Present and Future of Development Studies." *Third World Quarterly* 35, no. 6 (2014): 922–938.

Bennholdt-Thomsen, V., and M. Mies. *The Subsistence Perspective. beyond the Globalized Economy*. London: Zed Books, 1999.

Berger, M. T., and H. Weber. *Rethinking the Third World. International Development and World Politics*. Houndmills: Palgrave Macmillan, 2014.

Blumberg, R. L., and S. Cohn. *Development in Crisis. Threats to Human Well-Being in the Global South and Global North*. London: Routledge, 2016.

Booth, D. "Marxism and Development Sociology: Interpreting the Impasse." *World Development* 13, no. 7 (1985): 761–787.

Booth, D. *Rethinking Social Development. Theory, Research and Practice*. Harlow: Longman, 1994.

Brigg, M. "Post-Development, Foucault and the Colonisation Metaphor." *Third World Quarterly* 23, no. 3 (2002): 421–436.

Chari, S., and S. Corbridge, eds. *The Development Reader*. London: Routledge, 2008.

Corbridge, S., ed. *Development Studies. a Reader*. London: Edward Arnold, 1995.

Corbridge, S. "'beneath the Pavement Only Soil': The Poverty of Post-Development." *Journal of Development Studies* 34, no. 6 (1998): 138–148.

Cowen, M. P., and R. W. Shenton. *Doctrines of Development*. London: Routledge, 1996.

Elliott, J. A. *An Introduction to Sustainable Development*. 4th ed. London: Routledge, 2012.

Escobar, A. *Encountering Development. the Making and Unmaking of the Third World*. Princeton: Princeton University Press, 1995.

Esteva, G. "Development: Metaphor, Myth, Threat." *Development: Seeds of Change* 3 (1985): 78–79.

Esteva, G. "Development." In *The Development Dictionary. a Guide to Knowledge as Power*, edited by Wolfgang Sachs, 6–25. London: Zed Books, 1992.

Ferguson, J. *The Anti-Politics Machine. 'Development', Depoliticization and Bureaucratic Power in Lesotho*. Minneapolis, MN: University of Minnesota Press, 1994.

Greig, A., D. Hulme, and M. Turner. *Challenging Global Inequality. Development Theory and Practice in the 21st Century*. Houndmills: Palgrave, 2007.

Haslam, P. A., J. Schafer, and P. Beaudet, eds. *Introduction to International Development*. Oxford: Oxford University Press, 2009.

Haynes, J. *Politics in the Developing World. a Concise Introduction*. Oxford: Blackwell, 2002.

Haynes, J. *Development Studies*. Cambridge: Polity Press, 2008.

Hettne, B. *Development Theory and the Three Worlds. towards an International Political Economy of Development*. 2nd ed. Harlow: Longman, 1995.

Hoogvelt, A. *Globalization and the Postcolonial World. the New Political Economy of Development*. Baltimore, MD: Johns Hopkins University Press, 1997.

Hopper, P. *Understanding Development*. London: Polity Press, 2012.

Johnson, C. *Arresting Development. the Power of Knowledge for Social Change*. London: Routledge, 2009.

Kambhampati, U. S. *Development and the Developing World*. Cambridge: Polity, 2004.

Kiely, R. *Sociology and Development: The Impasse and beyond*. London: Routledge, 1995.

Kiely, R. "The Last Refuge of the Noble Savage? A Critical Assessment of Post-Development Theory." *The European Journal of Development Research* 11, no. 1 (1999): 30–55.

Kingsbury, D., J. McKay, J. Hunt, M. McGillivray, and M. Clarke. *International Development. Issues and Challenges*. Houndmills: Palgrave Macmillan, 2008.

Knippenberg, L., and F. Schuurmann. "Blinded by Rainbows: Anti-Modernist and Modernist Deconstructions of Development." In *Current Issues in Development Studies. Global Aspects of Agency and Structure*, Nimegen Studies in Development and social change 21 vols, edited by F. Schuurman, 90–106. Saarbruecken: Verlag fuer Entwicklungspolitik Breitenbach, 1994.

Kothari, U., and M. Minogue, eds. *Development Theory and Practice. Critical Perspectives*. Houndmills: Palgrave, 2002.

Li, T. M. *The Will to Improve. Governmentality, Development, and the Practice of Politics*. Durham: Duke University Press, 2007.

Lind, A. "Feminist Post-Development Thought: 'Women in Development' and the Gendered Paradoxes of Survival in Bolivia." *Women's Studies Quarterly* 31, no. 3/4 (2003): 227–246.

Martinussen, J. *Society, State and Market. a Guide to Competing Theories of Development*. London: Zed Books, 1997.

Matthews, S. "Post-Development Theory and the Question of Alternatives: A View from Africa." *Third World Quarterly* 25, no. 2 (2004): 373–384.

Mavrotas, G., and A. Shorrocks, eds. *Advancing Development. Core Themes in Global Economics*. Houndmills: Palgrave Macmillan, 2007.

Mies, M., and V. Shiva. *Ecofeminism*. London: Zed Books, 1993.

Muia, D. M., and J. E. Otiende, eds. *Introduction to Development Studies for Africa*. Nairobi: Acacia Publishers, 2004.

Nanda, M. "Who Needs Post-Development? Discourses of Difference, Green Revolution and Agrarian Populism in India." *Journal of Developing Societies* 15 (1999): 5–31.

Nederveen Pieterse, J. *Development Theory: Deconstructions/Reconstructions*. London: Sage, 2001.

Nustad, K. "Development: The Devil We Know?" *Third World Quarterly* 22, no. 4 (2001): 479–489.

Olivier de Sardan, J.-P. *Anthropology and Development: Understanding Contemporary Social Change*. London: Zed Books, 2005.

Peet, R., and E. Hartwick. *Theories of Development. Contentions, Arguments, Alternatives*. 2nd ed. New York: Guilford Press, 2009.

Petras, J. *The New Development Politics. the Age of Empire Building and New Social Movements*. Aldershot: Ashgate, 2003.

Pieterse, J. "My Paradigm or Yours? Alternative Development, Post-Development, Reflexive Development." *Development and Change* 29 (1998): 343–373.

Pieterse, J. "After Post-Development." *Third World Quarterly* 20, no. 1 (2000): 175–191.

Pieterse, J. *Development Theory: Deconstructions/Reconstructions*. 2nd ed. London: Sage, 2010.

Potter, R. B., T. Binns, J. A. Elliott, and D. Smith. *Geographies of Development. an Introduction to Development Studies*. 3rd ed. Harlow: Pearson, 2008.

Rahnema, M., and V. Bawtree. *The Post-Development Reader*. London: Zed Books, 1997.

Rahnema, M. "Introduction." In *The Post-Development Reader*, edited by Majid Rahnema with Victoria Bawtree, ix–xix. London: Zed Books, 1997.

Redclift, Michael, and Delyse Springett, eds. *Routledge International Handbook of Sustainable Development*. London: Routledge, 2015.

Rist, G. *The History of Development. from Western Origins to Global Faith*. London: Zed Books, 1997.

Roberts, J. T., and A. Hite, eds. *From Modernization to Globalization: Social Perspectives on International Development*. Oxford: Blackwell, 2000.

Sachs, W. "Introduction." In *The Development Dictionary. a Guide to Knowledge as Power*, edited by Wolfgang Sachs, 1–5. London: Zed Books, 1992.

Saunders, K. *Feminist Post-Development Thought. Rethinking Modernity, Post-Colonialism and Representation*. London: Zed Books, 2002.

Schuurman, F., ed. *Beyond the Impasse. New Directions in Development Theory*. London: Zed Books, 1993.

Schuurman, F. "The Impasse in Development Studies." In *The Companion to Development Studies*, edited by V. Desai and R. Potter, 12–15. London: Routledge, 2013.

Sen, A. *Development as Freedom*. New York: Anchor Books, 2000.

Shiva, V. *Staying Alive. Women, Ecology, and Survical in India*. London: Zed Books, 1989.

Shiva, V. "Resources." In *The Development Dictionary. a Guide to Knowledge as Power*, edited by Wolfgang Sachs, 206–218. London: Zed Books, 1992.

Simon, D. "Separated by Common Ground? Bringing (Post)Development and (Post)Colonialism Together." *The Geographical Journal* 172, no. 1 (2006): 10–21.

Simon, D., ed. *Fifty Key Thinkers on Development*. London: Routledge, 2006.

Sittirak, S. *The Daughters of Development. Women in a Changing Environment*. London: Zed Books, 1998.

Storey, A. "Post-Development Theory: Romanticism and Pontius Pilate Politics." *Development* 43, no. 4 (2000): 40–46.

Swanepoel, H., and F. De Beer, eds. *Introduction to Development Studies*. Johannesburg: International Thomson Publishing, 1997.

Webster, A. *Introduction to the Sociology of Development*. 2n ed. Houndmills: Macmillan, 1990.

Williams, D. *International Development and Global Politics. History, Theory and Practice*. London: Routledge, 2012.

Willis, K. *Theories and Practices of Development*. 2nd ed. London: Routledge, 2011.

Ziai, A. "The Ambivalence of Post-Development: Between Reactionary Populism and Radical Democracy." *Third World Quarterly* 25, no. 6 (2004): 1045–1060.

Ziai, A. "Post-Development: Premature Burials and Haunting Ghosts." *Development and Change* 46, no. 4 (2015): 833–854.

Index

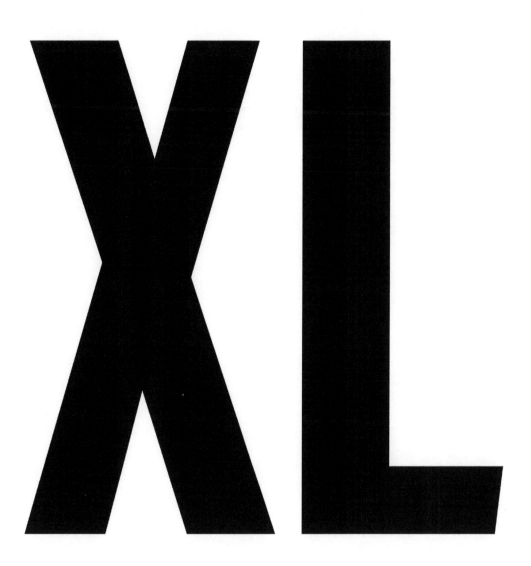

ZED

Forty years of publishing on the politcs of development
www.zedbooks.net
@ZedBooks

For Product Safety Concerns and Information please contact our EU
representative GPSR@taylorandfrancis.com
Taylor & Francis Verlag GmbH, Kaufingerstraße 24, 80331 München, Germany

www.ingramcontent.com/pod-product-compliance
Ingram Content Group UK Ltd.
Pitfield, Milton Keynes, MK11 3LW, UK
UKHW051832180425
457613UK00022B/1210